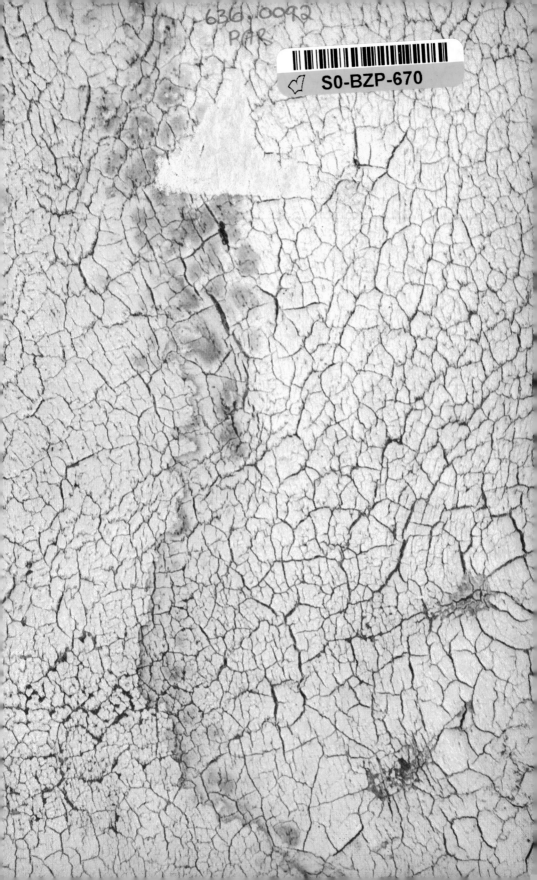

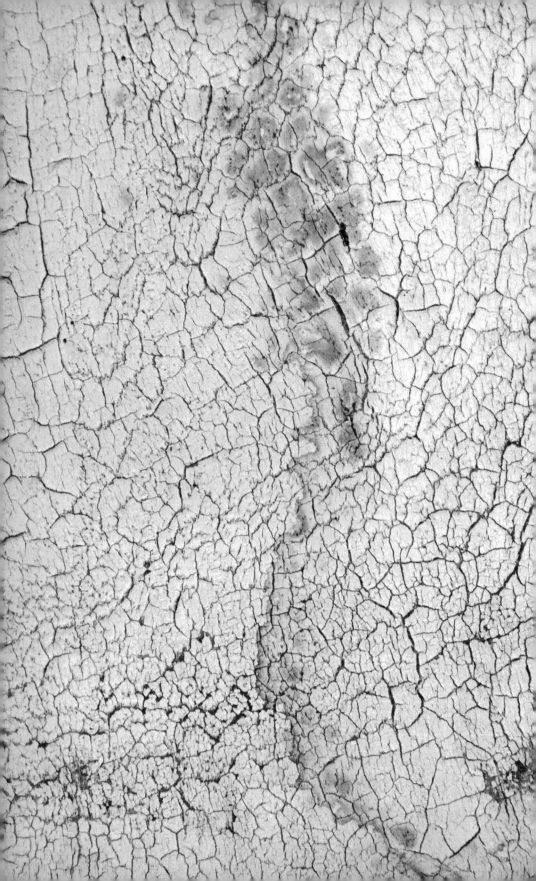

A Youth Not Wasted
Ian Parkes

FOURTH ESTATE

WARNING: Aboriginal and Torres Strait Islander readers are
warned that the following stories contain images, names
and words of deceased persons.

AUTHOR'S NOTE: Some names have been changed to protect people's privacy.

Fourth Estate

An imprint of HarperCollins*Publishers*

First published in Australia in 2012
by HarperCollins*Publishers* Australia Pty Limited
ABN 36 009 913 517
harpercollins.com.au

HarperCollins*Publishers*
Level 13, 201 Elizabeth Street, Sydney NSW 2000, Australia
31 View Road, Glenfield, Auckland 0627, New Zealand
A 53, Sector 57, Noida, UP, India
77–85 Fulham Palace Road, London W6 8JB, United Kingdom
2 Bloor Street East, 20th floor, Toronto, Ontario M4W 1A8, Canada
10 East 53rd Street, New York NY 10022, USA

National Library of Cataloguing-in-Publication data:

Parkes, Ian.
  A youth not wasted/Ian Parkes.
  ISBN: 978 0 7322 9534 9 (pbk.)
  Parkes, Ian.
  Jackeroos – Australia – Biography.
  Stockmen – Australia – Biography.
636.0092

Cover and internal design by Matt Stanton, HarperCollins Design Studio
Cover image © Christian Fletcher
Inside cover image and internal background images by shutterstock.com
Maps by Matt Stanton, HarperCollins Design Studio
Internal photographs courtesy of Ian Parkes
Typeset in 11/16pt Sabon by Kirby Jones
Printed and bound in Australia by Griffin Press
60gsm Hi Bulk Book Cream used by HarperCollins*Publishers* is a natural, recyclable product
made from wood grown in sustainable forests. The manufacturing processes conform to the
environmental regulations in the country of origin, Finland.

5 4 3 2 1   12 13 14 15

For Jody, Emma, Sophie, Candice.

And for Ben and Barbara.

Contents

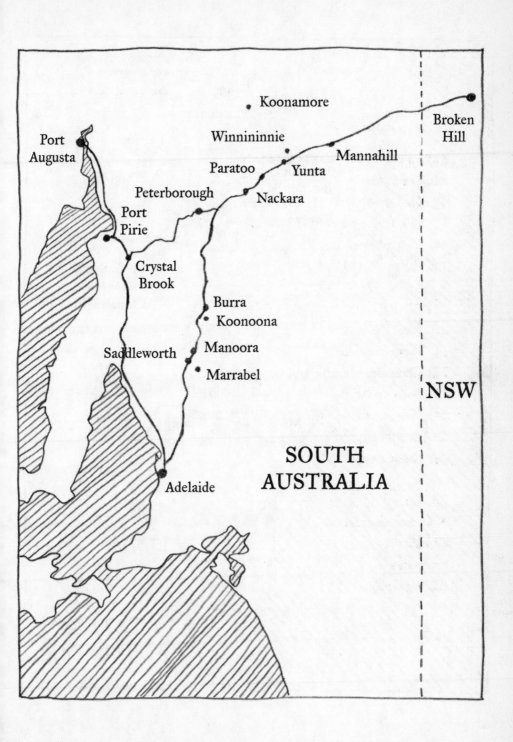

Koonamore

Broken
Hill

Port
Augusta

Winnininnie

Mannahill

Paratoo

Yunta

Peterborough

Nackara

Port
Pirie

Crystal
Brook

Burra

Koonoona

Manoora

Saddleworth

Marrabel

NSW

Adelaide

SOUTH
AUSTRALIA

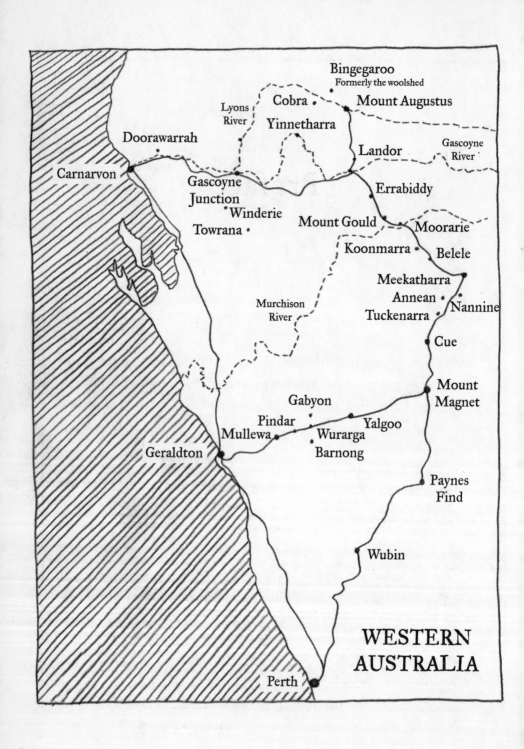

Bingegaroo
Formerly the woolshed

Lyons
River

Cobra

Mount Augustus

Yinnetharra

Doorawarrah

Landor

Gascoyne
River

Carnarvon

Gascoyne
Junction

Errabiddy

Winderie

Mount Gould

Moorarie

Towrana

Koonmarra

Belele

Meekatharra

Annean

Nannine

Murchison
River

Tuckenarra

Cue

Mount
Magnet

Gabyon

Pindar

Yalgoo

Mullewa

Wurarga

Barnong

Geraldton

Paynes
Find

Wubin

WESTERN
AUSTRALIA

Perth

Preface

For well over a hundred years, the wool industry was integral to the identity of Australia. Towards the end of the nineteenth century, Australia was the world's biggest supplier of wool. After the setbacks resulting from the depression of 1890 and the First World War, wool resumed its position as the major force in Australia's economy. Later, in 1946, there was a dramatic five-year run when top-quality wool was fetching 240 pence or more per pound, hence the old catchphrase 'a pound for a pound'. The average price was equivalent to ten times today's prices.

In 1950–51, wool production increased to 56 per cent of the total value of all agricultural production. It was no wonder that in the decades leading up to 1950, Australia was said to be 'riding on the sheep's back'.

On the vast pastoral leases, outback sheep stations prospered, as did wheat and sheep farmers. They were supported by an Australia-wide infrastructure that included stock and station agents such as Dalgety, Goldsbrough Mort, Elders, Wesfarmers and others. Those were the halcyon days when successful station owners and farmers had an exalted status in the eyes of many city people.

In 1952, for a variety of reasons, including competition from synthetics, wool prices suddenly fell and continued to fall over ensuing decades. Sheep ceased to be viable on outback stations. The shearing sheds disintegrated through disuse. Dalgety and Goldsbrough Mort disappeared from the scene. Station populations dwindled to a fraction of what they had been. The way of life that I experienced in Western Australia in the fifties has vanished. This book will give you a glimpse of what it was like.

Prologue

When I began my youthful passage, my expectations were simple: to learn to be a sheep station manager and to enjoy a life in which horses would play a major part. I had no idea what would unfold or where my inclinations would lead me. I learned and I enjoyed, but somewhere along the way, the country crept inside me and took root.

In South Australia, I began to know it and to feel it. But when I went to Western Australia's Upper Gascoyne and Upper Murchison, the country's power increased – and I began to love it. Love? Such a hackneyed word, but I can't think of a better one. What else can it possibly be? When my gaze passed over and through the landscape, I felt a frisson of excitement, of exquisite pleasure. How can mere red dirt and stones and scrubby trees and shrubs and rises and falls in the land and haze and a vast blue sky be so potent? Such was its power, even in intense heat, even at night – sometimes, especially at night – the landscape seized you. And what held together and enclosed all the elements was the enveloping silence, a soothing emptiness of noise. Yes, there were sounds, but they were the life-affirming murmurs of the movement of air, of the calls of birds, of the shuffle of leaves. Human sound is noise – and noisome. How sweet to be away from it.

When I listened to the silence and the stillness of the country, there was communication. Writing this now, seeing in my mind's eye the country that I learned to love, the old frisson stirs afresh. People who truly live in the outback listen to it. What they hear, I do not know. What I hear, I will not try to tell you. What the country says is beyond words. You feel it – or you don't.

So I discovered something I was not looking for, something profoundly important and beautiful. How grateful I am that I listened. And when people ask me why I wasted my youth working on sheep stations in the vast Australian outback, all I can say is that my youth was not wasted. It was not – wasted.

In 2009, I went back, yet again, into the country where I was forged. I camped alone on the bank of the dry bed of the Upper Gascoyne River. The place is called Teamarra Pool. I had camped there back when the pool had water for half a mile. I settled at my usual spot, at the base of an ancestor river gum. The night was pleasantly warm. Clothes seemed superfluous, irrelevant. I lay naked on my swag, which was unrolled on the ground beneath my tree's vast, spreading branches. I removed my watch. I disengaged from everything in my life but the country. I was back. The connection was back. There was no moon; the night was intensely dark. Stars flickered on and off as the leaves wafted. Soft, cool breaths of air came and went across my body, with intermittent, long-drawn-out periods of stillness.

I lay lightly on my back, looking up, feeling the earth's weight beneath me, observing the infinite firmament above through the thin veil of foliage. As I listened to the creak of the ancient tree's branches and the flicker of its leaves and the soft tumbles of the campfire coals, I asked myself if this is where I would like to die. Could I close my eyes and pass on here? Fade away, as the campfire faded out? Could I? Well, yes, I could. I felt at ease here. What greater feeling can a country give you than to set you free to pass on in its embrace. Alone, tracks dispersed by the wind, mind emptied, scattered traces, a final passage, no more rites. Knowing I could accept my death, my appetite for life surged and flooded me with urgency. The country is alive! I am alive! I am not ready to end the partnership. If we do not take a firm grip on life, it will slip through our fingers.

When I was there in my youth, Death did reach out to me and seek to take me. I was sustained by the strength the country had given me. Through long dark days and nights, I heard the whispers and the reminders, and I listened.

Two hours into that night alone at Teamarra Pool, the full moon emerged and lit the floodplain with pale light. Eventually I slept; and in the morning, I brought the fire back to life to boil my billy, and I packed up and drove slowly away from the river to the road. I skimmed down that soft dirt track through miles and miles of flat wanderrie country, trying, as always, to imprint in my memory the landscape I was watching. But the details of memories fade. All that remain are impressions and feelings – and a sadness at the loss. There is only one solution – to return.

PART ONE

JACKEROO

A trainee on a sheep or cattle station

I

The seeds

In 1949, at fifteen years of age, I was clearly the unquestioning product of my family's background. My mother's father was a sheep station man all his life, as was his son, Jack. My father, who grew up in Onslow, Western Australia, surrounded by sheep stations, also worked for a time as a station hand – and never really got the outback out of his system.

To own a sheep station was a worthy and potentially profitable aspiration. From the late 1800s through to when I had to decide what I wanted to be in life, the wool industry was prominent in the consciousness of nearly all Australians, and there I was, bred to it.

Onslow was a frontier port on the northwest coast – and that's where my mother and father met. My mother's father, James Porter Henderson, was managing a sheep station called Peedamulla, not far from town. My father's father, Herbert Maurice Parkes, had established a fleet of pearling luggers in the 1890s, and he was also the Onslow agent for Dalgety, a major stock and station supplier. He also had a store that serviced the pearling and fishing boats.

The Hendersons had started life in South Australia and moved to Western Australia in 1930, buying a farming property at Darkan, south of Perth. The Great Depression put paid to that venture so they walked off – as did so many other would-be farmers. My grandfather returned to what he knew best, managing a sheep station. That was how he and his wife, Lilian; son, Jack; and daughter, Margaret, came to be at Peedamulla in 1932.

My parents were married on 11 May 1933, when the Great Depression was theoretically over. But the times were still tough as the world slowly recovered. The pearling industry ran aground when synthetics took over from mother-of-pearl for the making of buttons. Sheep stations and the wool industry were still in recovery mode. My father decided his prospects were better in Perth, so he studied accountancy by correspondence. He found a job as a clerk at the Swan Brewery, continued studying and went on to become a fully qualified accountant and company secretary. To augment his income, he taught accountancy at night at a business school.

In the late 1930s, my mother's parents moved to Mundaring, twenty-one miles east of Perth. It was then a small country town, surrounded by orchards and small farms, with a large timber mill in the main street. The main transportation to and from Perth was the train, and the trip took one and a quarter hours. Few people could afford a car. My grandparents ran a small tearoom and shop and lived in the rooms behind. My grandmother was a busy cook. She made pies and pasties and sandwiches for the primary school children, as well as cakes and scones for travellers passing through and needing a tea break.

My grandmother had a large garden at the back and fertilised the plants with urine diluted with water. To obtain the urine, she made my grandfather relieve himself in a pot, while she ignored his grumbling and complaining.

During the Second World War, when my father was serving in the air force elsewhere in Australia and in the Far East, my mother rented a house just down the street from the shop. At Christmas in 1942, when I was eight years old, I received more presents than I deserved. The four of us were in the kitchen-cum-dining room, and when my mother and grandmother went into the back room, leaving my grandfather and me alone, he took the opportunity to say, 'You know what I think?'

'No,' I answered.

'I think you're a bloody spoiled brat.'

I had no reply. It stung, but I didn't cry. I looked through the window at a big old pine tree just outside. I thought about what he'd said, and I thought he was probably right.

In 1944, after my grandfather sold the shop, we shared my grandparents' new home, called Wyndalia, in Hartung Street, not far down the slope from the Anglican church. My grandmother, the dedicated gardener, had my grandfather build an extensive collection of raised garden beds and trellises for climbing roses. She kept the Anglican church decorated with flowers for the services every Sunday. Even after they retired, she continued to be a great cook. Her only facilities were a Coolgardie safe and a Metters wood oven and stove – and a ready supply of chopped wood. There were no electrical appliances. Apart from the lights, the only item in the house that used electricity was the wireless. In any case, the privately owned power station frequently broke down – and it did not operate between ten o'clock at night and six o'clock in the morning.

A lot of my time was spent with my grandfather, helping build yards for the chooks, repairing fences, burning off and doing other odd jobs. His talk revolved around politics (he was an ardent Liberal); cricket (he took me to see Don Bradman play on the Esplanade in Perth); and endless reminiscences of station life, mostly at Koonamore, north of Peterborough, in South Australia. Although he lived in Western Australia from the age of sixty-one to eighty-eight, he remained a South Australian to the core. In those days, parochialism was considered a virtue and people took pride in clinging to their roots. My grandfather went to St Peter's College, in the suburb of the same name in Adelaide. It was, of course, the best school in Australia. And Adelaide was Australia's most civilised and beautiful city. Nothing, absolutely nothing, about Perth and Western Australia could compare favourably with South Australia. My mother embraced the same outlook. I think my grandfather felt that for all of his twenty-seven years in Western Australia he was in exile.

There was much reference to his three maiden sisters, my great aunts, in Adelaide. They lived in a large house called Poltoonga, in Harrow Road, St Peters, ten minutes from the centre of the city. Throughout their lives, Mary, Maggie and Dorothy had supported themselves by conducting a school at Poltoonga. They became the keepers of the family archives for the Henderson clan in Australia. The maiden aunts were part of my life long before I ever met them.

When my father returned from the war, my parents and I went to live in Perth, where my father could be closer to work and I could be closer to Hale School, where my father spent eight years of his boyhood. But my grandparents' home in Mundaring remained a focal point in our lives. We congregated there, especially when my uncle Jack came down from up north.

It was mainly my grandfather's influence that led me to choose to be a sheep station man. I dreamed of being an overseer at nineteen, as my grandfather had been. I was impressed that someone so young would be given such a responsible job. My mother could think of nothing better than for me to work on sheep stations. My father was all in favour because he had hankered after the same thing in his youth.

And my uncle Jack? He was a sheep station man. If my grandfather was my guiding light, my uncle was my hero. And my mother worshipped him. Jack was six feet two inches tall. Always rangy, always fit, always wearing a moustache that was almost Errol Flynnish, always cheeky, always dashing – and a great horseman. He and my father were good friends. When Jack was in Perth, the two of them went to the races at Ascot on a Saturday afternoon and then to the trots at Gloucester Park that evening. They would burst into the house late at night, not drunk but well lubricated, and my mother put up with it because she loved them both, although she found it easier to forgive my uncle than my father.

As much as Jack loved horses and the ladies, he also loved high-powered motor vehicles. He couldn't see the point in driving at anything less than high speed – as fast as the vehicle and the conditions would allow. Of course, there were speed limits in Perth, but those were the days before speeding was seriously policed. And as far as the bush was concerned – what speed limits? What police? He was known far and wide as Galloping Jack.

Inevitably, my big dream was to emulate my grandfather and my uncle and do what my father had always regretted not doing.

Another of my dreams was to be a horseman like Jack. My mother and I had spent seven weeks with him at a station called Elliott Creek in 1941, when I was seven. My mother was there to chaperone Lindsay Thomson, whom Jack was contemplating marrying. Lindsay was a lady from a farming family in Moora. Jack had been married before and had a daughter, Penelope. His first wife had died soon after Penny was born.

In 1949, I also spent school holidays with Jack when he was managing a station called Moorarie, on the road from Meekatharra to Mount Augustus. By this time he was well and truly married to Lindsay. Penny was a boarder at Perth College, and Jack collected the pair of us and drove us to Moorarie. The homestead and its various buildings and yards were scattered along the north bank of the Murchison River.

He taught me to ride a brown gelding called Robin. When I stood beside Robin's flanks to put my left foot in the stirrup to mount, Jack roared at me and said, 'Any self-respecting horse will kick you in the arse if you stand there.' He then commanded me to stand alongside Robin's shoulder. He showed me how to hold the reins in my left hand and place that hand on the pony's neck. With my right hand gripping the pommel and my left foot in the stirrup, I hopped up and down on my right leg and then swung up and around and on. Penny sat on her horse and giggled because she knew what to do and I didn't. This was embarrassing, because Penny was five years younger than me – and much smaller.

Penny and I rode for hours, sometimes mustering, more often just riding along tracks through the bush. I was fourteen, Penny was nine and we had a lot to learn. Jack blasted both of us when we returned from a ride at a gallop, pulling up in a cloud of dust at the stables. 'Don't you ever do that again,' he raged. 'You're not bloody American cowboys. Australian stockmen walk the last couple of miles home. You gallop back and you'll teach the buggers bad habits. Christ almighty, learn to think of your horses and come home quietly.'

Then there were the interludes with Jack alone, at dusk, in the stockyards when there was a mob of horses in the big main yard. We stood very still, leaning back against the post-and-rail fence, taking it all in, talking, murmuring really, with the mob shuffling and milling in the dust. When an unbroken colt stepped cautiously across the yard and tentatively put its head out to smell me, Jack told me to stay stock-still. The colt took another step closer and nuzzled my shirt where it was loose above my belt buckle. 'Don't move,' Jack whispered. 'If you move or shift your weight, he'll back off like the dickens. Let him take his own time.'

I stopped breathing until the colt lost interest and turned away.

It used to be common practice for the owners of stations to send adolescent sons to other stations for experience – well away from home. This was called jackerooing and the lads were known as jackeroos. There was usually a prearranged period of time for a jackeroo to work at a host property, anything from several months to two years. His wages were a pittance, if he received any at all. It was often said that 'jackeroos were paid from the waistcoat pocket of the manager', the implication being that jackeroos were in a separate class to general station hands, which was true. For one thing, they were not permanent employees. For another, they often enjoyed privileges, such as separate accommodation from the men's quarters.

There was an understanding that the host station was performing a favour for the jackeroo and his parents. Consequently, such an arrangement was made between people who knew each other and were confident that the jackeroo would know his place and be well behaved.

When my grandfather was managing Koonamore he had many jackeroos over the years. One of them, Len Boothby, was now the manager of a prominent merino sheep stud, Koonoona, at Burra, in South Australia.

In 1949, wool prices were higher than they'd ever been and high-quality merino rams sold for a premium. Koonoona was a rung down from the top three merino studs in Australia, but it commanded respect and had a strong reputation. The premier studs were Peppin, near Deniliquin, in New South Wales; and Collinsville and Bungaree, both in the Clare Valley, in South Australia. Koonoona was a thirty-minute drive northeast of both these studs.

My grandfather urged my parents to see if Len Boothby would take me on as a jackeroo. My father was strongly in favour. He saw it as an opportunity for me to learn about top-class merino rams.

In September 1949, my parents and I met with Len Boothby at the Perth Royal Showgrounds. He and the stud master, Glen Hawkes, had brought twelve selected stud rams all the way from Burra to be shown and sold. In effect, this small collection of rams was a sample around which they could hold discussions with breeders and woolgrowers from all over the state. Most of the rams presented by the country's top studs at the shows around Australia were bought by local studs, which then sold their progeny to farmers and pastoralists. This introduced fresh blood into their breeding flocks and enabled them to change or vary the strength of the wool in their fleeces.

My mother reminded Mr Boothby of Koonamore days. They talked about the good times they'd had and how my grandparents were in retirement in Mundaring. The rams, laden with their heavy wool burden, stood patiently in the pens. I listened and looked, picking up the heavy, acrid smell of the ram shed and its guests. My parents explained that I wanted to follow in the footsteps of my grandfather and uncle. The starting point? Jackerooing at Koonoona.

'How old is he?' Mr Boothby asked.

'He'll be fifteen this October,' my father said.

'Good, just the right age. When can he come?'

'Well, not right away. We want him to do his Junior Certificate next year.'

'Hmm, I'd rather get hold of him now. It's better when they're young.' There was a pause. 'I'll think about it and let you know.'

Softly, my mother said, 'I think you were about seventeen when you went to Koonamore. That was all right then.' I looked away from them and held my breath. But I was listening.

'True . . . yes . . . you're right,' he conceded.

And then it was settled. I would go to South Australia in January 1951.

In 1950, my last year at school, encouraged by my father, I did a wool-classing course at Perth Technical College in the evenings. This gave me the beginnings of technical knowledge about the qualities and categories of wool as it comes off the sheep's backs.

I did not fully understand what lay ahead, but I was more excited than I was apprehensive.

One evening in the week before I went to Koonoona, my father asked me to go for a walk with him. We were living in a flat in Merlin Court, in St Georges Terrace.

We went down Spring Street, past the Emu Brewery on the west side, and we crossed over Mounts Bay Road. We walked across the wide lawns and under the big trees of the Swan River foreshore, towards the Narrows. When he spoke, his voice was soft, not at all threatening, but it was firm. 'You know, you could find yourself in a spot of trouble one day.'

Really? I thought instantly: what trouble?

'I don't know what it might be,' he said, as if reading my thoughts. 'Could be anything. I don't know. Anyway, the point is this . . . things happen and . . . well, I want you to know that whatever happens, you must tell me.'

I didn't know what to say.

'Don't ever be ashamed to tell me if you've ever done anything wrong,' he said. 'I mean – anything that means you're in trouble. Anything.'

We stopped walking, and we looked at each other, and I looked across the river and then back to him. He was still looking at me.

'Will you do that?' he asked. 'Will you do that for me?'

'Sure,' I said.

'Because,' he said, 'I will always be here to help you. No matter what. Don't ever forget.'

'Sure, Dad,' I said.

I felt as though we had just made a pact, a deeply personal pact. It was sobering. I smiled at him to show that I knew what he was saying, that I understood. He smiled in return. The pact was sealed.

We continued our walk and continued our talk – his talk. We walked slowly now, pausing to look around and at each other. 'Jum,' he said. Jum was my parents' favourite nickname for me, and exclusively theirs. 'Jum, when you become a station manager, you won't have to know all there is to know about the workings of windmills – you'll employ windmill men. You won't have to be an expert mechanic to fix cars and trucks – you'll employ mechanics. It will be your job to be a manager.'

I understood what he was saying. What neither of us realised was that his thinking belonged to an era that was about to be left behind. The situation was to change dramatically in a few more years. Today's stations do not have the luxury of employing specialists for specific areas. But at the time, the principle of what he was saying was sensible.

'And remember what I've told you before,' he said, 'to ask and not order.'

'I will,' I said. 'I will remember.'

It was easy to say – but would prove to be a lot harder to put into practice at all times.

It felt like much later, although it was only about three years, that I visited Perth and spent two days with my grandparents in Mundaring. Sitting by the fire, yarning with my grandfather about my experiences in South Australia and up north in Western Australia, just the two of us, my grandfather said, 'I'll give you some advice. When you're out in a mustering camp, wash your feet and your arsehole every day. Oh, and your hands too. Doesn't matter about the rest. You want to stay healthy, do what I tell you.'

My grandmother was in the kitchen making cakes for the next day. Dinner was finished and we were warming each other with stories of station life.

'Now, sonno,' he said. 'Keep your wits about you. There was a time on Koonamore once when I had an argument with a carpenter in one of the workshops. He was a foreign bastard. I'm sure he was German. There were lots of Germans in South Australia in those days. Well, when I turned to walk away, I heard a noise that made me spin round, and there was this bloke about to stab me in the back with a bloody chisel. It would have been really bloody if he'd succeeded, but I grabbed his wrist and I bent his arm back until he dropped it. By this time, three of the other blokes woke up and came running and one of them wrapped his arm round his neck and put him in a headlock.'

'Bloody hell,' I said.

'So I warned this joker. I said, "Try that again and I'll belt the living bloody daylights out of you."'

'Then what happened?'

'Nothing happened. I never heard another peep out of him from that day on.'

'What was the blue about?'

'Nothing really. It was bloody stupid. Some joker, thinking he was being funny, told him I'd been giving his wife the once-over. Which I hadn't. He said it just to stir the silly bastard up.'

My grandmother came in and said, 'I wish you wouldn't swear. You shouldn't use language like that with Ian.'

My grandfather gave me the merest flicker of a wink. He looked up at my grandmother standing there expectantly. 'Well,' he said. 'What do you want?'

'Do you two want a cup of tea and some sponge?'

'Of course we do. And thank you,' he said.

When she was preoccupied back in the kitchen I asked him: 'How come you had a carpenter on the station?'

'A carpenter? We had three carpenters. And we had blacksmiths and mechanics and stonemasons – and we had a plumber. And we had station hands, of course, and cooks and a bookkeeper. We even had a few cottages for the married ones. Some of the wives worked in the house or the kitchens. All up, I had more than fifty people working there. Koonamore was a big station.'

'I've never seen a station with that many people. There were a lot at Koonoona, at Burra, but nowhere near that many,' I said.

'Sonno,' he said, 'Koonamore was so big they cut it up into ten independent stations and sold them off – and that's when I decided to leave. That was 1929. That's when your grandmother and your mum and your uncle Jack and I packed up and came to Western Australia and bought that bloody farm down at Darkan. It was the worst thing we ever did.'

I had heard a lot about the farm at Darkan and I didn't want to hear any more. Besides, I wasn't interested in farms. My interest lay in the open spaces of the pastoral country. 'Tell me about Peedamulla,' I asked, although I had been hearing about Peedamulla, like Koonamore, for years.

'Peedamulla,' he said, looking into the distance as he relit his pipe. 'Not a bad place, but you just couldn't compare it with the saltbush plains out from Peterborough. Now, that was strong country. Saltbush country can carry you through drought after drought, not like the Ashburton. No, Western Australia can't be compared with South Australia. In some ways, I'm sorry your mother and father brought you back. You won't have as good a future here as you would there. But I'm glad you're here.'

The tea and sponge cake arrived. My grandmother sat down with us and we sipped our tea and stared into the fire. I was dying to tell my grandfather about something that happened to me on Mount Augustus, but while she was there I couldn't tell the story the way he would have liked to hear it.

I loved talking with him about my life up north. He loved to hear my stories about horses, especially Mount Augustus horses. He laughed at the stories about shearers and he was curious about my relationships with two blackfellas called Mitchell and Gilbert. Whenever I was in Perth, which was no more than twice a year, I always spent time with him and my grandmother. We had many evening meals followed by long yarns in front of the fire in winter or sitting outside watching the sunset in summer.

On one occasion, when there was a quiet lull, he looked at me and said, 'You're going to be a top station man one day.'

'I hope so,' I said.

'Yes, you will be,' he said. 'I know. It's in your blood.'

All through my youth I felt his presence. He did not do it deliberately, but he set a marker for me when he told me he was an overseer when he was only nineteen. I was impressed – and awed. I did not set out to emulate him, but the standard had been set. He presided over my life. His values were my values. I learned so much from him: the straightness of his thinking, his determination, the knowledge he had accumulated. He was not demonstrative with his affection. It could be said that he erred on the side of sternness. I cherished his company, as I think he cherished mine. We were proud of each other – and we didn't hide it.

I was with him two days before he died, on 17 January 1957. He was eighty-eight and he was a frail shell. His mind was wandering and he could not understand why my mother (Babe, to him) was wearing a wedding ring.

2

Len Boothby

How was I to travel to Koonoona? And why was there any question about this? Well, in those days, travelling from Perth to the eastern states usually meant going by train, which took two or three days. The second option was to travel by ship. The third option was to drive, but people were reluctant to do that. Between Port Augusta, in South Australia, and Southern Cross, in Western Australia, the only route was the Trans Australia Highway (as it was known then), and it was an arduous dirt-road expedition. Bituminisation was not completed until 1976.

My parents decided that it would be quicker and simpler for me to have the luxury of flying overnight to Adelaide, where I would stay a day with my mother's maiden aunts at Poltoonga, and then take the train to Burra. In those days, domestic flights landed at Parafield, north of the city. From there I took the transit bus into town, where I was met by Great-aunt Dorothy. She was so small I felt like a giant standing next to her. Her welcome was bright and warm, and we slipped into a relationship that felt as if it had been going for years. I suppose, in a way, it had been. She was my grandfather's beloved sister, and she was fully informed about me and what I was doing.

At Poltoonga, Mary and Maggie were waiting impatiently. They fussed around me as though I were a young prince the moment I stepped onto the front veranda. The three of them were the same height and I felt I had been captured by a trio of affectionate gnomes. It did not take long to see that Mary was the boss. Not only did the aunts fascinate me, their house fascinated me too. Every room was full of antiques. It was all neat and tidy – and crammed with interest.

My stay was only until mid-afternoon, when I caught the train to Koonoona. But I was to return several times and spend many days with the gracious ladies who had so much to offer me.

As a dutiful son, I wrote to my parents quite regularly. When my mother died in 2001, I found a bundle of my letters in a box. This extract from one tells the story of my introduction to Koonoona:

11 January 1951

I caught the train by myself and the only seat I could get was opposite an old man who started talking immediately. He must have worked on every type of job in Australia. He was going to Sydney, via Broken Hill. He told me an awful lot, but all I said of importance was I was going to Burra to work. Another young chap joined us and as he came from N.S.W. and the old man from Queensland we made a mixed trio.

Mr Boothby was not waiting for me, but an old chap called Colin Williams was. We went out to the station in a Land Rover. Mr Boothby has just bought a house in Adelaide and the other day £100 was stolen from his wife's purse. He had gone to Adelaide to fix things up.

I am in a room with two other men of twenty. The rest of the men are married, living up to an average 1 to 8 miles away in houses on the station's property.

At Koonoona proper there are about 11 men. It is a five day week from 7.30 to 5.30.

One of the chaps is a real cowboy, with a fancy shirt and American high heeled boots and blue jeans.

The Boothby's house is very nice with beautiful gardens and a TENNIS COURT upon which we are ALLOWED TO PLAY. Nobody plays because it is too far to come from their homes, but one of my room mates said he would play, so would you please send my racket over.

Koonoona was not at all what I expected. Life on a merino stud situated in farming country bore little relationship to life on a station. For a start, it was only a few thousand acres, not hundreds of thousands of acres. It was cropped intensively. Apart from the wheat and oats that were sold, much of the crop was used to hard feed the pedigree rams. Hard feed meant chaff and oats and some mineral additives.

There were five lots of forty or fifty rams, each fulfilling criteria laid down by Glen Hawkes, the stud master. Selections from each of these lots would be sent to the annual agricultural shows in every capital city. The criteria related to the needs of each state, hence they were known as the Queensland Lot, the New South Wales Lot, and so on. Each lot had its own paddock. In each paddock there was a large shed, raised three or four feet above ground, where the rams were housed at night. On a regular basis, the rams were inspected and weighed and had their hooves trimmed. This meant walking them into the main shed at the homestead. The station hands and the jackeroos had to take the rams from a pen, one by one, and drag them by the horns to where Glen Hawkes and Len Boothby would check the condition of the fleece and the state of the mouth. The ram holders held the rams by the horns, like handles, with the rams' noses in their groins. Mostly, the rams stood still, but sometimes they were restless and pushed forward with all their strength. If you could feel it coming, you could brace yourself and bear down on their horns. But you didn't always feel it coming and they'd get you by surprise – and that was unpleasant.

Len Boothby was a somewhat remote figure. He was very visible during shearing and at key times, such as when we regularly monitored the progress of the selected lots, and at lamb marking. Otherwise, he was in his office or travelling to talk with clients – the other sheep studs that produced rams in large quantities for farmers and pastoralists. Thus the quality bloodlines were filtered through the breeding system.

Most mornings, the station hands and the jackeroos would gather in the open space outside the workshop, and Gil Moxham, the overseer, would tell us what each of us would be doing that day. Some discussions went on for twenty minutes. We'd all stand around, or squat, and wait. Gil's brother, Derek, always had a couple of sheepdogs with him, messing around, playing. It was quite common for one of the dogs to cock his leg behind Derek's leg, and when that happened someone would yell, 'Hey, Derek. One of yer bloody dogs is pissing on yer trousers.'

Derek would just stand – and he'd say, 'Yeah, bloody mongrel bastard does that all the time.'

From my visits to Moorarie Station with my uncle Jack, I had visualised myself spending most of my time riding a good horse in open country, mustering stock. At Koonoona, my first task was to work with the overseer and his brother in building an above-ground sheep-spray tank. Sheep were annually dipped in a solution that would keep pests at bay. The base of the tank had concrete perimeter walls, and the inside was filled with gravel and topped with a concrete floor. There were channels in the floor for the spray to run back into a below-ground tank, from which it was pumped and recycled. We dug the hole for the below-ground tank by hand. We mixed the concrete by hand. A large sheet of tin was laid on the ground, and on that we mixed sand, gravel and cement with shovels.

The sand and gravel were dug out of creek beds and watercourses that ran out from the low-lying hills nearby. I spent several days on the end of a shovel, working with Gil Moxham and his brother, Derek. Mixing the concrete was hard and tedious. Digging gravel out of the creek beds and heaving it up and onto the back of the truck was worse. The gravel was water-washed stones, some of them big enough to stop my shovel as I thrust it in. The sudden jolt when the shovel, with my weight and strength behind it, came to an abrupt halt jarred my stomach muscles as if I'd been hit by a heavyweight boxer. I hated it. And all the while, Gil and his brother kept up a steady pace, digging and shovelling, as if it were child's play. Their hands were big and callused; their bodies were strong and hardened by years of this sort of work. I struggled to keep up, especially as the blisters on both my hands multiplied through the day. It was no wonder I died every night after dinner.

The spray tank was finished just in time for shearing. Then I worked in the yards with the others. The tank was set up about three feet above ground level. We drove the sheep up a ramp and packed them into the tank. With the doors at both ends closed, the sheep were sprayed from jets above. When they were thoroughly soaked they were let out the other side and the next batch then followed them in.

Compared to mixing concrete by hand, working with the rams was easy. But it was only a lull, a brief period of restoration before the next physical challenge: cutting chaff.

A team of us drove to an old farmhouse about ten minutes from the main homestead. The farmhouse was set up for chaff cutting. Nobody told me what to expect. All information and instructions were left until the last moment. The chaffcutter was in a back room and the chaff was discharged through a chute into a front room. The chute was divided into two outlets, which went straight down into the bags. When one was open the other was closed, so a full bag could be removed and the flow of chaff directed to the other side. It took just over a minute for a bag to fill, during which time the two men on the sewing had no time to scratch themselves. The air was clouded with dust and chaff particles, which permeated their clothes. If they failed to sew a bag in time and get a new bag in place, there would be chaff piling up on the floor and the overseer would be all over them, giving them hell. Two other men hovered in the background, grabbing the bags as they were sewn up and stacking them in another room.

Gil Moxham worked in the back room, guiding the sheaves of hay onto the conveyor and cutting and removing the twine that bound each sheaf. I was outside on the haystack, in the sun, pitchfork in hand, flicking the sheaves headfirst onto the start of the conveyor belt. To begin with, it was pleasant work: driving the fork into the sheaf, just behind the twine that bound it together, and then swinging the pitchfork with the sheaf on the end and tossing it over to the chaffcutter, facing the right way, in the right place, so Gil could grab it and place it on the belt.

Yes, it was very pleasant at the start of the day, with the smell of new-mown hay, a long, slender-handled pitchfork in my hands, a warm sun and a rhythmic task. It didn't stay pleasant. After an hour the blisters returned. After two hours, when it was time for smoko, my arms and shoulders were aching. There was no way to ease the pressure. I was out there, on the stack, the sole supplier of sheaves of hay for that damned chaffcutter and its insatiable appetite. If I slowed for a moment, I got a rocket from the overseer.

The hours we worked were the same as in the shearing sheds:

7.30	to	9.30	work
9.30	to	10.00	morning smoko
10.00	to	12.00	work
12.00	to	1.00	lunch break
1.00	to	3.00	work
3.00	to	3.30	afternoon smoko
3.30	to	5.30	work

At the lunch-time break I was so tired I felt I couldn't continue. My whole body ached. The blisters on my hands had burst and the skin was red raw. On top of that, I was being burned by the sun and the wind in spite of my broad-brimmed hat. I wanted to crawl away somewhere and hide. I was in despair. I couldn't see how I could work through the afternoon. I didn't dare say a word to anyone about how I felt – although, in retrospect, I think Gil and everyone else could see my distress. They would have shrugged their shoulders and said to themselves: he'll learn.

But as I sat there on the concrete floor with the rest of the men, in the cool of the bag-sewing room, eating my lunch and drinking cold, weak, unsweetened black tea from a flagon, I gradually recovered my spirits. Then, in the blink of an eye, the hour's break was over and it was all go again. Reluctantly, I went outside into the full heat of the day and up onto the haystack. I picked up the pitchfork and thought about how I could hold it and use it in a way that minimised the blistering.

By the time we stopped for the afternoon smoko, my despair had changed to a combination of depression and panic. How was I going to tell Gil I couldn't continue? I hated the hay; I hated the chaff; I hated Gil Moxham and everyone else on the team. But I still had to keep my mouth shut. Then, in the fourth and final two-hour session of the day, a strange thing happened: my exhaustion began to evaporate, the blisters hurt less, the sheaves of hay seemed lighter, I enjoyed the rhythm of swinging and tossing the sheaves, and I started to like Gil Moxham again. I had stopped calling him names under my breath. But I was glad when the work had finished and the clattering chaffcutter was shut down and there was stillness and silence.

Those of us who lived at the homestead were returned there, and those who lived elsewhere went to their cottages. Gil Moxham always spent half an hour with Len Boothby, reporting on the day's production and whatever other matters overseers talked to the boss about. I showered and changed into clean clothes for dinner. There was a men's dining room adjoining the kitchen, and I ate there with the other station hands and the other jackeroo, Bob Money, plus the cook and her husband, who was the yardman. After a day of work, like mixing concrete by hand, I would head straight to bed. At other times, when the day had been less exhausting, we'd play cards. They taught me to play poker and pontoon, and we played for small change.

16 January 1951

On Saturday afternoon, Colin and I went for a ride. On Sunday afternoon we had a water fight with Arthur, the overseer's son. That night Mr Boothby came home. I had to work hard yesterday, shovelling sand and gravel. We didn't stop work till 6.30. Today we spent chaff cutting. Just because it's my first time we had to do 345 bags, 100 more than the previous record.

Would you please send over my saddle cloth, mirror and running shoes?

There is a race meeting at Black Springs and they have a 100 yards foot race for which I will enter.

22 January 1951

On Friday night, a new chap arrived from W.A. He is Jack Money's son Bob. He had five suitcases in which were five suits, one of them a dinner suit. Since he has arrived here he hasn't lifted a hand to help himself and all the time says 'Ian, you're the youngest, you go & do it.' He is a stone heavier & much stronger than I and I nearly got bashed because I wouldn't get him any ice water last night when he ORDERED me to. I've had him already.

Bob Money and I were moved from the men's quarters to a room in a small building alongside the south veranda of the homestead. The western end of this veranda led to the back of the building, and the entrance to the kitchen and the men's dining room. Our room had no flyscreen on the window and no flywire door. On hot nights it was too stifling to keep the door and window shut – and that was an open invitation to the mosquitoes. They swarmed in. Bob and I sought refuge under sheets, but they still got to us. They bit me on my feet, ankles and hands, and the irritation woke me in the middle of the night. Then I went outside to a tap and ran cold water over my feet and hands until the itching went away. Bob mostly slept through the night and didn't feel a thing.

No-one at Koonoona became a special friend, least of all Bob Money. But I had allies and, of all my allies, the one who always gave me attention was the cook. Perhaps she felt I needed mothering. She was thin and bony, and she neglected her appearance. But she was always clean. Her hair was grey and wispy, and she didn't wear make-up. She smoked – and coughed. She had a penchant for crème de menthe, which she drank from small liqueur glasses in the hotel favoured by the Koonoona mob when we went to Burra on Saturdays. She seemed to own a corner of the main bar, where there was a table and chairs, and she held court with her mates from town. She liked to beckon me over from where I was standing, leaning on the bar with the men, drinking beer. She'd make me sit down and taste her crème de menthe and have a few words with her middle-aged lady friends. That stretched my patience, because I wanted to be back at the bar with my schooner of beer and not wasting time with the old biddies. She had a croaky voice and she liked to say, 'I've actually got a very good singing voice – it's just got a rough passage out.'

Her eyes were dark brown, almost black. Whether I was at the bar with the men or in the dining room at Koonoona or getting in the way in the kitchen, whenever I glanced in her direction, our eyes would meet. Sometimes she'd smile, but not always.

In my aloneness as a sixteen-year-old boy, I drew comfort from my occasional contact with Len Boothby, not that he gave me much time to chat. But when we were alone he gave me his full attention and I felt we connected in some way.

He frightened the life out of me one evening, though. We'd had an afternoon handling the rams, and they had been taken down from the shed through the yards and out onto the road. Everyone had gone except for the two of us. As two horsemen herded the rams to their paddock, Mr Boothby and I turned to walk back through one yard after another to get to the shed, to tidy up. I was following a few yards behind him. When we went through the first gate, he suddenly turned and faced me and shook his walking stick at me. I thought, shit, he's going to belt me; what have I done? It seemed to me he was glaring at me. Then, with a heavy tone, he said, 'Ian. Always remember to close every gate behind you.'

And with that, he turned and continued to limp through the yards with the aid of his stick. I was shaken. He offered no explanation, but I didn't need one. I worked out why. As we went through yard after yard, I closed every gate behind us. And to this day I have a compulsion to close every open gate I see.

Len Boothby certainly had a knack for getting his message across. I think he made an impact on me because he probably chose his moment to deliver his messages: it was always a quiet time; there were only ever the two of us; there were no distractions; he got my attention; and he did not repeat himself. No wonder I respected him.

After I had been at Koonoona for two months, Mr Boothby called me into his office late one afternoon. He told me to sit down. He then told me that 'they' were very pleased with me and 'they' were going to increase my pay from £2 10s a week to £3. No-one else was getting a pay rise, so I was asked to keep it to myself. He went on to say, 'People tell me you're always very civil. That's good, Ian. Keep it that way.' He used the word *civil* very deliberately.

I hadn't been conscious that I was being particularly polite: I simply behaved the way I had been taught, especially by my father. As I walked away along the veranda, I could hardly contain the thrill of the pay rise. Another ten shillings a week! I thought, what am I going to do with all that extra money?

In late March we did a week of lamb marking. All the young lambs had their ears notched with a distinctive shape that identified them, their tails were docked, and the males that had a flaw somewhere were castrated. Len Boothby, Glen Hawkes and Gil Moxham did the work with the knives. The station hands and the jackeroos picked up the lambs and, holding the front and back legs together on each side, rested the lambs' rumps on a wide plank fixed to the top rail of one side of a yard. This presented the tails and the scrotums, better known as purses, to the three men on the other side. In

1951, elastrators were just being introduced, but the Koonoona philosophy was to stick with the tried and true. It was simple and quick. A razor-sharp knife, a slice through the second joint in the tail, and it was done. The lamb was then placed carefully on the ground, with a thin stream of blood from the stump squirting out about eighteen inches. The flow soon slowed and stopped, and in about a week the stump was healed. For the female lambs that was all there was to it. For the males it was another story.

Every male lamb was checked by Glen Hawkes. He examined its wool, what there was of it. He checked for physical deformities, especially in the mouth: undershot or overshot jaws were not acceptable. And he checked for blemishes such as brown or black marks or spots. A purebred Merino ram had to have a pure white fleece. He couldn't see the back of the lamb because it was resting up against the holder – but the holder could see when he picked it up, and he had to tell Mr Hawkes if there was a mark.

If he found a problem, he castrated first and then docked the tail. This was sensible, because if he did the tail first, there would be a stream of blood coming at him while he worked on the purse. Mr Hawkes used his teeth to pull the testicles out. This technique was effective and was widespread around Australia. The top of the purse was sliced off, and a forefinger and thumb squeezed the bottom to stop the testicles retreating. Then they were removed by the teeth, one by one. An alternative was to use fingers, but this was difficult because the testicles were slimy and slippery. Another alternative was to use a knife with a special hook at the end of the handle to grip the cord at the base of the testicle. Neither of these alternatives was practical for Mr Hawkes because he only had one hand: the other arm was amputated from low on the forearm. Although he managed to use the stump of his arm to good effect, without two hands Mr Hawkes had no alternative but to use his teeth.

While he was busy checking for defects, the man holding the lamb often let his attention drift, sometimes exchanging comments with whoever was beside him holding for Mr Boothby or Gil. At least once, but not more than twice, every lamb-tailing session, one of the men would wake from his reverie and, as Glen Hawkes finished his inspection and docked the tail, the holder would say, 'Aw shit, boss. This little bugger's got a black spot on his back. Sorry. I forgot to tell yer.'

Mr Hawkes would curse and bend over and slice off the top of the purse and pull the testicles out with his teeth. The spurt of blood from the stump of the tail spattered his face and glasses as he bent down, and it made a bloody patch on the front of his shirt. He could never be sure if it was really an oversight on the part of the man holding the lamb – or whether it was deliberate. All the men kept a straight face, but when they joked about it at the end of the day I learned that Mr Hawkes had been set up. They thought it was a big laugh. It wasn't that they disliked him or wanted to pay him back for some offence, although he was pretty stuffy at times. But they didn't ever play that trick on Mr Boothby or Gil. They had too much respect for Mr Boothby – and Gil, well, I suspect Gil was a wake-up to the joke and it would have been unwise to do it to him.

Being young and raw, I was often the butt of practical jokes. It was never malicious, just harmless baiting. When we were working in the small shearing shed at the homestead (the main shearing shed was seven miles away), I was sent to the blacksmith's shop, up the rise, a quarter of a mile away, to bring back a left-handed hammer – or a sky hook, or some other nonexistent tool. Then I had to suffer gibes from the blacksmith. His reply never explained that I had been sent on a wild-goose chase. It was, 'Tell those pricks at the shearing shed to get their own sky hook.' I trudged back down the slope and passed on the message, and this was followed by cackling and smirking and a variety of smart-aleck comments that I struggled to comprehend.

'Don't worry, mate. Roll yerself a smoke,' someone said with a grin, offering me the makings. I declined politely.

'Aw, come on, for Christ's sake, roll yerself a smoke.'

'No thanks,' I said. 'I just don't like smoking.' It wasn't a question of feeling as though I would be doing something wrong or unhealthy: we were not aware at that time of the health issues. It was simply that I didn't like the taste of cigarettes.

'Jesus, you're bloody unsociable,' some bloke said.

'You'll smoke. Everyone does,' someone else said.

'No. I don't want to. I don't like it,' I said, digging in.

'Tell yer what, mate. The loneliness of the bush'll git to yer and then yer'll smoke.'

But I didn't ever smoke. And the loneliness of the bush never did get to me.

There were times when I wondered whether I was there to learn about merino sheep or there as a labourer. So much of what I did was sheer physical hard work – like wheat pickling, a process that prevents rust, a fungal disease. Two of us were assigned to do the lumping for the contract wheat pickler. The mobile wheat pickler was set up outside a large shed with a mountain of bags of seed wheat inside. Our job was to heave one of the 180-pound bags onto a shoulder to carry it, hurry to the pickler, put the bag on the ground, slash the string that closed the bag and then tip the contents into a bin. From there, the wheat was sucked through the pickler and back out into a bag, which was then sewn up. We then had to hoick the bag up from the ground and put it in a new stack. The other chap and I were on the run all day. As the eight hours of picking up and carrying 180-pound bags of wheat progressed, the bags got heavier and heavier. Rolling a bag from a head-high stack onto your shoulder was easy. But when the stack had been whittled away until the bags were below waist level, it was harder. The technique for lifting big bags off the ground was to stand the bag on one end, lean it against your legs, bend over and put your arms around the bottom of the bag, close to the ground, and in one movement, pivoting the top of the bag in your belly, swing the bottom up and over your shoulder. I wasn't conscious of it at the time, but I was getting stronger and fitter by the day.

* * *

Over the weekend before Easter in 1951 it rained heavily and those of us living at the Koonoona homestead played cards for hours. We played in the men's dining room. It had two doors. One gave access from outside, the other opened into the kitchen – and stayed open. Mostly we played poker, with jackpots. This meant someone must have at least a pair of jacks before the players could discard and draw new cards. Maybe that's where the term jackpot originated. It was a new world for me: in the company of adults, playing cards for money. The stakes were just high enough for me to feel fearful when the bidding was competitive and I was holding a hand that was problematic. To my delight, by Sunday night I was in front by about four pounds, more than a week's wages. I was very pleased with myself. I could hardly wait to spend some or all of my winnings. I wrote to Aunt Mary and asked if I could go to Adelaide for Easter and stay at Poltoonga. Her reply arrived in time for me to catch the late train on Thursday.

The aunts were curious about this sudden turn of events and I enthusiastically told them of my good fortune. Being card players themselves, they would be impressed, I figured. Their reaction, I thought, was subdued, even disappointed. The best Aunt Mary could say was, 'That's very nice, dear.'

After my success at Koonoona, I thought my new-found card-playing skills would help me to defeat the trio of maiden aunts around the rummy table. But again I was no match for them. I consoled myself with the thought that my poker skills were different from the skills needed for rummy.

In the ease of our growing familiarity, I stopped thinking of them as 'great aunts'. In any case, 'great-aunt' was too much of a mouthful for everyday conversation, and, like my mother, I referred to them as 'aunts' or 'the aunts in Adelaide'. In this relaxed ambience, on Easter Sunday, Aunt Mary created an opportunity to talk to me alone on the front veranda. 'Dear,' she said, 'you know we love seeing you and you're welcome here whenever you want to come. But we do wish you wouldn't play cards for money.'

I couldn't find anything to say, except 'OK.' Meaning: I hear you. Aunt Mary was so sweet and so earnest that I certainly wasn't going to protest. And I wasn't going to make any promises I had no intention of keeping. So we left it at that. Of course, I didn't agree with her, but I loved her all the more for her concern.

Shortly after Easter, Len Boothby called me into his office and said, 'You've done three months jackerooing. Now it's time for you to learn about being a station hand.'

I just looked at him, waiting.

'Yes,' he said. 'I'm going to take you up to Winnininnie and you can work there for a while.'

Winnininnie was a station owned by Koonoona, seventy-odd miles northeast of Peterborough, on the road to Broken Hill. And this was getting into Koonamore territory; this was getting close to that place of family legends and memories; this was a whole new adventure.

Later, I realised that Koonoona was really a finishing school. Other jackeroos were born to the life, but I was city raised and a couple of school holidays at Moorarie didn't count as real experience. Now I was to learn the fundamentals that other jackeroos already knew.

Mr Boothby drove me up to Winnininnie in his Chev ute. That ute always seemed to me to be a very powerful motor vehicle. It was solid and had plenty of grunt, and Mr Boothby liked to put his foot down and let it surge. From time to time I'd glance at him – lolling back in his seat, left hand on the wheel, right elbow resting in the open window, cigarette in the corner of his mouth – and I'd think, this ute and he suit each other. He spoke very little, his mind elsewhere. But he did interrupt his train of thought now and then as we rolled along the highway, with the railway track just to our right. We passed a road going to the west, with a sign pointing to 'Peterborough', and he said, 'Peterborough's the nearest big town to Winnininnie. It was where your grandfather did business when he was running Koonamore.'

As the ute swallowed the miles, the country graduated from cultivated farms to the open pastoral lands of stations, and I had my first sighting of the legendary blue-grey saltbush plains. Sixty miles from Peterborough, we cruised through Yunta. I caught a glimpse of the pub and the scattering of buildings: houses and sheds. 'Twelve miles to go,' he said.

A mile or so from the turn off, Mr Boothby pointed to a clutch of white buildings to the left, two miles from the highway, huddled at the base of a long, dark range of hills. 'There it is,' he said. 'Winnininnie.'

We turned onto a gravel road that dipped down into a flat watercourse before rising up a long slope to the homestead. The manager was Ken Wade. He and his wife occupied the homestead along with their only child, a son called Ian, who was mostly at boarding school. Winnininnie was a small station. It was rough and stony, and in many places the hills were too steep to ride a horse over. Considering the hills and ranges over most of the property, if it had been ironed out flat it would have been twice the size. Between the ranges there were vast saltbush flats.

Ken Wade came out to greet us. Then we all headed inside for the ritual cup of tea, me lugging my suitcase. Just as we got to the door, a lanky young bloke joined us. This was Bill Moxham, a son of Gil Moxham. He was nineteen and, by my standards, an old hand. Although we didn't think in such terms then, Bill was to be my guide and mentor. Most of his guidance took me in the right direction, but some of it didn't. Although we didn't come to any harm, we could have been in trouble several times.

Sitting around the table drinking tea was not where I wanted to be. It didn't suit Bill either, and he said, 'D'you reckon I should take this bloke over to 'is quarters?'

Len Boothby nodded and said, 'Keep up the good work, Ian.'

We shook hands for the last time and I went with Bill.

3

Bill Moxham

It felt as though I was putting more and more distance between me and my parents: going first to Adelaide and the aunts, then to Burra and Koonoona, and now here – a hundred miles from Broken Hill, almost to the border of New South Wales. No sooner had I connected to Len Boothby than he sent me off to start again with strangers.

Well, Ken Wade and his wife looked like kind people. They were in their late thirties, which seemed old to me. Bill Moxham had a rough feel about him. He was loose-limbed and gangly but there was nothing loose or gangly about the way he talked. He was sure of himself and of his authority over me.

Between the homestead and the men's quarters, there was a wide, deep, dry creek bed. We walked along a track that took us down into the creek and up the other side. I'd never seen such a stony place and, wonder of wonders, right in the middle of the creek there was a six-foot-high structure built entirely of stone. It was long and narrow and came to a point where it faced floods coming out of the hills. It looked like a solid stone boat stuck in the middle of nowhere. Up on top, in the middle of this mound, there was a windmill. Bill told me later that the mill pumped water from a well 180 feet deep and all the rock that was dug out of the well was used to build the structure that would protect the well and the mill against floods. No-one could ever explain to me why it was necessary to dig a well in the middle of a creek bed and not somewhere else nearby.

On the bank on the other side was a long, whitewashed stone building. It had three rooms, each with a door opening onto a three-foot-wide ledge that ran the length of the building. It was too narrow to call a veranda. Three steps of stone took you from ground level to the ledge. This was the men's quarters and Bill and I were to share a room there, fortunately one with a fireplace. I loved the old stone walls and the feel of the place immediately. But my first priority was to get the measure of Bill.

Over the following months, Bill and I grew easy with each other. Our room became home and I slipped into a sense of belonging. It was very familiar and reassuring to walk down through the creek and over to the homestead for breakfast and dinner, prepared by Mrs Wade. The table we ate at had a small forest of sauce bottles and condiments and jam jars in the middle. No matter how much we ate for dinner, we always finished off with a slice of bread and jam.

The original settlement at Winnininnie was a police station. The stone building was quite substantial and was 200 yards up towards the hills from the homestead. It was in good condition but it wasn't used. Bill reckoned the history of the place kept people out of it. He showed me several graves. 'This is where they buried the copper and his wife and their kids. Poor bastards died of ptomaine poisoning from eating canned fish that'd been open too long,' he said.

I took his word for it. I didn't believe in ghosts, but after hearing that story, the building always had an ominous look about it to me. Maybe that was just because it was standing there, isolated, empty in a barren landscape. There was no glass in the windows to give off reflections, and the interior was dark, even on a sunny summer's day. I often had the feeling someone was inside, in the shadows, looking out, watching.

You may wonder why a police station was located in such a godforsaken place. There was a permanent spring in the foothills just behind, as there were in many places on Winnininnie. But the water supply couldn't have been good enough or reliable enough to meet the needs of a small population when they built the homestead, else why dig a well through almost solid rock in the middle of the creek?

Anyway, the water from the well at the homestead was not good enough to drink, which was why the homestead and the men's quarters had rainwater tanks for drinking water. The same was true of nearly all the bores and wells dotted around the station: the water was unfit for human consumption. There were also many dams, but these weren't much use to us either, because it was quite common to find the floating carcass of a sheep or a kangaroo or, on one occasion, a dead horse in a partly decomposed state.

When we were mustering, we tried carrying water in a water bag that was shaped to fit under the neck and against the chest of the horse. It was secured by a leather strap around the base of the neck and by another strap that went between the front legs to the girth. That was not very successful, because the horses didn't like it, especially when they had to trot or canter. Winnininnie horses were quick to put their heads down and pig-root. When one did that with me, the stopper jerked out of the water-bag spout and water splashed over the horse's head and into its ears. That just made it buck all the harder until the bag was empty.

At Winnininnie, I began my education as a stockman and as a horseman. But it was an education lacking in quality horsemanship, as I was to discover later at Mount Augustus. Meanwhile, not knowing any better, I accepted the situation at Winnininnie: horses that were a very mixed bunch in terms of their breeding – and worse, horses that had not been well handled and schooled. Nearly all of them bucked or pig-rooted when we mounted up in the morning and every second time we dismounted to open and close a gate. No matter how long the day had been, they still found the energy to try and dump us on the way home. Several times they caught me by surprise. Just when I thought my horse was settled and content to stroll home, down went the head and the buck was on. Up he'd go, coming back down on four stiff legs that jolted me loose in the saddle and jarred my teeth. If I was unprepared, there was a mad scramble to gather up the reins, get hold of the monkey grip and hang on until it stopped. On four occasions the horse won and I lost. Losing meant trudging back to the homestead in my high-heeled riding boots and having to put up with jeers from Bill and Mr Wade at the horse yards, my horse having arrived back long before. Did they consider going to look for me? I don't think so. When I got to about a mile away, I knew they could see me coming up the slope, and I knew they wouldn't jump in a vehicle and fetch me.

Until I went to Winnininnie, I had never seen a monkey grip on a saddle. A monkey grip is a home-made handle that a rider can grasp with his right hand to brace himself against falling off when a horse bucks. It was made from a long leather thong that was connected to a D-ring on the right side of the pommel, ran to another D four inches away and then back through the first D, and so on until there were about five strands. The remainder of the thong was wound tightly round these strands so many times you couldn't see the strands. Then it was knotted to the first D. It was a snug fit for the four fingers of your right hand but you had to be careful not to lose skin off your knuckles.

Before we mounted up in the morning, to ease the tension we walked our horses at least 150 yards before tightening the girth and surcingle. That usually prompted a few pig-roots. When that was over, we made sure we had a firm grip of the reins and the monkey grip before swinging up. Usually – especially on cold mornings, when the temperature was around four degrees – the horses tried to buck. That's when our knuckles, white with the cold, lost some skin. Did we think of wearing gloves? Not at all: we were Australian stockmen, not American cowboys! We reckoned riding gloves were just for show. But without the monkey grips, there is no doubt we would have been pelted many times more than we were.

Our only concession to vanity was to buy R.M. Williams riding boots with the highest heels available. I thought the Santa Fe boots were the best – much more stylish than the regular round-toed boots with the Cuban heel. When the boots arrived from mail order, Bill and I brought out the last, the hammer, the tacks, the sharp knife and the thick sole leather and increased the height of the heels by another inch. Thus shod, we tottered around admiring each other and ourselves. We put up with the inconvenience of hobbling along on rough ground, but it's a wonder we didn't break an ankle.

On one of my few trips to Adelaide as a bushie-in-the-making, I felt compelled to visit the R.M. Williams emporium. For a young stockman always half-drunk on the romance of the bush, it was a treasure trove. The smell of leather hit me the moment I walked in the door. There were racks of saddles, pegs dripping with bridles and head collars, displays of saddlebags and quart-pot carriers and stockwhips and belts – and shelf upon shelf of boots, the best boots in the world. And clothing: moleskin and gabardine trousers, cotton shirts, leather coats. And hats, broad brimmed, medium brimmed, short brimmed, high crowned, low crowned, grey, brown, black, white. There was equipment for racing, camping, polo and hunting. There were knives, saddlery tools, even books and jewellery. I realised why the name R.M. Williams was legendary.

Wearing R.M. Williams boots – with the little pull-on tags at the front and the back, bearing the name R.M. Williams and the address (5 Percy St. Prospect, Sth. Australia) – supplied instantly recognisable identity, anywhere in Australia. If you thought a bloke might be from the bush, a quick glance at his boots and trousers gave you the answer.

In the early fifties, country Australians were just beginning to concede that American jeans might be acceptable here. To many people, jeans were a corrosion of dyed-in-the-wool Australian culture, yet another Americanisation of our values. I agreed with that. But R.M. Williams accepted the dictates of the market and started making and selling jeans. It was a long time before I capitulated and stepped out of my moleskins and into denim. It felt like treason. Apart from that, compared to moleskins, denim was stiff and hard until it had been washed about fifty times. Moleskins are also stiff after you've washed them, but they soften up more quickly than jeans.

I wanted to buy a pair of moleskin trousers but I had trouble getting a size to fit. The shop assistant came up with the right answer. 'Why don't we make you a couple of pairs to measure?' he asked.

'Made to measure? Do you do that? How much more will that cost?'

'We do it all the time. No extra cost. I'll get the tape measure.'

When the trouser measuring was done and the details recorded, he then said, 'Now, what about boots? Why don't we measure you up for boots?'

'Sure,' I said. 'Why not?'

It was heady stuff. I embraced the concept of clothes made to measure for me. I felt very important. Tailor-made moleskins, tailor-made boots – what next? With my details in their files, R.M. Williams continued to make my trousers and boots to measure. Moleskin trousers cost £4 7s 9d, and Santa Fe boots cost £4 5s 9d. When we converted to decimalised currency, a pound was the equivalent of two dollars. I ordered off their 1952 catalogue, which I still have. It has fifty-two pages of every conceivable thing a bushie could want. Well, almost everything.

When I first mustered the northwesternmost corner of Winnininnie it was at shearing time and there were two extra stockmen to help out. One was a fellow called David Grant, from Geraldton – another jackeroo from Koonoona.

It had taken us two and a half hours to ride to Wattle paddock, and Bill sent us off separately to muster. An hour later, from where I sat on my horse, Koonamore homestead was about twenty-five miles further north, as the crow flies across the saltbush plains.

Somewhere out there was that place of legend. I paused for a few minutes, sending my mind on a journey of its own, way out into the distance. But all I could see through the haze were vague images from family photos. And I could hear my grandfather's voice and I could see him, sucking on his pipe, and I wanted to tell him, 'I'm nearly there, Granddad. I'm nearly there.'

The day was stinking hot. There was not the slightest breeze to cool the sweat on my forehead. In my saddlebag, the water in the metal water bottle was hot. Although it was only mid-morning, I could feel my arms already burning in the relentless sun. Foolishly, just to be like the other blokes, I'd made the mistake of tearing off the sleeves of my shirt at the shoulders.

To my right, I could see far off the motionless fans of the windmill and the sun glinting on the water in the tank, where we were to meet. I stirred my horse and worked through the country I'd been told to muster. Hills, stones, dry creek beds with white-trunked eucalypts, saltbush where the hills gave way to undulating country that gradually flattened out to the plains that went on through the shimmer to the horizon – and Koonamore. Heat pressed down from on high. Heat came back off the stones and the earth. Heat came off my horse. Sweat saturated my hat where it gripped my forehead. A dense black assembly of flies competed for space on the sweat patch on my back.

A small mob of sheep, clustered in some filtered shade, reluctantly moved out at my insistence. They picked their way out of the hills and I headed them towards the windmill. When I arrived, the others were already there. The collection so far, about 120 out of the 650 we had to move. The mob, such as it was, sniffed the water in the trough and stood, waiting. Bill, David and the fourth member of our team, Wally Childers, sat hunched in the narrow shade of the tank. There was no campfire on which to boil a billy – fires were banned for fear of starting a bushfire. I took my crib out of my saddlebag, along with the metal bottle of hot water, and joined them. Bill was pissed off.

'Jesus, this fuckin water tastes shithouse.'

'You can say that again,' said Wally. 'Beats me how the bloody sheep can drink it. It's gotta be the worst water in the fuckin world. I can't drink it. And m'water bottle is so bloody hot I can't hardly hold it.'

David said, 'I reckon it's salt. Too much salt.'

'I don't give a shit what it is,' said Wally. 'You'd think the boss would fix us up with something drinkable. But he doesn't give a bugger.'

'And these bloody flies,' said Bill. 'I'm fed up with them.'

David was tall and rangy, a good-looking young bloke. Wally was a little bit older than the rest of us. He was a station hand, employed to help out during shearing. After that he'd go to some other station. It wasn't hard to find work in those days. Bill was in charge, because he was permanent and knew the station.

After we'd had a spell, Bill roused us up. We reset the saddles on the horses, tightened the girths and surcingles, mounted and headed out, taking the line that Bill told us to. 'We'll go up this way north and when we get to the corner we'll swing west. We'll come back across the line of those hills. My guess is that the big mob will be out there to our left. We'll pick em up and collect this lot by the windmill. They won't go far from here. Ian, you muster in from the fence again. David, you muster in from Ian. Wal, you know where to go. See you lot back here in about two hours.'

Four o'clock in the afternoon and it was still baking hot. We opened the gate into the next paddock and pushed the mob through. There they were free to go where they liked. From a management point of view, they were one paddock closer to the shearing shed and would be mustered again and moved closer, paddock by paddock.

The four of us set off on the two-and-a-half-hour ride south to the homestead, mostly walking, sometimes trotting, and occasionally cantering. As the sun sank lower and lower, it seemed to stay suspended on the horizon and to get bigger and closer. The heat on my right arm intensified. My upper arm was scarlet and already blistered – the price I paid for having fair skin. It was torture. There was no escape, no protection. The others, with their brown, suntanned skin, were indifferent. Our route took us through miles of saltbush and scattered, spindly gumtrees and bushes, until we came to where the plateau ended at the edge of a steep drop down to the homestead buildings clustered on both sides of the rocky creek bed.

By seven o'clock, the horses were unsaddled, hosed down and fed. By 7.30 we were at the table having dinner. We'd ridden out at 7.30 in the morning. Ken Wade sat with us for a while, wanting to know exactly how many sheep we'd moved, was the windmill pumping OK, were the horses OK? Then we walked back down and across the creek and up the other side to our rooms. We listened to the radio and talked for a while, and turned in. The next day I wore a shirt with long sleeves.

We listened to the radio a lot. At night, we could pick up radio stations in Queensland, New South Wales, Victoria and South Australia. The dial of the radio was crowded with signals, but there were a couple of country-and-western stations in New South Wales we listened to the most. We heard the songs of Slim Dusty, Tex Morton, Smoky Dawson, Buddy Williams, Reg Lindsay, Wilf Carter, Hank Williams, Roy Acuff and many other greats whose names I can't remember. We heard them so often we memorised the words, and I taught myself to yodel.

My big favourite was Harry Torrani. His recording career ended in 1942 but a decade later his music was still being played regularly. Harry Torrani was English and he was renowned as the world's greatest yodeller, even better than the Swiss. His songs were interspersed with long passages of yodelling that were inventive and imaginative. Riding along in the paddock in the course of a muster, I sang my heart out. I sang the same songs over and over until I was word perfect and yodel perfect. To my ear, my yodels were an echo of the best. What better life could I have? I rode willing horses through the saltbush and stands of mulga and eucalypts in the bright, warm sun – singing at the top of my voice. In my mind I wasn't just entertaining myself, I was entertaining all those people who had come to hear me and I was giving it to them with all the feeling I could raise. Mr Wade asked me late one afternoon why I was sounding a bit hoarse when I spoke.

As at Koonoona, there was plenty of hard yakka at Winnininnie. Again I had to work on a spray dip, this time digging the hole in the ground for the cistern. It was six feet deep and six feet in diameter, and every square inch had to be chipped out with a crowbar. It took us two days. However, we didn't have to do the concreting and build the thing. That was done by a contractor with a team of blokes.

Bill taught me how to kill a sheep and dress it. He and Ken Wade taught me how to build fences. We branded and cut cattle, throwing the beasts on the ground and roping them and holding their heads down. We toiled in the heat and we slogged it out in the wind and the sleet. And it was all good. I relished everything.

Of all the different kinds of work I did at Winnininnie, I enjoyed mustering the most. One of the joys of mustering was discovery. Because I was new to Winnininnie, every paddock was new country for exploration. I was always heading off into the unknown. Sometimes, as I rode along, I had saltbush plains in front and, beyond that, layer upon layer of ranges painted in washed-out blues and purples. At other times I rode through deep, narrow valleys and gorges. One of the paddocks in the middle of the station was called Federation, and this was the roughest of all. And pretty much in the middle of Federation, a spring emanated from a hillside, in a gorge with almost perpendicular rocky sides. There was a thick, white sandy patch of ground around a deep, clear pool with a handful of white-trunked eucalypts along one side. It was such a beautiful place I wanted to live there. And it was such a contrast to the saltbush plains across much of the station that I felt I was in another state, like the Northern Territory.

In this country we mustered long-legged wethers that could outrun our horses in the hills. They'd take one look at us and they'd be off, usually straight up the side of a hill, skipping blithely from rock to rock, pausing at the crest to look back at us and sneer, before disappearing over the other side. It was folly to follow them. That meant dismounting and leading my horse, with both of us scrambling to find a way up. I tried it once and it was terrifying. Three times my horse stumbled and went down on its knees, and my heart was in my mouth because I thought we'd both tumble the forty yards to the bottom. We learned to abandon the chase and, instead, ride around the hill and block the sheep as they got to the bottom on the other side. But you had to be quick to head them off before they went up the next hill, which was very close. It was frustrating, but it was also fun and exhilarating because it involved hard, fast riding over very rough ground.

In the winter, the country was so cold I felt the winds were blowing all the way from the Snowy Mountains. At times we rode through fog so dense I could see only fifty yards in any direction. When we found sheep, it was by accident. You may well ask, why muster when the fog is like that? The answer is that it wasn't like that when we started; it could descend on you as if it were a vast cloud floating down to rest on the ground. Sometimes it was patchy and thin. And sometimes the wind would rise, and the fog would be swept away like wispy smoke, and the sun and the vista would break through. And always the cold was biting, especially if there was wind. I rode with my right hand thrust into a coat pocket, leaving the other hand exposed, holding the reins. After a while, I wouldn't be able to move my fingers and unlock my grip: I would have to withdraw my right hand, prise loose my frozen fingers, white with cold, and massage them back to life. As Bill used to say, 'It's so fuckin cold it'd freeze the balls off a brass monkey.'

Another part of my horse education that was seriously at odds with my later experience at Mount Augustus was the business of shoeing. As is usually the case when you're young and you're learning about something for the first time, you accept what you're taught without question. Nevertheless, the way they handled shoeing at Winnininnie was very daunting and even complicated. Watching what was going on made me wonder if I would ever be able to master the task.

Bill and Mr Wade did the shoeing. I held the horses and tried to keep them still. If they misbehaved when they were ridden, they were worse when it came to being shod. Most of them had to be roped up to some degree. With several, it was a case of tying a rope around the fetlock, holding the hoof up off the ground so it could be worked on. Some were thrown on the ground and roped so they couldn't get up and couldn't kick. It was a lot more difficult to shoe a horse lying down but Mr Wade managed it somehow. Later I learned that all of that could be avoided.

But Mr Wade was good at shaping shoes to fit the hoof. The Winnininnie blacksmith shop had a charcoal forge in which the shoes were heated until they were soft enough to knock into shape. I can still smell the pungent odour of singeing hoof as he laid a red-hot shoe on it to ensure a perfectly flat contact. In the hands of someone inexperienced, like me, a horse's hoof can suffer damage that might take weeks to heal. Too much rasping will take the hoof down to the blood line. Nails that go into the sole instead of out through the wall will prick the hoof. Both mistakes draw blood and the horse may be lame. Only towards the end of my time was I allowed to even rasp a horse's hoof and make my first attempts at actually nailing shoes on. Until then, it was bring the horses up to the blacksmith shop, one by one, hold them while they were shod, watch closely what Bill and Mr Wade were doing, wind the handle on the blower of the forge until my arms ached – and do what I was told immediately.

My days on Winnininnie were the most carefree of my life. I loved it there. I had a good boss, good living conditions – and a great mate. Bill and I shared a room and never had a blue. We spent hours in that room, especially in winter. We kept the fire going all day and night on weekends. Bill had a theory that, since they were gas, farts would burn. He was eager to find out. When he felt a good-sized fart coming on, he dropped his trousers and poked his bare bum as close to the fire as he could bear. My job was to poke my head halfway into the fireplace to where I could see and report on the result. There was no result. He was too far away. Bill saved his wind until he thought he had enough volume, and he bent over and put his backside so far into the fireplace I thought he'd be scorched. When he was two inches away from the flames, he let go and, sure enough, the fart ignited with a pale blue flash. Bill moved away and rubbed his backside with one hand. 'Bloody hell,' he said. 'That was fuckin hot.'

'Yeah,' I said. 'You've burned all the hair off your bum and the back of your legs.'

'Well, now we know. But I'm not doing that again.'

While I was at Winnininnie, I bought my first rifle. It was a .22 single shot made by Sporting Arms, in Adelaide. I chose it because I liked the pistol grip. It wasn't long before the front sight fell out of its slot and I lost it. Mr Wade took me into the workshop and found a small piece of solid brass. He helped me to cut it roughly into shape with a hacksaw and then finish it off with a file. We locked the gun in a vice and fired off several rounds to true the sights. Mr Wade then used a touch of solder to fix it in the slot. It wasn't perfect but it was good enough and it served me well.

Guns became an important part of our lives. We spent hour after hour traipsing through the hills behind the homestead trying to shoot roos. Though we rarely got close enough, we kept at it, summer and winter. But we didn't hunt together: Bill went one way and I another. I returned to the men's quarters late one afternoon to find Bill treating a wound on his left forearm. He had shot a roo, and while he was skinning it, holding the skin out and away from the body in his left hand, he accidentally slashed himself. The cut was about three inches long and quite deep. It looked pretty bad to me. Bill scoffed at the idea of going to the doctor and told me to help him put on a tight bandage. It eventually healed, but it left an ugly, wide scar.

We took a lot of pride in our guns. We dismantled them and cleaned them meticulously after every shoot. It was very pleasant, working away in our room, talking quietly and concentrating on what we were doing. But Bill's concentration lapsed one afternoon, because his gun went off and the bullet went under my bed, where I was sitting, and whacked into the stone wall. Bill said, 'Shit, mate. Sorry. I didn't realise there was a cartridge in the breech.' We had another beer and laughed about it.

We were curious to know what would happen if we put live cartridges in the fire. We tossed a .22 bullet into the middle of the coals and in a few seconds it popped loudly and blew ash around, which we thought was very disappointing.

Fortunately, unlike men on many other stations, we worked only Monday to Friday, unless it was shearing time. That gave us two whole days to ourselves. Many times, as if we hadn't used enough of our youthful energies after a week of hard work, we battled it out on the clay tennis court on a Saturday or a Sunday. Bill and I were closely matched and we always needed five sets to determine the winner. We served as fast as we could and we ran like hairy goats from one side of the court to the other. When a ball was in our zone we hit it with all the force we had. We finished every match physically exhausted, especially when the temperature was around a hundred degrees. But we enjoyed it.

We also enjoyed killing rats in the chaff room, shooting them with shanghais. The chaff room at the stables was just that – a room full of chaff. There was a small door high up in an outside wall, a platform level with it. When chaff was delivered, the bags were opened on the platform and the contents were tipped straight down into the room. There was never enough to totally fill the room, which left some bearers in the walls exposed. Rats ran along these bearers, and Bill and I would sneak in, pockets bulging with the right-sized stones. We'd fire off at the rats as they scurried for safety, but they didn't all make it. We got very good at hitting them and knocking them to the floor, where we could kill them. We cheered and yelled every time we got one. What a life for a sixteen-year-old.

If I was content with where I was and with what I was doing, Bill was starting to get restless. He had been at Winnininnie for a couple of years and was ready for a change. He already had his option lined up. He reckoned there was a job waiting for him at a station at Tibooburra, a small town in the northwest corner of New South Wales. It was 120 miles north of Broken Hill, a few miles from the Queensland and South Australian borders. He'd been told it was hard, dry country but he was keen to give it a go. He wanted to get deep into Australia's outback and eventually see what Queensland had to offer. He was still at Winnininnie when I left, but I had a strong feeling he wouldn't be there for long.

Bill's pride and joy was a 1930 Citroën, which he bought in late 1951, and some Saturdays we'd drive into Yunta to spend the day at the pub. No-one asked any questions about my age; they simply served the schooners of beer and let us get drunk. But Bill's getting drunk gave me a problem. It was always the same: he'd empty his schooner and turn it upside down on the bar, move his stool back a little and stare round the room, swaying slightly as he sat there, trying to look fierce. Turning a glass upside down was a signal that you were prepared to fight anyone in the bar. Bill couldn't fight his way out of a paper bag, as they used to say, or, if you were really hopeless, a wet paper bag. Every time it was the same routine. I'd hastily turn his glass back up the right way. Bill would turn it upside down again and I'd reverse it again. 'For Christ's sake, Bill, cut it out,' I'd say. 'You can't bloody well fight and you'll get a belting.'

'Bullshit,' Bill would retort. 'Just let some bastard try and I'll knock his bloody block off.'

Then I'd get angry and say, 'Bloody stop it, Bill.' And I'd glare right into his face and keep hold of his glass. There were two possible outcomes. The first was that he would settle down and we would continue drinking with occasional rumbles from Bill; the second was that I would have to manhandle him and bundle him out of the bar and into the Citroën and make him drive us home, veering from one side of the road to the other.

In the meantime, to take his mind off fighting, I would try to get him to focus on something more pleasant. 'You don't see many girls around Yunta, do you?' I said one day.

'Mate,' he said, 'there's a handful of em, but they never poke their noses out – and good-lookin ones are as scarce as rockin' 'orse shit.'

Even back at the station, with just the two of us in the men's quarters, when he was drunk he wanted to fight. We used to bring back bottles of West End beer and bottles of Penfolds port. Bill's favourite poison was fifty-fifty beer and port in a quart-pot mug. Why he liked such a sickening brew was beyond me, but it got him drunk more quickly than anything else. On one occasion in our room, he challenged me to go outside and fight him.

'Come on, you bastard,' he growled. 'Come out and fight.'

'I don't want to fight you. Why would I want to fight you?'

'Doesn't fuckin matter why. Just get outside.'

Bill wobbled around, with his fists up, making out like a boxer. He kicked my bed, where I was sitting. 'Get up and fuckin come outside and fight, you gutless wonder,' he roared.

'No, Bill. Bugger off,' I said. I watched him warily because I thought there was a chance he might have a go at me while I was sitting there.

'Jesus, you're gutless,' he said. 'I've got to have a fight. It'll only take yer one punch and that'll be the end of me.'

I thought about that. He was probably right. Bill was so drunk he was staggering and couldn't stand up straight. But of course I didn't want to hit him – and I told him to give up and sit down. Grumbling and swearing at me, he did give up, and peace and quiet returned.

If Bill drunk was a problem, albeit a small problem, Bill in other areas was a great mate. In late winter 1951, he taught me to trap rabbits. Winnininnie had a traditional old grey mare that was harness broken. We hooked her up to a cart, and we rattled down the long drive towards the highway and stopped off in the widespread watercourse, which was a maze of rabbit warrens. We made camp in the middle of it, unharnessed the mare and tied her up to a tree with a big feed tin and a big bucket of water. We had a dozen traps each and we set these in the mouths of well-used burrows. We lit a campfire, using the only wood available, which was soft and burned out too quickly, so we had to keep putting more wood on through the night. But also through the night we checked our traps. We tried to get some sleep in between, but the best we could do was doze. So we talked and drank tea and looked at the stars in the clear sky. It was a good time.

It was good fun for both of us. We helped each other, especially if one of us had a fox or a cat in a trap. Take my advice, don't ever try to deal with a wild cat with your bare hands: they have twelve legs, three mouths and a backbone that can flex in five directions at once. And the claws and the teeth are needle sharp. Ounce for ounce, wild cats are probably the fiercest and most uncontrollable animals on earth. So we shot them – and skinned them. We didn't like skinning the cats because of the unpleasant smell of their flesh, but we did it because we picked up money for the pelts.

We checked the traps about every two hours. To leave it longer meant the foxes would get the trapped rabbits, or the rabbits would freeze to death, making them too difficult, if not impossible, to gut. We generally overcame both problems by setting each trap just inside the mouth of a burrow so the trapped rabbit could get some protection. When we gutted them, we linked them together in pairs by pushing the hind legs of one between the hamstrings and the bones of another's hind legs. Like that, they were easy to hang up and easy to carry. First thing Monday morning, a chiller truck came to collect our catch. They paid cash: two bob a pair. For Bill and me it was good extra money.

When Ken Wade and his wife were away, taking Ian back to school or picking him up, Bill and I had the whole of Winnininnie to ourselves. Being young and stupid, we tried shooting kangaroos from horseback, not only with the horse standing still but also at full gallop. With the horse stationary we had the glimmer of a chance, but we had not a hope in hell at the gallop. In order to aim, I had to have the rifle in both hands, with the butt at my shoulder. This meant I had to hook the reins loosely over one arm, abdicate control and rely on the horse to run straight. It was fun but as a roo-shooting exercise it was a failure. So we only tried it on horseback the once. Shooting from Bill's Citroën, bouncing along on twisting, uneven tracks, was equally unsuccessful.

The big event of the year locally was the Yunta races. One of the races was for station hacks ridden by stockmen and I entered with an old grey gelding called Bluey. Considering Bluey's age, I thought we did well to come third. Bill and I rode our horses from Winnininnie to Yunta in the morning and back home again later that night. During the day, we drank beer, bet with the bookies, chatted with some girls and generally behaved like a couple of cocky young upstarts. Riding home, I thought I probably looked rather impressive in my white moleskins, extra-high-heeled boots, blue shirt and broad-brimmed Akubra hat, and on the back of an upstanding grey thoroughbred that would rear on command.

The Yunta races paled into insignificance when Bill and I went to the Marrabel Rodeo. Marrabel is a small town just off the Adelaide to Broken Hill highway, south of Burra. It was October 1951 and my first rodeo. I was amazed. I thought Winnininnie horses could buck, but they were nothing compared to the horses at Marrabel. And the roughriders, how impressive were they? Compared to them, Bill and I were boys. These men were hard and tough and strong and no bullshit. They went about their work with professional ease. Their confidence showed in every step they took, in every gesture and in the expression on their faces.

Rodeo riding is serious business. The highlight of the day was the invitation ride on a grey mare called Curio. This horse was famous throughout the Australian rodeo world. She was seven years old and no-one had been able to ride the required ten seconds on her. She had graduated from being just another horse in the buckjumping string to being the star attraction. A tall rider called Johnny Roberts won the right to challenge her. I was behind the chutes, watching him prepare. He wore white cowboy boots and I thought that was a bit flash. As he climbed up on top of the chute, I ducked around to where I could get a place in the stand. It was packed with people. I squeezed into a space, close to the chute.

As Curio exploded out of the gate it was clear that she was in another league compared to all the other buckjumpers. She could twist her body like no other horse. She exuded violent energy and authority. She was majestic. Johnny Roberts had the ride of his life – for a whole six seconds – and then he was in the dust and all you could see of him were flashes of white from his boots. Curio had triumphed again – and I was glad.

Bill and I stayed on after the rodeo finished. We mingled with the crowd that was drinking and celebrating. We eyed off the girls, who were as lovely as those we saw pictures of in *Pix* and *People* magazines. We were awed and tongue-tied and all we could do was look. And look we did – though gawk might be a better word. One or two noticed us and offered a half-smile, which gave us shivers of excitement. We wished we had the charisma of the roughriders. We envied them. We were so ordinary – pathetically, painfully ordinary. As the evening wore on we realised there was no action for us at Marrabel. 'You're not gunna get anywhere near them sheilas as long as your arse points to the ground,' Bill said.

So we drove back to Winnininnie, half-drunk, still enthused and exuberant. Our destinies had now shifted course. We were going to be roughriders. No more sheep. No more shovels and axes. We were going to follow the rodeo circuit and we'd do it together and we'd look after each other and we'd be mates forever, and sooner or later we'd each get a girl and do what everyone else was doing and what we only talked about.

We went west to Saddleworth and then swung right. Bill had his foot flat to the boards. The Citroën was flying along at forty-five miles an hour. At least it seemed like flying. There were no side windows and the canvas roof was flapping and the body was vibrating and we felt as though we were outside in the open. Cars and trucks flew past and tooted derisively as they went. We whooped and waved and told them to get stuffed – but they couldn't hear us. We sang all the cowboy songs we knew. Over and over, I sang a song about the strawberry roan: 'Oh that strawberry roan, he bucked t'wards the west and he bucked t'wards the east, oh that strawberry roan.' And I sang Hank Williams's 'Lovesick Blues' again and again and did all the beautiful yodelling bits to a T. We tore up the highway, through Manoora and Burra, past Peterborough out in the west. Just past Nackara we stopped to relieve ourselves and refuel the Citroën from the spare fuel Bill carried in cans in the back, then we went straight through dark, dead Paratoo and dark, dead Yunta, and finally we turned off the highway and roared into Winnininnie homestead at midnight, three hours after leaving Marrabel. We staggered and stumbled to our room and fell asleep in our clothes.

We talked about the rodeo every night for days on end to begin with. Then our enthusiasm for following the circuit waned and died. It was many years later that I rode in my first rodeo, at Mobrup, south of Kojonup, in Western Australia. As for Curio, she met her match in 1953 with a rider named Alan Woods. His ride is considered to be one of the greatest rodeo rides of all time, though there was a dispute about whether or not it was legitimate. His moment of glory was captured in a thrilling photograph that was used as the inspiration for a life-sized bronze statue outside the rodeo ground. To prove it was no fluke, he rode her again in 1954 and everyone agreed it was a clean ride.

While I was at Winnininnie, I had two trips to Adelaide to stay with the maiden aunts for a few days. My only means of transport was the train from Broken Hill to Adelaide. It came through

Winnininnie siding late at night, usually loaded with miners from Broken Hill heading for holidays in Adelaide and elsewhere in South Australia. They drank and played cards all the way. The return trip was especially inconvenient. The train dropped me off at the siding at two o'clock in the morning, and I had to sleep on a bench in a small shed, open on one side, until someone drove down from the station to pick me up. On these occasions, waiting for the train or waiting for a lift, I got to know some of the Dutch migrants working as fettlers on the railway and living in a line of tents. When the weather was cold, they warmed their tents with tins of red-hot coals. To me, it was so cold the tins of coals didn't make any difference, but the fettlers persisted.

Just as I was really getting into the swing of things and enjoying life at Winnininnie, my mother wrote to say that she and my father wanted me back in Western Australia, that I had to resign and pack up and meet her in Adelaide. It was March 1952. Mr Wade gave me a good reference.

The regret I've carried all my life is that I did not get to visit Koonamore. I was almost within sight of the place and I didn't close the gap. It would have set the seal on my time in South Australia if, somehow, I had found a way of getting to walk on the hallowed ground and stand on the veranda of the homestead I had studied so often in photographs.

Bill and I promised to stay in touch, but we didn't. I've often wondered if he went to Tibooburra and what eventuated in his life.

4

Mary, Maggie and Dorothy

In 1951 the aunts and Poltoonga drew me to Adelaide at Easter (March), in September and again at Christmas. In April 1952, when my mother came to Adelaide, I was with them for the last time. It's hard to connect impressions and incidents with any one particular visit. The visits merged and felt like one long visit. Each one picked up where the other left off, the same as when you meet someone after a long gap and it's as if you saw them only yesterday. What I'm about to say now may seem odd. There I was in South Australia, a seventeen-year-old who didn't grow enough fuzz on his chin to warrant shaving, living a toughish life on an outback sheep station, enjoying boozing with my mate Bill, indulging in all the wild things I would never tell my parents about, and then I was transposed to a suburban house inhabited by three elderly maiden ladies – and I loved it. I bent down and hugged each one. I could never get enough of them.

Poltoonga was much bigger than it appeared from the street. There were rooms at the back that had been used as classrooms when it had been a private school with a limited intake of students. In the late 1800s and in the first half of the twentieth century, private schools were quite common and, generally, exclusive. What are now called private schools were originally called public schools, because they were not exclusive to anyone who could afford the fees.

Despite the age gap, I enjoyed the aunts' company. They were well read in the classics – novels and poetry. Their sense of humour leaned towards banter and flashes of wit. They loved to tease and they never for a minute let me take myself too seriously. At the dinner table, Aunt Mary and Aunt Maggie were always teasing Aunt Dorothy. When they did, Aunt Dorothy would look at me and wink, as if to say, 'I don't care in the least.'

At the card table at Easter, playing rummy, Aunt Dorothy discarded an eight, which I, being on her left, pounced on. 'Oh, Dorothy,' said Aunt Mary. 'Surely you're aware that Ian is saving eights?'

'Poor dear. He hasn't won a game yet,' said Aunt Dorothy.

'So what!' said Aunt Maggie.

'Don't take any notice of *them*,' Aunt Dorothy said, as she turned slightly and looked at me with a knowing smile.

To me the ladies were gems, living gems. Those three women had a delicious balance of formality and playfulness. Maybe that was a product of having been teachers for so many years – and surrogate mothers to some. I could see my grandfather in them – and them in him. The instant closeness I felt when I first arrived in Adelaide grew stronger with every visit. In January 1951, Mary was eighty-one, Maggie was seventy-six and Dorothy was seventy.

It was totally unexpected when Dorothy died of acute bronchitis, on 15 August 1951. It was after the funeral that Mary wrote to tell me. That was a shock. It was my first experience of a death in the family, and the loss was especially painful because, of the three maiden aunts, Dorothy was my sweetheart. And now the dear bright spark was gone.

Many hours in Adelaide were spent listening to the aunts talk about their lives and their school, my grandfather and my other great-uncles and great-aunts. From time to time, we were joined by Great-aunt Jane, whose married name was Blondell. She was a widow and she lived with a paid companion. My grandfather had eight siblings. I got to know only five of them; the fifth was Great-uncle Edgar, who lived in Mundaring, near my grandparents. The aunts took me back in time to the 1800s and 1700s, with stories about Irish and Scottish ancestors. Mostly it was Aunt Mary who cast the spells and lit my imagination. She was aided by the environment. Poltoonga was a house full of treasure – rooms containing furniture inherited from their parents, and memorabilia in every cupboard and every drawer. The book shelves were packed. There were many thick scrapbooks with cuttings from Irish newspapers featuring stories about the Porters, from whom the family was descended. They had collections of letters and albums of sepia photographs: being in Poltoonga was a step back into the past, the chequered history of the Porters and the Hendersons lying there, unread or not looked at for years and years.

Aunt Mary opened up the cupboards hoarding family memorabilia from as far back as the early 1800s. I read about an Irish ancestor whose name was James Porter. He was a writer who was active in producing what were called political pamphlets, railing against the occupying, hated British. He was caught, charged, tried and convicted of sedition. The British hanged him on a hill on the outskirts of Dublin, and they carted his wife and children out to see what happened to traitors. But the British could not eliminate his name. It was carried on through succeeding generations and ended up with my grandfather, James Porter Henderson. My grandfather's stock brand was JP and, inevitably, JP became my stock brand.

Another JP was Jane Porter, another writer. Her family was an extension of the Irish Porters, but she was born in Durham, England, in 1776. She was raised in Edinburgh but she spent most of her life south of London. Her most renowned book was a historical novel, *The Scottish Chiefs* (1809). It was acclaimed as the greatest historical novel ever written. The story was about the Scottish fight for independence. The hero was William Wallace. The book is said to have inspired Andrew Jackson, a commander in America's 1812 war against the British. He too became a hero and, ultimately, president of the United States. Jane was awarded literary honours, and I have a framed head and shoulders drawing of her wearing nun-like robes, required for her investiture.

Another scrapbook had articles from newspapers from around 1905, warning of the dangers from Asian hordes. There was a story with a map with a thick black arrow curving and sweeping from the region of Manchuria and Japan all the way down to the northernmost tip of Australia. 'Beware the yellow peril,' screamed the headline.

We drank tea. We ate fresh scones. They introduced me to mint julep, with home-grown mint. We talked and talked. I think they saw in me a repository for the family's history and, more importantly, an agent for the continuation of Porter and Henderson values and culture. Some years later, my mother told me that the aunts worked on her to persuade me to give up sheep station life and get a university education instead. 'He's wasting his potential,' Aunt Mary allegedly said. She would not have received any support from my grandfather.

It was my grandfather's sisters who laid the foundations for my reading and my hoard of books and, probably in their minds, my education. The oldest book I have was printed in 1838 and nearly all were printed in the mid- to late 1800s. Most of them were school prizes; several were gifts they'd received and two were given to my grandfather by his father.

Even though I was not conscious of my grandfather being a great reader, he gave me several treasures: *Robinson Crusoe*, by Daniel Defoe; in two separate volumes, the complete works of Cowper, Longfellow and Milton; and *A Course of Lectures on Fine Painting*, which he received as a school prize in 1884.

The aunts gave me, individually and collectively: *The Waverley Novels* of Sir Walter Scott, *The Complete Works of William Wordsworth*, *The Works of Alfred Lord Tennyson*, Lamb's *Tales from Shakespeare* and *The Treasury of Geography*, printed in 1872.

Aunt Maggie also gave me her Bible and her Book of Common Prayer. She had had the Bible since 1892. Did she feel my need was greater than hers? If I had said that to Maggie she would have replied, with a twinkle in her eye, 'Of course, dear.' For Aunt Maggie, it was as personal a gift as she could make. I was moved – and honoured.

The book I valued the most was Aunt Dorothy's *The Works of William Shakspeare* (the spelling of Shakespeare's name has varied over time). It had been awarded to her as a prize when she was a schoolgirl. Mary and Maggie gave it to me at Christmas 1951, after Dorothy's death.

All these books were beautifully printed and bound. They each have an inscription inside the front cover, showing why it was presented and by which school or person. In my talks with the aunts, it was clear they were familiar with the contents. They could discuss the relative merits of Wordsworth and Tennyson. Because they valued them so highly, I felt that each book placed in my hands was a token, handed to me to pass to another generation. What a lot that says about the times they were born into. In my grandparents' time, such works were standard reading. Pioneers such as the Duracks carried literature with them in their saddlebags and read by the light of a campfire. Now, in remote outback places people watch satellite television.

The primary reason for visiting Adelaide was to be with the aunts, but the major bookshop in Adelaide was another attraction. Aunt Mary had told me about it and where to find it, suggesting books I should read and urging me to take a good collection back to the station. I browsed endlessly. Then I bought Charles Dickens's *Christmas Books*, Charles Reade's *The Cloister and the Hearth*, H.G. Wells's *The Invisible Man*, Wilkie Collins's *The Woman in White*, Conan Doyle's *Sherlock Holmes: Selected Stories* and Alexandre Dumas's *The Count of Monte Cristo*.

And I flirted with the attractive young lady assistant. When she asked for my address so the bookshop could send me newsletters,

I took delight in saying 'Winnininnie Station' so quickly I had to spell it for her. Even then I rattled it off – W – I – double N – I – N – I – double N – I – E – with a flourishing lift at the end. She was bewildered, but she smiled daintily and glanced up at me as she wrote.

Another attraction was the Art Gallery of South Australia. Drawing and painting had always appealed to me and I tried my hand at watercolours. I tried to capture the magic of the saltbush plains at Winnininnie, but I wasn't pleased or inspired by my efforts.

I was frequently startled by the aunts' directness. We were gathered in the living room one afternoon in April 1952 when Mary said to me, 'Now dear, we want you to look all around this house and tell us which things you'd like us to leave to you when we're gone.'

I couldn't think of her and Maggie as being 'gone'. I felt like a grave robber before the graves were even dug. Aunt Mary said, 'You don't have to tell us right now. Take your time. Look around. You choose what you want. And as much as you want.'

Our conversation wandered around the subject and then they drifted off, leaving me uncomfortable and uneasy. I struggled to think about an answer, but my mind would not deal with it. I mooched through the rooms and dawdled in the living room and, finally, I made my choices. Even then I was still reluctant to speak and they had to drag it out of me. For my birthday in October 1951, Mary and Maggie had given me a copy of Lowell Thomas's *With Lawrence in Arabia*, and this had whetted my appetite for more about T.E. Lawrence. I had my eye on *Seven Pillars of Wisdom*, a second impression printed in August 1935, so I asked for that. I also asked for a splendid bookcase-cum-cupboard. After Aunt Mary died in 1961 both items duly arrived. I still have them and I use the bookcase for the books I value most.

When you think of their view that I was wasting my time on sheep stations, it is ironic that, probably, I would never have met them if I had not gone to South Australia as a jackeroo. In their own dear ways, they taught me things I would not otherwise have been aware of. Being with them was a highlight of my life, albeit far too brief.

Saying goodbye to Aunt Mary and Aunt Maggie, I felt that as they were my introduction to Adelaide and South Australia, they were the conclusion too. There was a sweet fittingness about that. As my mother and I left on the train to head back across the continent, I was vaguely aware that I was leaving behind my young youth. I was no longer the boy I had been when I went there. I was a youth on the threshold of being a young man. I could not imagine what lay ahead. For now, I was again in the shadow of my parents. I loved my parents, but they constricted me, both deliberately and unconsciously. It would be a while yet before I threw off the leash.

After Aunt Maggie died, in October 1958, Aunt Mary was left alone at Poltoonga. The last contact I had with her was a long letter she wrote in November 1958. Her handwriting was strong and very legible, especially for someone at eighty-eight. The sadness of what she had to say was so poignant that even now it still affects me.

My Dear Ian,

I know it is a long time since I wrote to you because your Aunt Maggie for a long time has not been able to write or read so I have had to answer all her letters for her and also to read to her. She has been ill for so long, the last three weeks of her life being dreadfully sad for she suffered too much. I shall and do miss her very much as we shared all our joys and sorrows, the deaths of many of our friends this year saddened her, for most were sudden . . .

I am all alone in this big house, but hope to get a tenant for the three inside rooms and the kitchen soon . . .

Much love, my dear Ian, Aunt Mary

Three years later she too was gone.

5

Ian Bridson

The seemingly interminable train journey from Adelaide to Perth was the perfect situation for mother and son to talk. As the train rattled up through Whyalla, across the Nullarbor and on to Kalgoorlie, it gave my mother the opportunity to talk about our little family and its future. This was not the stuff she could write in a letter. It needed to be said directly, mother to son – and some matters considered and revisited.

In early 1950, my father left the Swan Brewery, where he had risen to chief accountant, and bought an accountancy practice in Bunbury. By the end of 1950, the business had foundered and my parents had lost everything. For the second time in her life, my mother was dependent on someone who was broke. All of that I knew, just as I was well aware that my father had taken a position managing a sheep station north of Carnarvon. Now, in April 1952, he was about to start work as overseer at Doorawarrah Station, just east of Carnarvon – and I was to join my parents there. What I had not known, or realised, was how much my parents were shaping their lives around me and my aspirations.

The wool industry was booming. My father's son had an exciting future ahead of him, so why not join him, he reasoned, and be part of it? Father and son together – and, who knows, one day they might be able to make the transition from station managers to station owners. How they would find the capital was an issue that might be dealt with when the opportunity arose. In the meantime, we would be at Doorawarrah as a family – and take it from there.

We settled into a small cottage near the main homestead, but it wasn't long before my father was looking for a new job: my mother did not get on with the owner's wife; nor did she like being restricted to the confines of the cottage.

By the end of June, we were in Carnarvon, staying at the Gascoyne Hotel. There, I met a young man named Ian Bridson, about three years older than I. He was working for his uncle, who was a water-boring contractor. Because his uncle was ill with diabetes and had to be flown to Perth for treatment, Ian was now looking for someone to work the boring plant with him until his uncle returned. He asked me. I liked him and I liked the idea. My parents thought it would be a good experience. My father put a high value on experience as an essential part of one's education.

My mother and father secured a position at Mount Augustus Station, a cattle and sheep property 300-odd miles east of Carnarvon. My father was to manage the sheep side and I would join them when Ian Bridson no longer needed me.

Ian was working on a contract at Winderie Station, south of Gascoyne Junction – and Gascoyne Junction was nearly halfway to Mount Augustus, so, in outback terms, my parents and I were in the same area. For me it was an adventure. There was something about Ian that excited me. He was more intelligent and more self-assured than any other young bloke I'd met.

Still only seventeen, I headed off into unknown territory to do a job I knew nothing about, with a young man I didn't really know. Perhaps that's why I asked my father if I could take his dog, Smokey, with me. He hesitated and gave me a searching look and said, 'OK. But look after him. I want him back in one piece.'

Smokey was a very handsome dog and well behaved. With his dingo-like looks and his obedient nature, he attracted attention and interest. In spite of his pale yellow coat, he was officially a Red Cloud breed. I was very proud to have a dog like that in my possession, even though he was borrowed.

Early one morning, we left Carnarvon and drove the 120 miles to Gascoyne Junction. Our vehicle was an ex-army 4 x 4 – a blitz wagon, with no side windows and little or no suspension. It felt bigger and heavier than it really was, and the engine made so much noise it was difficult to hear yourself think. We stopped at the pub at the Junction for a couple of beers before driving the twenty-five miles to Winderie.

Gascoyne Junction is so called because that's where the Lyons and Gascoyne rivers meet, having collected waters from various tributaries. The pub was built of corrugated iron and the huge back yard was fenced in by stacks of bottles. Thousands and thousands of bottles, mostly green, were neatly piled about four feet high and two feet wide. The two sides were fifty yards or more long, and the end was forty yards across. I suppose it was one way of making empty bottles useful – the fence was certainly effective.

Everything about the pub was old. It wasn't dilapidated, but it was heading that way. Structural timbers were warping, floorboards in the passage down the middle bowed and creaked with every passing foot, and some of the sheets of corrugated iron were loose at the ends. Inside it had a dark feeling – not just from a lack of light but also because what was once white was now yellowed with age and there was a lot of dark timber. Two of the customers, so old and so settled in, looked as though they had been there since the pub first opened.

It was common in outback places like Gascoyne Junction, Carnarvon and Meekatharra to find odd characters like these perched on stools in the pub. Many stations employed men in their sixties and seventies as outcamp men or gardeners or yardmen. Usually they were homeless and spent their two-week annual holiday drinking their way through the money they had saved during the year. The oft-told story was that these old blokes would slap their pay-out cheque on the bar and say to the publican, 'Here you go. Let me know when it's cut out.' After two weeks of drinking and meals and accommodation, the money always happened to dry up on the last day.

When the bar closed, the publican helped them stagger down the passage to a room or to a bed on a veranda, where they slept off the day's consumption. Next day they started all over again. It was no wonder the fence of bottles was so big. At the end of their stay, they returned to where they worked to live out another year until they were sent off on holiday again.

For Ian and me, our visit to Gascoyne Junction was but a fleeting break. Ian was all business and responsibility and did not dawdle. We went to Winderie and settled in to the shearers' quarters: a room each and a functional kitchen was a very civilised situation. The half-finished bore we were to work on was close to the homestead, and we checked that everything was in place to start work the following morning.

But when the next day dawned, the sky was full of thick, grey clouds, the sun lurking behind. Ian mooched around in his overalls, glancing at the sky, muttering to himself.

'We're buggered,' he said. 'Can't run the boring plant when I can't see.'

'Eh?'

'Aw, shit, I've gotta see what's going on at the bottom of the bore hole. The only way I can do that is to use a mirror and reflect the sunlight down. Bugger it.'

So that was that – until the clouds cleared. Although he couldn't see to recommence drilling, Ian started the motor and dropped the sludge pump down the bore to get a feel for what was happening deep below. After three tests, he announced that too much sand was falling in. Most of the way down, the drilling was through hard ground. But right at the bottom, there was a narrow stratum of sand giving a problem because we weren't casing as we went. We tipped two bags of cement down the bore hole to try to set the sand and stop it from caving in.

There was nothing else we could do now: the plant was in good condition and there was charcoal on hand for when the drill bits had to be sharpened again. So we returned to the shearers' quarters, where we sat on rotten, white-ant-eaten benches and drank tea and wondered how we would fill in the time. I had been singing the praises of *The Wind in the Willows* and Ian suggested I read it aloud. I did – nearly all day. Ian gave up sitting on the rickety bench and he sprawled on the stone floor. In the afternoon, he said, 'After this chapter we'll test that cement.'

With my elbows resting on the dirty wooden table, I went on reading. There was no other sound outside or in, just my voice bringing to life green English meadows and tiny unfamiliar animals. It was so hushed you'd think a willy-willy had blown every living thing clean off the earth, leaving just the two of us in a mud-walled hut, with the skinny mulgas standing twisted outside in that dry, droughty country.

That story took such a hold that when I finished the chapter, we sat for fifteen minutes, staring into space, forgetting completely what it was we intended to do. Picture this: two rough-looking young blokes who hadn't shaved or bathed for two days, caught in the magic of Kenneth Grahame's story for children. I thought that if ever there was a tribute to a writer it was us.

Ten days later, the bore was finished. There was good water at 160 feet. It had been a heavy slog to get through the earth's tough crust to find it.

In idle moments we gave our guns some exercise. I had my Sporting Arms .22 with the pistol grip, and Ian had an 1892-model .32-20 Winchester carbine that had been reconstructed. He had found it in a shed somewhere and took it to a gunsmith in Perth, who replaced the barrel and cleaned up all the metalwork. It was a lovely gun.

It was a classic gun. It was the kind of gun you saw in Western films, where the hero pulled it out from a scabbard attached to the saddle and, after levering a cartridge into the breech, raised it to his shoulder and shot an Indian on a galloping horse 150 yards away. From my experience at Winnininnie, I knew the impossibility of such marksmanship. It was accurate up to not much more than a hundred yards, providing you were standing on the ground and had a steady brace for the gun – and the target was stationary. But it was a satisfying weapon to feel and use. When Ian eventually went back to live in Perth, he sold it to me – and I still have it, and it still works perfectly.

With the work at Winderie completed, we moved another fifteen miles south, to a station called Towrana. The site where we had to drill was another twelve to fifteen miles further south again. The country was hard and desolate. The scrub was tough and desiccated. There were no features to relieve the monotony of the landscape. It was as dreary and uninspiring as any country I'd ever seen. We uncoupled the boring plant from the tow ball on the back of the truck and set it up. This took time, because the plant had to be braced, and the head had to be raised and locked in place, and the engine that drove the winch had to be serviced. We also had to set up camp. This time our accommodation was a tent and our kitchen was a roughly cleared patch of ground with a campfire.

One of my jobs was to maintain a water supply for the drill by taking the blitz wagon to fetch water in 44-gallon drums from a mill five miles back the way we'd come. As the drill bit thumped its way down, breaking up the rock-hard soil and, sometimes, actual rock, water was used to create slurry so that all the waste could be sucked up and out with a sludge pump.

Maintaining a supply of charcoal was another of my responsibilities. This required a pit, four feet deep, which I dug using a crowbar and a shovel. Large quantities of mulga were burned in this hole. When the wood was a mass of bright-red coals, I placed sheets of tin over the hole and covered it with loose soil, making sure the edges of the tin were sealed. Next day, the soil and the tin were removed and, lo and behold, the hole was full of black, crisp charcoal.

This was used in a portable forge to heat the drill bits until they were red-hot and malleable. Then they could be hammered and belted back into their original shape. Sharpening the bit was a two-man job. I had to brace the bit by holding it in place with one foot on top and one foot at the end, with both hands holding a crowbar jammed against the side. Ian swung the sledgehammer and pounded it into shape. To achieve the final result, the bit had to be put back in the forge several times and reheated until it was malleable again. As at the blacksmith shop at Winnininnie, attached to the forge there was a blower, which forced air onto the charcoal to increase the heat – and I was the one who had to keep turning the handle on the blower, until I thought my arms would drop off.

My other jobs included cooking, keeping the camp clean and tidy, maintaining the fuel supply for the fire, keeping the water bags full and making billies of tea for Ian throughout the day. He was a tough boss. He was highly disciplined and hated wasted time. He was fanatical about cleanliness, to the point where I had to scrub the cooking pots and pans, inside and out, until they showed no trace of ever having been used for cooking, let alone cooking over an open fire. This was not as hard as it sounds, because Ian taught me to cook on beds of coals and not over flames. It's the flames that cause the black, sooty burn marks. To begin with, Ian inspected my work and gave me his frank criticism. That eased up after the message finally sank in. The one exception to his scrutiny was the billy. The billy was usually brought to the boil with fire all around it.

My mother had taught me the rudiments of cooking using a wood stove but a campfire was different technology, though not difficult. Under Ian's tuition, my cooking expertise improved, but we did not have the produce or the condiments to be creative.

However, I did become proficient at making damper. This was important. We ate damper for breakfast and lunch and used it to mop up our gravy at dinner. Every second day I made a damper in a camp oven, a round cast-iron pot with a slightly domed lid. One of the secrets is to make the dough barely moist – not wet. If it's too wet, the damper comes out soggy. Another secret is getting the heat just right. The camp oven is placed in a hole just wide enough for it to fit in and deep enough for it to sit on a dense bed of coals at the bottom, so the hole becomes an oven. The lid is covered with coals shovelled from the fire nearby. Three-quarters of an hour later, the coals are shovelled aside, the lid is lifted and a dry stick is poked into the damper right to the bottom. If the stick comes out dry, with little or no dough adhering, the damper is cooked. Then the oven is removed and the damper is tipped out and left to cool. After several weeks of applying myself to producing the perfect damper, I reckon I got pretty close. Like riding a bike, it's one of those things you never forget.

In the evenings, we didn't sit by the fire for long, because the nights were cold and, if there was a wind, the tent gave us some protection. Ian's stretcher was on one side, mine on the other. Between us, there was a long trestle table. We sat or lay on the stretchers and wrote letters, or read or talked. Mostly we talked. Rather, Ian talked and I listened.

He came from a well-educated family. His father was a headmaster. His elder brother became a dentist and his elder sister married a teacher. Ian was educated at Perth Modern School and the University of Western Australia, where he majored in English. He was infinitely better and more widely read than I was, and, more to the point, he understood what he was reading, whereas too often I didn't.

Ian was about six feet tall, slim, fit, but not athletic. We did have fun at times, but mostly he was serious and intense. His aura of self-assurance bordered on arrogance and it disturbed some people. He didn't really care if he offended anyone and sometimes he did. But to me, his knowledge and appreciation of literature was impressive, and I didn't mind his authoritarian attitude – I was ripe for learning.

In the camp at Towrana, in the light of a pressure lamp, with blankets around our knees, we read a range of books. In particular, we read and examined the subtleties and meanings of Shakespeare's sonnets and Robert Browning's poetry. It was a revelation to me. We read aloud. Ian read. I read, and he corrected my timing and emphases. We paused at certain lines and phrases and examined them. We started with the sonnets, because one of the books I had with me was Aunt Dorothy's *The Works of William Shakspeare*. We lingered over many, but of all of them, the one we came back to again and again was number 73:

> That time of year thou mayest in me behold
> When yellow leaves, or none, or few, do hang
> Upon those boughs which shake against the cold,
> Bare ruin'd choirs, where late the sweet birds sang.
> In me thou seest the twilight of such day
> As after sunset fadeth in the west;
> Which by and by black night doth take away,
> Death's second self, that seals up all in rest.
> In me thou seest the glowing of such fire,
> That on the ashes of his youth doth lie,
> As the death-bed whereon it must expire,
> Consum'd with that which it was nourish'd by.
> This thou perceiv'st, which makes thy love more strong,
> To love that well which thou must leave ere long.[1]

What were we thinking, two youths alone in an isolated tent, steeped in the words and rhythms and images of long-gone poets? What relevance did their words have for us? I doubt that we fully understood what we were reading and mulling over. But we felt the feeling. Years later, a Portuguese naval architect made a remark to me that was relevant. He said, 'They can follow it without understanding it.' What he said had nothing to do with poetry, but it might as well have.

It has been said that Shakespeare's sonnets were private thoughts. Whether or not that was true, he gave us hours of pleasure; we slowly savoured his words, quietly contemplating their significance.

So too with Robert Browning. Ian had a volume of his poetry and verse writings, which I had never read. In the poem 'Andrea del Sarto (Called "The Faultless Painter")', Ian uncovered the ageing painter's painful awareness of his limitations as an artist and the sadness and futility of his relationship with his young mistress, Lucrezia. Del Sarto was very conscious that his painterly skills were superior to those of Rafael (Raphael) and Michel Agnolo (Michelangelo) but recognised that they had a soul that he did not possess. Thus, del Sarto described 'this low-pulsed forthright craftsman's hand of mine'. And about Rafael he said:

To Rafael's! – And indeed the arm is wrong.
I hardly dare . . . yet only you to see,
Give the chalk here – quick, thus the line should go!
Ay, but the soul! he's Rafael! rub it out![2]

I learned what Browning meant when he had Andrea del Sarto say, 'Well, less is more . . .'

I learned what was meant in, 'Ah, but a man's reach should exceed his grasp.' Browning's lines became talismans for me. They are as potent today as they were then, in that desolate spot at Towrana, or when they were written.

So, our cold tent was suffused with the warmth and atmosphere of Florence and Renaissance painters and Renaissance poetry. Did ever a youth fall on his feet when he was found by Ian Bridson?

As for Smokey, I think he was bored out of his mind. Hanging around with me, he had nothing to do. He enjoyed travelling in the blitz wagon but he was a sheepdog, born to work, and there was no work for him at a camp site in the bush.

Then it rained. It rained for two days and it stopped as abruptly as it had started. The land all around us was awash. Then the water drained off through shallow watercourses and left behind a surface of slippery, sloppy mud. This dried out, but slowly. Ian wouldn't operate the boring plant when the rain was heavy, and there was not a lot of other work we could do. Fortunately, rain only wets the outside of wood and the inside remains dry and burnable – once you get it going. We could cook and make tea, ducking out and back in between showers – and we could read, lying in our swags on the stretchers in the tent.

When the weather cleared, it was back to work to make up for the lost time. Our 44-gallon drums were empty and Ian sent me off to fill them. The track was slippery and the blitz wagon was hard to control. It slid like a skater on ice when I applied the brakes. I drove slowly and tried to pick the firmest ground. When I was nearly at the mill and the tank, the front wheels broke through the crust and dropped down to the axle. I was bogged and helpless. I walked back to the camp and told Ian. We both walked to the truck with shovels, but our digging only made the situation worse. We could do two things: sit and wait for the ground to dry out or walk to the homestead and get help. We chose the latter.

Hours later, we were back with the manager, who also had a 4 x 4 blitz wagon like ours. Without too much effort, we managed to get that vehicle bogged as well. Although it was not bogged as deeply as ours, it was still immoveable for the time being. The three of us stood and contemplated the scene. Ian and the manager discussed the options. What options? They both came to the same conclusion: even if we got the trucks out from where they were bogged, we were highly likely to get bogged somewhere else. It was decided: we would come back in two days, providing there was no more rain. Ian and I trudged back to our camp. Our walk was about an hour and a quarter, but the manager's walk was more than two hours. We got the idea he was not impressed with us.

In the bush, we had no communication with the outside world: no telephone, no radio. Our postal address was care of the post office in Carnarvon, and that's where we went for mail and news. There was a telephone at Towrana homestead, but it was unattended most of the time, so no-one left messages for us. Even if they did get a message through, it would mean that the manager would have to drive out to tell us – and that was stretching the friendship.

To try to find out what was happening with Ian's uncle we went to Gascoyne Junction to phone. Generally, that was no use when there was no-one at home at the other end. So, hoping there would be news in the mail, we drove the four hours from the camp to Carnarvon. We collected the mail, bought a few stores, had a few beers, and drove four hours back again. With no side windows in the truck, it was hard to endure driving at night when the weather was cold.

Eventually, Ian received a letter from his uncle to say that he was out of hospital and to set the date for when he expected to be back in Carnarvon. That gave us time to finish the bore at Towrana and pack up. You can never really know for sure how deep you will have to go to get a decent supply of good water – or whether you'll get any water at all. But we'd had promising indications and soon hit water. We cased the bore, cleaned up the camp site, packed up, and left the boring rig at Gascoyne Junction, where Ian and his uncle could pick it up and take it to their next contract.

In Carnarvon, Ian paid me off and we hung around at the Gascoyne Hotel for nearly a week while he waited for his uncle. Smokey and I waited for the next mail-truck run that would take us to Mount Augustus. We found other blokes at a loose end, and the days and nights drifted by in a blur of beer drinking and card playing. This was not good preparation for what lay ahead.

PART TWO

STOCKMAN

Employed primarily to do
cattle or sheep work

6

The dominion of Mount Augustus

It was a relief to end the waiting and take my gear to Gascoyne Traders and find a place on the weekly mail truck. Besides, I was almost out of money and I couldn't afford to stay a minute longer. The journey from Carnarvon to Mount Augustus was 294 miles. I figured I'd be there by the end of the day. But no, we left early on a Saturday morning, and I arrived at the Mount Augustus sheep homestead on Monday morning.

The load on the mail truck was five feet high. The driver had two other passengers in front, so a young bloke and his dog travelled outside, on top. The load was rearranged to make a small depression for Smokey and me to lie in so we didn't fall off.

The road ran parallel to the Gascoyne River. It was a road with a history. In its beginnings, it was a route that led into the unknown: an unknown world to the early explorers and prospectors – and, for me too, an unknown future. After two station stops, we arrived at Gascoyne Junction at midday. We pulled up outside the pub. I climbed down off the load. When I called him, Smokey jumped off the top into my arms, and I lowered him down. How could you not love a dog like that?

I asked the driver how long we would be there. 'Till some time termorra,' he grunted.

'Why?' I asked.

'Because it's the bloody Gascoyne Races this arvo and I'm going and I'll be on the piss tonight.'

Then he went into the pub and left me wondering what to do with myself. With only a few shillings in my pocket and with a dog to look after, the racecourse was no place for me. That suited the mail-truck driver. After a few drinks, he emerged from the pub and told me to get in the truck. It was an hour before the races were due to start, and the pub was going to shut down the booze supply so everyone had to go out to the racecourse for a drink.

He drove up to the police station, about half a mile away. He parked the truck just outside the police compound. He handed me a metal bracket and said, 'See how this bastard's twisted outa shape. Use this hammer and file to get it straight again. I'll need it before we get going termorra. OK?'

'OK,' I said. I had no idea what the bracket was used for – and I didn't ask.

'Good. Now, here're the keys of the truck. Stay here and keep your eye on everything. Sleep inside the cab if ya want, but don't let no other bastard in.'

As he said that, a ute arrived with the usual cloud of dust and he got in the back with two other blokes. 'See ya later,' he said. Then they were gone – to the racecourse way over the other side of the pub.

The truck suddenly seemed very big, very bulky, very long – and very silent. 'Righto, Smoke,' I said. 'We might as well get started.' For the next hour and a half, I hammered and banged at the bracket until it was as right as I could get it.

When I stopped, I heard the quiet – one of the things I liked about the bush. But there are different kinds of quiet. Sometimes silence was simply the stillness of the bush. At times like this, outside the police station, it was different. It was an uneasy silence. Was there anyone around, or wasn't there? The driver had told me that the policeman rented out the lock-up cells for people to stay in overnight. I wondered what he would do if the festivities got too lively and he had to arrest someone. I started to feel edgy. I decided to see what food I could afford for Smokey and me.

We followed the dirt road to the pub. The place appeared deserted. I stepped onto the veranda and walked into the bar. There was no-one there. 'Anybody here?' I called out.

'Yeah. Whaddaya want?' The owner of the voice shuffled through a doorway. 'Well. Whaddaya want?' he demanded.

It turned out that all I could afford was a tin of sardines and a packet of saloon crackers. Smokey and I walked back to the truck. Everything was as it should be. There was a tap in the police compound from which we could get a drink. We ate all the sardines and half the biscuits, and I saved the other half for breakfast.

The driver turned up next day, unshaven but in a cheerful mood. Smokey and I rode on top of the load again. The road took us through Bidgemia, Dairy Creek, Mooloo Downs, Yinnetharra and Mount Phillip, and, finally, just as the sun set, we arrived at Cobra Station. This was the easternmost point of the Carnarvon mail run, even though Mount Augustus homestead was only another twenty-five miles further on. Mount Augustus was served by the mail run out of Meekatharra. There was no-one to meet me at Cobra so I was obliged to stay the night.

Cobra, otherwise known as Bangemall, was owned by Ben Wilson and his brother, Jack. I suppose Ben was in his fifties. He was lean, grey haired and burnt from years in the sun. He was a kind man and he treated me and Smokey hospitably, giving us a big dinner. He told me that someone, he didn't say whom, would pick me up in the morning to take me to Mount Augustus.

Ben filled the evening with the Bangemall story. The homestead had once been the Bangemall Inn, its thick stone walls completed in

1896. He described how prospectors travelled here by steamer from Fremantle to Carnarvon and then by coach the final 270 miles.

He talked about Charles Kingsford Smith. Until 1924, regular mail and supplies were carted from Carnarvon by camel trains to stations and mines throughout the region. Kingsford Smith saw an opportunity and started the Gascoyne Transport Company. One of the contracts they secured was the run from Carnarvon to the Bangemall goldfields.

I was just one more traveller following the beaten track.

Monday, as soon as the sun was up, we were up. After breakfast an old Land Rover appeared, slowly coming over the creek bed and on up to the homestead. The driver sat at the wheel for half a minute and then got out and slammed the door shut with the singular clanging noise that Land Rover doors make. He appeared to me to be elderly. He walked with a slight stoop. He was wearing khaki trousers and a khaki shirt, flat-heeled elastic-sided boots and a battered khaki hat. He wore spectacles and he had a very direct way of looking at you. Judging by his age and appearance, I wondered if he was the yardman from Mount Augustus.

He spoke to Ben and Jack, and then he glanced at me and said, 'Get your gear and put it in the Land Rover, son.' I did – and waited by the vehicle. The old bloke finished his conversation with Ben and Jack and then we were on our way. The gruff old driver quizzed me about where I had been and what I'd done.

'Can yer ride?' he asked.

'Of course.'

'How many times have yer fallen off?'

I gave it some thought and said, 'About twelve.'

'Well, yer can't bloody well ride then, can yer?'

'Why? Because I've fallen off that many times?'

He looked over at me and said, 'No. Because yer haven't fallen off enough. Yer can't ride until you've fallen off more than a hundred times.'

'Oh,' I murmured. I felt like giving him some sort of smart reply in return, but I didn't really know who he was, so I thought it would be wise to keep quiet.

Then he said, 'That dog of yours looks as though he's seen more dinner times than dinners.' Now I started to feel angry, but I kept my mouth shut.

The old fellow drove slowly and carefully, changing down at every watercourse and unhurriedly changing back up again. He drove at fifteen miles an hour. He said he always drove at fifteen miles an hour. He said you didn't have to change the oil so often if you drove slowly. Forty minutes after leaving Cobra, I had opened and closed half a dozen gates. We drove slowly around the gently sloping side of a low hill and down a fence line, and, in front, I saw a small homestead, a woolshed and a collection of corrugated-iron buildings. As we got closer, my mother and father came out of the homestead to meet us. They each greeted the old fellow with, 'Good morning, Mr Potts.' So that's his name, I thought.

Smokey and Dad had a very big reunion, and I went inside with my mother and my gear. 'Who's the old bloke?' I asked.

'Mr Potts,' she said, somewhat surprised at my question.

'Yeah, I know that. I just found out. But who's Mr Potts when he's at home?'

'Don't you know? He's the manager of Mount Augustus. He's the boss.' She paused. 'And he's a grumpy old sod.'

Of course, it was time for a cup of tea and a catch-up on all the news, but Mr Potts, Mr Ernest Potts, did not stay. He said his terse goodbyes and drove away so slowly you could barely hear the sound of the Land Rover's engine, which was a feat in itself.

Later in the morning, my father asked me casually if I knew how to shoe, and I said yes, not realising the point of his question. Perhaps I should have said no, because he showed me out to the horse yards where five horses were waiting. He handed me a box with shoes, nails, a hammer, a rasp and pincers, and told me to get on with it. With that he turned and walked off.

There was nothing for it but to get started. I was praying that these horses would be easier to handle than the horses on Winnininnie. And I was racking my mind to remember the full procedure. It is one thing to watch dozens of horses being shod and quite another to actually do it. Very soon I started feeling the effects of the time off in Carnarvon. The sweat was pouring off me. By lunch, I managed to get one horse shod, and then it was straight back to the other four. The day felt endless. It was dark when I finished, and no-one had come to ask if I needed a hand. It was backbreaking work if you didn't really know what you were doing. By the time I got to the last horse, my work was looking less than workmanlike. There was skin missing off several of my knuckles. That night I wondered whether station life was really what I wanted. It was too hard, too hard.

So began a year and a half of living in the shadow of Mount Augustus – and Mr Potts. Mount Augustus was always referred to as The Mount. Behind his back, Mr Potts was always referred to as Pottsy. Man and mountain, they were both landmarks. The authority of The Mount seemed to endorse the authority that Pottsy stamped on the country when he first arrived in 1921. You couldn't think of one without the other. They both demanded integrity of those who came in contact with them.

The Mount killed those who treated it lightly. For some, being ill prepared to tackle the climb resulted in death. For others, to be the butt of Pottsy's scorn for what he perceived as incompetence didn't exactly make you wish you were dead, but you certainly felt excoriated. Were they both that harsh all the time? No, not all the time. Pottsy had his mellow moments, although these were not easy to detect unless you knew him well.

The Mount can be beautiful, with exquisite pale pastel colouring that slowly becomes richly dark as the light changes late in the day. It rises 2,300 feet above the surrounding landscape. This is 3,600 feet above sea level – not very high as mountains go, but more than high enough to have a commanding presence. It stands alone. It can be seen from ground level as far as forty miles away and even from that distance it claims your attention. It fascinates. It lures. It beckons. You don't just look at it – you watch it, as if it were alive. You scan it from top to bottom; you examine the rock formations along its sides, the scrub, the shadows, and the colours always changing hue and tone. You feel it doing something to you, reaching deep and invading your mind as well as your senses. It exudes a force, as if to say, 'Respect me.' Its effect alters you. Oh, how I wanted to climb to the top, up where the birds swirled in the air currents, far above the surrounding stony plains.

Mount Augustus Station was a focal point in the Upper Gascoyne. All roads seemed to lead there. Travellers on their way up from Meekatharra in the south headed east through Woodlands towards the Great Northern Highway about 200 miles away, or headed west towards Carnarvon.

But Mount Augustus was also a destination that attracted many who sought to be in Pottsy's aura. When it came to station management, cattle breeding and especially horse breeding, Mr Ernest Potts was an authoritative figure – and he knew it. Lunch at Mount Augustus, always on the dot of 11.45, could be a challenge for visiting station owners and managers, or the representatives of service companies such as Elders. If visitors were late, Pottsy started without them and then had something caustic to say about their tardiness. Pottsy did not suffer fools, and he was hard on people who in his opinion did not know what they were talking about. But visitors were usually rewarded with information or knowledge worth having.

The station was renowned too for its one million acres of good-quality river-flats country, about ninety miles from west to east. From one end of the station, in the east where it meets Woodlands Station, the Lyons River makes its way right through the property, parallel to The Mount and then out the western end. It was primarily a cattle station, running up to 17,000 head across maybe

80 per cent of the property, with 10,000 sheep on the remaining 20 per cent.

The homestead was near the base of the northeastern end of The Mount. There was a large house for the manager and a cluster of buildings for workshops, vehicles and men's quarters, and there was a shed for fodder for the horses and a tack room. The house was referred to as the homestead, but the whole collection of buildings was also referred to as the homestead. So if you were in one of the workshops and you asked where Mr Potts was, the answer would be, 'At the homestead', meaning the house.

The sheep run was started in 1926 at the western end and it was subdivided into several paddocks in the early 1940s. There was a small homestead there too, but to differentiate it from the main homestead, it was referred to as the woolshed, or sometimes the woolshed homestead. A woolshed is the same thing as a shearing shed; the names are interchangeable. At Belele it was always 'the shearing shed'.

Integral to Mount Augustus Station and its culture was the resident community of Aboriginal people. They referred to themselves as Yamatjis, the word *Yamatji* meaning 'Aboriginal man'. The Yamatjis' sense of belonging was respected by the pastoralists, and as manager, Pottsy supported and provided for them. Their numbers fluctuated but hovered around twenty. Although no more than half actually worked, they were all fed and clothed and their health was watched over. Those who worked were paid wages. Sick and injured Yamatjis were attended to by Pottsy's wife, Madeline. Like so many other women on stations, she had a close relationship with all of them – especially, of course, the women. She soothed them and listened with sympathy and understanding to what they were prepared to tell her. Matters that were strictly blackfella business stayed with the blackfellas.

The term *Yamatji* is well known and is used throughout the Murchison and the Gascoyne, an area of a million square kilometres. Beneath that umbrella nomenclature, there are twenty-four groups, each with their own culture, language and traditions. Those who belong to the area in the vicinity of The Mount call themselves Wadjari, as well as Yamatji.

To the Wadjari, The Mount is known as Burringurrah. For them it has deep spiritual significance. When I did eventually make the climb and looked into the dark, steep depths of its countless gullies and crevices, I could understand why. The feeling was eerie, disturbing. Just off the northwestern end of The Mount, in the bed of the Lyons River, lies a deep, permanent water called Cattle Pool. This too has great spiritual significance for the Wadjari.

For the Wadjari and everyone else who lived at The Mount, the dominating but unifying presence of Pottsy was felt everywhere. He was never out of our conversations for long. He was not well liked, which didn't seem to bother him, but he was respected and he was feared. Perhaps his reputation as a man who would rather have a fight than a feed preceded him, although the Pottsy I knew wielded his authority by the sheer force of his personality.

There was a frequently told story of Pottsy having a heated argument with a young drover named John Edney and how the blue escalated into a fight. Finding that the more energetic younger man was dancing around, just keeping out of his reach, trying to wear him out, Pottsy dropped his hands and said, 'Come with me.'

He led Edney up a small slope to an abandoned water tank with a ladder up the outside. Pottsy ordered him to get inside and then followed him in. 'Now run away from me, you young bastard,' he said. And he gave the younger man a thrashing.

Pottsy started his working life as a horse tailer in the Queensland outback, went to the First World War as a private and came out as a commissioned officer. He also came out with a .303 bullet embedded in his chest. As Sir Ernest Lee-Steere recalled in his memoirs, late in his life Pottsy was advised to have an X-ray of his chest. To everyone's surprise, including Pottsy's, the result was a clear picture of a bullet in the area of his lungs.

Sir Ernest also wrote, 'I rarely, if ever, heard him praise anyone.' Nevertheless, he said Pottsy was 'one of the markers by which I measured myself through life'.

At the same time as I was coming to terms with Pottsy, The Mount, the Yamatjis and all the unusual people coming and going, I found myself immersed in beautiful horses. Mount Augustus horses were the best in the Norwest. That's what I was told, time and time again, by horsemen from far and wide. Pottsy was legendary for all kinds of reasons, but especially because he was such a great horseman. He gave me high-quality thoroughbreds to ride and my relationships with horses went to a new, exciting level.

The memories and the influence of Pottsy and The Mount are part of who I am.

7

Two Dutchmen and a Norwegian

No-one could foresee that 1952 was the beginning of the end of the era of high wool prices. The pastoralists continued on as though all they had to contend with was the inevitable next drought. With wool still so profitable, stations could afford to employ many people. At the main homestead on Mount Augustus, apart from the thirty or so Yamatjis, there was Bris Ford, the full-time windmill man, plus an old fellow who was a mechanic and who also did plumbing work and odd jobs. White stockmen and station hands came and went.

At the woolshed, apart from my father, who was in charge, the population fluctuated, depending on the workload, but I was there permanently. Another young stockman, Albie Zilko, alternated between the woolshed and the main homestead. This was also the case with three Yamatjis – Mitchell and Gilbert Dooler, and old Snowball.

My mother was the unpaid cook who prepared three meals a day for everyone. Cooking on a wood stove was a tiring and seemingly never-ending trial in the long, hot summer.

Another member of our team was the outcamp man, but his shack was about twenty miles away and we saw him only once a week at the most.

Last but not least, there were two permanent station hands, Dutch migrants who had come to Australia on assisted passages. They were not at Mount Augustus by choice – it was conditional that for two years they worked wherever the government sent them. Their names were Pieter den Besten and Bill van Rijn.

Mount Augustus was a shock to Pieter and Bill in every way: the corrugated-iron men's quarters, the food, the heat, the work, the emptiness of the harsh, stony country, and especially the remoteness. Life on a sheep station was utterly alien to them. Fortunately, they both spoke fluent English. Pieter was fair haired and fair skinned. He was a good-looking fellow and he tackled his work with energy. Bill was tall and dark haired, with a slightly darker complexion. Bill was a thinker and he was slow moving. If they found Australia foreign and strange, to us they were exotic. Despite their accents, they spoke with more precision and clarity than we did with our Aussie drawl. Their focus on anything was more intense too. Part of my role was to teach them.

At the woolshed, we consumed a sheep every four or five days, and for that purpose we maintained a mob of seven or eight wethers in a small paddock. This was square, a mile by a mile, and it adjoined a paddock the same size, called the Cow paddock. These wethers were called killers, and when we killed one it was always late in the day so it could hang overnight in the meat room. This was a special small building with flywire walls to allow the cooler air of the night through so the meat would set. In the morning, the carcass would be butchered.

Teaching Bill the art of cutting a sheep's throat, bleeding it, skinning it and dressing it was as much of an experience for me as it was for him. I showed him how to lie the sheep on its side and bend its head back to make the cutting easier and faster. Bill knelt down and positioned himself above the sheep and, when he plunged in the narrow-bladed knife, he swore at the sheep. 'You bloody sheep, you. I kill you, you bastard.'

He was trembling and he behaved as if he was angry. Watching and listening, I was confused. For me, killing a sheep was routine. Bill's attitude was so uncharacteristic it unnerved me. Perhaps the act of killing a harmless sheep for the first time was so foreign to him that the only way he could handle it was to work up an anger. The moment passed and we continued with the lesson as if nothing had happened. He certainly did not behave that way again.

Driving with Bill in the truck one day, I stopped to shoot a kangaroo. A small mob was standing still, about sixty yards away. Bill had been pestering me for days to let him have a shot, so I handed him my rifle. While he was getting set, the kangaroos decided it was time to move on. Bill fired at one of the roos while it was hopping. 'Why are you shooting now? What do you expect to hit?' I asked.

'I'm shooting for the head,' he replied.

'While it's hopping?'

'Sure. Why not?'

Shooting a kangaroo while it's stationary is hard enough. While it's hopping, you might fluke hitting it in the body, but shooting it in the head is impossible. Bill was not convinced.

He and Pieter had many qualities I enjoyed, and I sensed they had much to offer me. Bill, in particular, attracted me. Before long, we were talking about books. Of all the writers he discussed, Dostoevsky snared my interest the most. We talked in the men's quarters after dinner, with the insects smacking against the glass of the pressure lamp on the veranda. When we grew dry from talking, we took a swig from the water bag hanging outside on the edge of the darkness.

His voice was sonorous as he described *Crime and Punishment*, *The Idiot* and *The Brothers Karamazov*. When he warned me that reading *Crime and Punishment* at too young an age might send me mad, it was an absorbing moment: sitting in a pool of light, enveloped by the intense blackness and silence of the night, with everyone else asleep. Nothing else existed.

Of course, I was compelled to see what effect the book would have. On my next trip to Perth, I went to Albert's Bookshop, in

Forrest Place, and bought it. I still have it. On the inside cover I wrote my name and the date I bought it: May 1953. The introduction was sobering:

> For the deepest essence of tragedy, though it avoid the final catastrophe – for the evocation, that is to say, of the profoundest feelings of pity and terror which can purge the reader's heart – there is, I believe, no work of literary fiction that can take its place by the side of Dostoevsky's *Crime and Punishment*. [The work of other writers] becomes but as a melting rushlight in the fierce glow of Dostoevsky's powers, in the vast and dreadful flickers of his imagination.[3]

Well, Bill did warn me – but I not only survived, I took a big step up the ladder in the world of real literature. Dickens and Walter Scott and Alexandre Dumas were a far cry from Dostoevsky, although Edgar Allan Poe's dark tones gave hints. *Crime and Punishment* was a new world of intensity and challenge, which, once tasted, demanded more involvement. It was the start of my love affair with Russian writers. Bill gave me far more than I was ever able to give to him.

Like every day in January, it was hot. Bill and Pieter and I had driven out to Clarke Well in the Commer truck (usually it was referred to simply as 'the Commer' or 'the truck') to repair a line of fence. This well was in a wide, shallow depression. The fence that needed repair ran east–west, and the track that took us to the well ran beside this fence. The last 200 yards or so were in the depression, where the ground was thick with clumps of coarse knee-high grass. It was here that we had to work on the fence.

The surrounding scrub stopped at the edge of the depression and started again on the other side. There was a scattering of straggly bushes in between, but not much. It was really quite a pretty, peaceful spot. The scrub contrasted with the emptiness of the depression and its sun-dried, yellow grass moving slightly in the fitful easterly breeze.

We set about the work, replacing rusted, broken wires and straining them tight. Simple things to me were confusing to Bill and Pieter but they were eager to learn and they took direction without hesitation. The word *strainer* had two meanings, the first was a heavy post to which the fence wires were fixed as they were strained tight. The second was an implement used to strain the wires. This was made from a stout piece of bush wood with a fork. The Y shape was ideal. The stem at the bottom of the Y had a hole, through which the end of the wire was passed. The top two ends of the Y served as handles. By turning the handles, the fence wire was wound around the stem. When it was tight enough, a thick steel punch was hammered into the hole in the strainer post, jamming the wire tight so it stayed put. Then the wire on the strainer tool was unwound and wrapped around the post three or four times and then fixed back on itself.

Bill and Pieter worked well. As the day advanced, the temperature climbed and the scorching easterly gained strength, and all three of us were sweating. By midday, it was time for a break and a billy of tea. I stopped what I was doing and said, 'Righto, boys, that'll do for a while.'

While the tools were being gathered together, Pieter straightened up and took the cigarette butt from his mouth and deftly flicked it a full ten yards out into the paddock.

It was as if the grass was lying in wait. The speed with which it ignited shocked me. By the time I reacted and ran to the fire, the wind had caught it and it was spreading fast. Bill and Pieter stood by the fence and watched. It was too much for me to stamp out. 'For Christ's sake,' I yelled. 'Grab some empty bags off the back of the truck and help me beat it out.'

Pieter said, 'Why we don't let it just burn?'

'Because it'll burn the whole bloody place,' I screamed.

For the next two hours we fought the fire. It was a miracle that we had empty hessian bags in the truck. I told Pieter to put an armful in the water trough to soak. We thrashed and beat at the flames until the bags dried out, and then we'd run to the trough and get more, stuffing the dried bags back into the water. At one point we had a front that was forty yards wide. Smoke was billowing into the sky. I did not dare to send Pieter or Bill to get help, because that would leave only two of us. I urged them on. I urged myself on. The smoke made our eyes sting. Our arms were aching and heavy. When the fire reached an area where the clumps of grass were thinner, we redoubled our efforts to get it under control. For half an hour we patrolled the dividing line between the blackened, burnt ground on one side and the waving, inviting, long-stemmed grasses on the other side.

Then, believe it or not, we lit another fire. This was in the shadow of the water tank, where we could boil a billy for tea. I looked at my two Dutch mates and saw their black-smudged faces – and their exhaustion. There was no point in giving them a lecture. They were as shocked as they were tired. Knowing the naiveté of these two, I figured I should have warned them. We did talk about it, though – but quietly.

It was a glaring day of white heat that seemed to pour out of the clear blue sky. There was relief under the bough roof of the stables. Two horses were standing by the overflowing trough waiting to be shod, while I procrastinated; they stood head to tail so they could swish away the flies from each other's eyes. An elderly man came walking down the track and over to where I was standing. He had a wizened, meagre body, dark as mahogany. His face was as gnarled and creased as a walnut. His very pale blue eyes looked exhausted. He was in his middle sixties. He introduced himself with a thick foreign accent. 'My name vas Andy. Andy Johansen. I am come to do vencing,' he said.

His manner was self-effacing, gentle. 'Have you got a cool drink of vater to spare?'

'Water bag's under that old veranda,' I said. I followed him over to the dust-choked bag dripping on the dirt floor.

That day, he had driven the twenty miles from the main homestead to the woolshed with two tyres that had perished tubes. He knew his repair kit might not last the distance to his camp, where he had spare tubes and patches, but he would not permit himself to ask Pottsy to help him out. After four hours of driving and many blowouts, he had run out of patches. He gathered handfuls of dry grass in his big, hard hands, and he stuffed the offending deflated tyres. Then, limping and chugging along at a full ten miles an hour, it got to the point where the radiator boiled. He could see the woolshed roof shimmering in the distance, so he walked in.

When the sweat had dried on his bony chest, he trudged out into the heat carrying two new tubes, a pocketful of patches and a two-gallon can of water that I had given him. It was a pretty bad feeling to watch him stumble along the stony road, swaying with the weight of the water can. My insistence that I should drive him back had fallen on deaf ears. He had looked at me reproachfully, as if I'd cast a slur on his character.

Much later, when Andy had to replace the clutch plate in his ute, he did it on his own, in the middle of a bare flat, under a scorching sun. He never complained, unless you offered to help him. He considered that he was his own responsibility – no-one else had any right to interfere in his personal tasks.

But on that first day, the ute, when it came slowly into view between the woolshed and the shearers' quarters, looked like a relic from the 1930s. It was moving so slowly there was little or no dust.

He camped out on the job, some ten or twelve miles away, and he told us, 'I von't bozzer you.' But when he came in to the woolshed homestead for fresh supplies of tea and flour, we made him join us in the dining room for a mug of tea. Gradually, we wore down his reserve. He told us about his girlfriend in Meekatharra and how she looked after him when he was in town; how she cooked for him and made cakes for him, which she sent out on the mail truck. He complained about the crows and how they would steal chunks from his damper if he left it in the open while he was working down the fence line.

Then, one afternoon, he noticed some mail on the dining room table. It had arrived that morning. He was not a stickybeak, but when he saw my father's name on some envelopes, he said, thoughtfully, 'Parkes. Mmmm.'

It was as if, seeing it written, the significance of our surname had suddenly dawned on him.

'So,' he said. 'I knew a man called Parkes vonce. Vorty years ago.' He had his right elbow on the table and he stroked his lips with his middle finger. We waited. 'Ya,' he said, 'in Onslow.'

My father looked quite startled. 'You mean Herbert Parkes?' he asked.

'Ya. I sink so.'

'Well, that was my father. How did you come to know him?'

'Zat vas a long story. I vas shipwrecked on ze Eighty Mile Beach. Zat vas just before ze First Vorld Var. After three days, ve vas found. Zen I had to look for vork. I go to Port Hedland. Zen I go to Roebourne. I stayed zere a vhile. Zen I vent to Onslow and Mr Parkes he give me a job. I like him. He vas a gentleman to me. I vorked for him a few years. Don't remember how many.'

He looked around the table at each of us in turn: my father, my mother and me. Suddenly, he stood up. He reached his hand out to my father and said, 'I must shake your hand again. So you are his son.'

He turned to me and reached for my hand, saying, 'So you must be his grandson. Vell, vell. All zis time. All zis time.'

Andy was Norwegian. He sailed on some of the last sailing ships that carried wool or grain, until he was washed ashore halfway between Broome and Port Hedland.

One day he told me about the time he was bitten by a redback spider. In his slow, matter-of-fact way of speaking, with his heavy Norwegian accent, he told me how he was sitting in the dunny at the shearers' quarters and was bitten on the head of his penis.

Dunnies were a favourite place for all kinds of spiders to lurk and we usually brushed them away if there were any too close to where we sat. Andy had neglected to do that – and he paid the price. At first there was only a bit of a sting but, as the day wore on, the pain grew extreme – and the head of his penis became swollen and red. That night he was desperate. He had no painkillers and very little first-aid material. So he used his shovel to drag a heap of red-hot coals away from the flames and he took off his pants and he knelt down as near as he could. He took hold of his penis and poked it almost into the pile of hot coals. And he kept it there until the pain from the heat of the coals was greater than the pain from the spider bite. When he couldn't stand it any longer, he leaned back and rested. Then he leaned forward and started the process again. He did this, over and over, through the night. Eventually, he went to bed and slept for many hours. When he woke, the pain and the swelling had reduced, but it was several days before his penis returned to normal.

In Andy's mind, his fire treatment had been effective. Who knows? His story impressed me greatly and the moment was intensely memorable. After that, I kept my eyes open for redbacks in dunnies.

8

Gilbert, Mitchell and Snowball

At Mount Augustus the Yamatjis befriended me: the young men and old men, in their own quiet, dignified way. Not so the women – they were not unfriendly, but they chose to stay shyly on the periphery. My special friends were Mitchell and Gilbert Dooler. Mitchell was tall, solid, well muscled and gentle. His brother Gilbert was not quite as tall and he carried a large pot. Gilbert was smart. He enjoyed banter and joking, including jokes at his own expense. Mitchell did too, but he was quieter and more reflective. Both of them were well presented, fastidiously clean, well mannered and well spoken. They set an example to the whitefellas. Before any meal, or morning or afternoon tea, they washed their faces and hands. The whitefellas didn't. They washed their clothes regularly. The whitefellas didn't. Some of the white employees didn't shower or bathe from one month's end to another. For a few weeks, there was an elderly man working at the woolshed on the plumbing in the shearers' kitchen and you could smell him from ten yards away.

Gilbert was more fun to talk with than most of the whitefellas. We were easy about referring to each other as a blackfella or a whitefella. For us, they were never pejorative terms. The implications always depend on the relationship and the context and the tone. Gilbert and Mitchell and I joked and laughed together so much I felt accepted – and I learned a lot from them.

Gilbert's humour was always at the ready. He loved to tease, to poke fun. He would chuckle from deep inside and his round face would crease up. So many times I watched him wipe the tears from his eyes, while I too was laughing. Even though the joke was on me, I had to laugh the day he took four horses out to Koorabooka paddock to spell. He went alone with the horses and, an hour or so later, I followed in the Commer and picked him up. When I arrived at the bore on the fence line between Deep Well and Koorabooka paddocks, Gilbert was sitting on the top rail of the post-and-rail enclosure around the bore and the windmill. 'I'm lookin for a blackfella called Gilbert. You seen him anywhere?' I asked.

'Nah. There's no blackfellas round here, mate,' he said.

'Well, you look a bit like a blackfella. You'll do.'

'Whatever yer reckon. Anyway, can yer gimme a lift?'

'Chuck your gear in the back and jump in.'

Gilbert put his saddle, bridle and saddle blanket in the back and got in the cab. As we turned and headed back to the woolshed, Gilbert said, 'Which way you come ere?'

'Whaddaya mean, "Which way?" There is only one way. Down through the Cow paddock and then through Deep Well.'

'No. You coulda come through the Killers paddock and then inta Deep Well.' And he started to laugh.

'What are you bloody laughing at?' I had to ask.

When he could hold his laughter back enough to speak, he said, 'I thought you'd come through the Cow paddock – and through the wooden gates.' And the laughter got the better of him again.

'For Christ's sake,' I said, 'what are you bloody laughing at?'

'I knew you'd come that way, I knew it, so I pissed all over the gate handle.' Then he laughed until his eyes were swimming and his whole body was shaking and I was infected by his laughter and I started laughing too. Of course I made a show of protesting and threatening to beat him up. Gilbert just laughed. We were still laughing and carrying on when we got back to the woolshed. Over the following days we continued to relive the joke. Every time we did, I would mock punch him and wrestle him, which simply made him laugh all the more.

Political activists would say that Gilbert's joke was the gesture of an Aboriginal letting the white man know what he thought of him. But that's not how it was. Gilbert would have done the same to a blackfella, even his own brother. Come to think of it, especially to Mitchell. Was it a problem for me? Not at all. What about the contamination of the cast-iron gate handle, the hygiene? What contamination? By the time I got there, the scorching sun had removed any trace of Gilbert's joke.

On another occasion, when Gilbert and I were riding together, we both felt the need for a leak. We stood a few yards apart, facing the same direction, with our horses behind us. As I was standing there, urinating into the dirt, Gilbert suddenly said, 'Hey. Look at that big white gumtree over there.'

He was on my left and pointed to his right. It seemed he was pointing past me, so I turned my head to see what he was looking at. 'What bloody gumtree?' I asked.

'The big white one you've got in your hand.'

With that he laughed until he cried.

Mitchell was tall and strongly built. I always thought of him as being powerful, not that I ever saw him do anything that required great strength. For all his size, or maybe because of it, he was gentle. He loved to hold a small puppy in his cupped hands – his large, strong, capable hands cradling a soft, helpless puppy.

Like Gilbert, Mitchell enjoyed a joke, but he did not laugh as much and he never played the same kind of practical jokes. He preferred to talk softly about himself and about his world. He told me about a girlfriend he had, somewhere near Gascoyne Junction. The Yamatji word for young woman is *coorie*. He always referred to her as 'this coorie'. He left us for a while, and when he came back, he told me he had been to see this coorie. We sat together on his wire stretcher late one night, just the two of us, and he described her to me. He told me how much he liked her, how much he wanted her. I asked him if he and she had a njeem on his last visit. *Njeem* was the Yamatji word for having sex. He said, 'Nah. She got da plowers.'

'What do you mean?'

'She got da plowers,' he insisted.

'I dunno what you're talking about.'

'Oh, I dunno,' he said. 'Don't you know what happen every month with a woman?'

'You mean periods?'

'Yeah. We call im plowers.'

'Plowers.'

'No. Plowers!'

And then I realised he was saying 'flowers' and in his Yamatji accent it was coming out 'pflowers'. I said, 'Oh, I get it. You mean flowers.'

'That's what I said,' Mitchell replied softly.

Mitchell and I were sent out to bring in a small mob of horses spelling in Deep Well paddock. Deep Well was mostly open country. Not much scrub grew on the crabhole flats. We agreed it would be quicker to go looking instead of trying to pick up tracks at a windmill. There was a rise on the south side which had enough elevation to provide a sweeping view. We stopped on the edge of this rise, where the ground fell away steeply. We scanned the country, looking for distant animal shapes and looking for movement. I was lost in thought and concentration when Mitchell, who had been looking to his left, suddenly turned his head and pointed straight past me to our right and said, 'There they are.'

When I looked to where he was pointing, there were the tiny figures of four horses grazing. In the distance, their shapes were insubstantial and vague. His discovery was so abrupt it took me by surprise. 'How come you suddenly turned and saw them like that?' I asked.

'While I was lookin over the other way, I felt you liftin up your whip and stickin out the handle to poke me in the eye. So I turned and straight way saw the horses.'

'But I didn't do that.'

'I know. But it felt like you were goin to.'

We clattered down the slope and trotted across the soft flats. We gathered up the four horses and brought them in to the woolshed. Later, several times, we talked about that moment when Mitchell felt a compulsion to look to his right and saw in a flash what we had spent ten minutes searching for. We figured that maybe he could sense the presence of the horses way out in the distance and that maybe that feeling was bringing their dark shapes closer and closer to his right eye. And his first thought was that it was horseplay from me. That's how we were: like young colts that play around, striking, kicking, biting, but rarely connecting. If colts do connect, it is never hard enough to really hurt.

If Gilbert and Mitchell were teachers, the professor was an old blackfella with a big, black, round stomach. His name was Snowball. Pottsy sent him out to the woolshed for a few weeks when Mitchell and Gilbert were away on blackfella business. The first day my father and I went mustering with him, the morning was crisp and fresh. He piled his saddle on his horse and went away to get his crib, stuffing it into his saddlebag as he came back. He tied the saddlebag to the dees on the saddle and flipped the reins over his horse's head. With great effort, he put his foot in the stirrup. Sighing and wheezing, he grabbed hold of the pommel to heave himself aboard. But he didn't make it. Instead he collapsed on the ground, on his back, with his legs and arms in the air – and the saddle on top of him. He had forgotten to tie the girth. It was a funny sight. Luckily he was unhurt, and we helped him to his feet and helped him saddle up.

Years earlier Snowball had caught a man who had stolen his woman and he had brained him with a nulla-nulla, which seemed fair enough at the time. But the man died and Snowball had to serve several years tracking for the police in Perth. After he'd served his time, he wandered away with a circus as a general hand. When he came back to the station country, he acquired another wife and had some sons and daughters. All his brood were as shy and timid as wild grey kangaroos.

One day we were drifting in the dust behind several hundred sheep that were straggling across the never-ending crabhole flats, making for a windmill on the fence line. It was called crabhole country, I suppose, because the whole area was pockmarked, like a giant crumpet, with holes, sort of round, about nine inches across and about a foot to eighteen inches deep. Horses not bred in that country sensed the problem and baulked at the edge. Horses that knew weren't bothered at all, even when the crust broke and one leg dropped down. The top layer was soft soil sitting on a hard, concrete-like base and, I think, the water drained away at the level of the base, leaving hollow spaces here and there.

Snowball rode over to the carcass of a sheep that was grossly swollen but was still without the smell of rot. He stood his horse alongside and read the ground. 'One dhu-dhu been kill this jeeboo,' he said.

'Yeah,' I said. There were dingo tracks in the dust. Bits of plucked-out wool tumbled in the wind.

'Poor fulla,' he said. 'Might be that government dogger fulla better clean up round this way.'

Next day we had to pass the same place and Snowball rode over to the carcass. He called me to join him. 'Hey,' he said. 'We shoulda been poison this jeeboo, you know. Six dhu-dhu been here last night and we'da killed them all, you know.'

How did he know six dogs had been there? Sure, I could see the dusty ground was all mixed up with dog tracks, but they all looked the same to me. Six? When I chatted with him about it, he was adamant that the number was correct. Snowball's authority being what it was, I accepted his word.

Snowball rarely spoke and when he did speak he was not easy to understand: his voice was so low and he barely moved his lips. My father was impatient with him and decided it was easier to let me be the go-between. Snowball and I accepted that and, from then on, he ignored anyone else who tried to give him instructions or extract a report from him. If he came in late from mustering, he would walk up to the homestead for his dinner and my father would say, 'Your mate's here. You better go and find out what's what.'

Sitting outside with him, as the last of the day faded quickly, I'd stay while he ate his dinner in the meagre light spilling out from the homestead. In between mouthfuls he would tell me how many sheep he'd mustered, what their condition was like and whether he'd noticed fencing or windmills that needed attention. I asked the questions. He mumbled his answers. Sitting with him was easy. In his unhurried way of being, he gave me the feeling he had a lot to give me – and probably would.

When he was back at the main homestead, Snowball was Pottsy's choice for someone to go with him to open the gates on his inspections round the station in the Land Rover. I think it was probably a semi-retirement job for Snowball. And company for Pottsy. I'm sure the two old men had a shared history. They seemed comfortable with each other. Well, maybe. I wasn't with them enough to really know. But it's what I like to think. Whenever I saw them driving around together, I felt they looked good. An old whitefella and an old blackfella who had known each other for many years. Neither of them had to prove anything to the other. I wouldn't call it intimacy, but I'd call it a kind of companionship. Pottsy was always the boss and Snowball always did as he was told, and Pottsy treated him with gruff courtesy. I saw no signs of friction between them.

There is something basic and rich in the heart of old blackfellas that white men find hard to understand. It is a simplicity and a purity and a respect for their instincts. But I think Pottsy was one who understood. He was a bit that way himself.

Snowball was the quietest native stockman I ever knew. He camped alone and ate alone and preferred to work alone. Actually, he preferred not to work. As he got older and his energy declined, he found it increasingly difficult to accept the fact that he had to work. Sometimes he'd fail to show up at the house for his evening meal. The other Yamatjis didn't worry about him. But I was worried the first time he did it to me. I went to his camp and found him lying on his bed, softly groaning. I said, 'Hullo Snowball, old fella. What's the matter with you?'

'Oh Chrishe, boss. I been killed. My tumack ache ohhhhhh.'

As I lifted up his shirt, I wondered what was going on inside that black mound. His voice was almost a whisper: 'Ohhhhhh, you not gonna make me work termorra are you?'

'Snowball,' I said. 'I think you've been eating too much bungarra. You'll be all right directly, and if you're not, we won't be able to give you any more tucker until that bungarra has passed right through.' And I grinned at him.

In the morning he came to breakfast with a very sour face. *Bungarra* is the Yamatji word for an Australian monitor lizard that grows up to five feet long. Elsewhere in Australia, bungarras are known as sand goannas. They are a favourite food of the Yamatjis.

Mustering with Snowball was not like mustering with anyone else. He said nothing unless he had to. He was never impatient. He set his own pace; he took his time saddling his horse and then shuffling down the track before mounting. It was an effort for him to get up into the saddle, but he did, on his own. We never gave him skittish young horses to ride; we all had a soft spot for the old man.

Every six or seven weeks, we brought in fresh horses, and on one occasion, Pottsy sent me out with Snowball to bring in six. Just the two of us. We headed for the windmill where the horses usually watered. We mooched around on the outskirts of the mill and the tank and the trough. I followed a few yards behind, giving Snowball space. It certainly wasn't my place to take the lead. He picked up tracks that he thought were those of the horses we were after. The mooching was over; Snowball let his horse pick up a quicker walk. For twenty minutes we followed the tracks, through sandy watercourses where the hoof prints caved in, across stone-strewn ground where it was sometimes difficult to see any mark, just a scuff on the surface, and all the while Snowball was thinking.

When he was in tune, he rode with his right arm out to the side, the upper arm almost at right angles to his body and his forearm hanging down parallel to his body. His right hand pivoted from the wrist and twisted and turned and swept, and with the back of his hand he seemed to indicate a direction. I rode behind him in silence, watching his arm and hand, watching the slow rhythm of his movements, looking at the ground to try to see what he could see. I imagined that he was anticipating where the mob was heading: maybe around that hill and then down towards another watercourse where there was a lot of dry feed. He knew the horses we were after. He knew their inclinations in that particular paddock. When he was ready, he paused and waited for me to catch up. I stopped alongside him, and he told me what he was expecting and what he wanted me to do when we found the mob.

We rode on, side by side, until we saw the mob and the mob saw us. Then we split, Snowball going one way, me going another. The mob took off and Snowball galloped to head them. With his stockwhip cracking, he turned them and wheeled them into a bunch that we could manage. The two of us brought them into the horse yards at the woolshed. We unsaddled our horses, washed their backs and let them roll. Then Snowball and I walked together up to the homestead for a mug of tea.

You can't put a price on that kind of experience.

When we were mustering sheep, of course, we would split up, and I might not set eyes on him until lunch camp or at the end of the day. Every stockman riding alone is a solitary figure in the landscape. But there was something about Snowball that made him look especially solitary. He sat straight and still in the saddle. He moved steadily, never pushing his horse. Maybe my awareness of his general silence heightened my feeling of his solitariness. A silent horseman moving silently through silent country.

9

Ernest Potts – the marker

One of the ironies of the outback was the dramatic rise in the kangaroo population with the coming of the white man and the development of the pastoral industry. Prior to the sinking of thousands of bores and wells and the creation of so many watering points, kangaroos had long distances to cover between permanent water holes and good feed. The average annual rainfall in the Murchison and the Upper Gascoyne was seven inches, and most years it was way less than that. The flow of the big rivers was usually years apart. When there were droughts, the water holes dried up one by one, and the kangaroos had to cover increasing distances between water and survival feed. This had two effects: there was a high death toll and it restricted breeding.

Even when dry, the native grasses still provided sustenance for the kangaroos and the white man's stock. And the kangaroos had a winning edge. Fences did not stop them the way they stopped sheep and cattle. The fences consisted of several strands of wire with, maybe, a barbed wire on top. Kangaroos simply crouched down and slipped between the wires, and they were on their way again, heading for better pasture. Whereas sheep and cattle could be rounded up and controlled, kangaroos were independent and uncontrollable. If they felt threatened, they got going and kept going as long as they felt the threat behind them. Sometimes they stopped and looked back, sized up the situation and then got going again, jumping straight over the fences if the need was urgent.

In the sheep country on Mount Augustus, kangaroos were in plague proportions. Their numbers were incalculable. They were everywhere, particularly along the river flats of the Lyons River and along Koorabooka Creek. They were thick in the Cow paddock and the Killers paddock. As one way of reducing the numbers, Pottsy invited a team of roo shooters to shoot in Deep Well paddock. In four weeks they took off 3,000 kangaroos – and it didn't seem to make one iota of difference to the numbers, or to the equanimity of the surviving roos. They were indifferent to the slaughter. We found it difficult to believe that 3,000 kangaroos had been removed. The roo shooters laughed at our disbelief and assured us that their vans and trucks were fully loaded, week after week.

For some time, whenever I had the chance, I shot roos for the skins. This was good for pocket money. Because I wanted to get the best possible prices, I was selective and only shot big adults. The larger, thicker skins were the most valuable. Mostly, I shot from the truck while doing a windmill round. I also shot most evenings, when I fetched the milking cow and her calf from the Cow paddock and locked the cow in a small yard to prevent the calf from stripping her udder. I was on foot and had no means of bracing the rifle. Instead, I lined up a roo ahead of the cow, and I kept the cow between me and the roo as we walked closer and closer. The roo, of course, did not feel threatened by the cow, but it would usually be quite wary. When I got to within thirty or forty yards of the roo, I stood still and brought the rifle to my shoulder. As the cow walked on, the roo was exposed – and so was I. If I kept perfectly still, the roo didn't notice me – until it was too late. Rarely did I miss those shots.

At night, the roos came in to drink at the trough at the woolshed. The trough was close to the tank, which was on a very high stand. On bright moonlit nights, I waited in the shadows and listened. The windmill creaked and the blades of the fan responded to the slight breeze and the pump rod worked silently up and down and water gushed from the outlet from the column and gurgled into the tank. There were no other sounds. The widespread land all around me was silent and bright with the light of the full moon.

When I heard the faint pat, pat, pat of young kangaroos' feet as they hopped in and then stopped, I stayed still and listened intently. A minute or so later, I heard the bump, bump, bump of bigger kangaroos coming in behind the young ones. They too stopped and took stock. This procedure repeated itself until the small kangaroos reached the trough and started to drink. Then, and only then, would the adult kangaroos join them. That's when I shot from a distance of about ten yards. When a kangaroo was hit and it dropped, it created chaos. The mob couldn't see me and they didn't know which way to go. They hopped this way and that, stopping and looking. This usually gave me the opportunity to get a second one. When they were gone and the dust had settled, I set about the task of skinning and then disposing of the carcasses.

After I finished, I stood still and collected my thoughts. At my feet there would be two skins rolled up into two parcels. The skins from the hind legs were on the outside and were wrapped around and knotted to tie the pelts into neat bundles. The knotted ends served as handles.

There was a big variation in prices between good hides and not-so-good hides. The difference lay in the skinning. The best hides had no nicks or cuts, had no residues of flesh still attached and were a reasonably square shape. The trick was to use a razor-sharp knife to make the necessary cuts and to punch the skin off in front and along the sides, pulling it up and off the back, the same as we did with sheep. To dry the skins, I pegged them out on the wooden floor of the woolshed and painted them with weevil paint. This was fine until Pottsy turned up on one of his inspection tours.

He stood in the wide doorway and called me over. Oh no, I thought apprehensively as I walked across. I had four skins pegged out inside and he must have found them. 'What the fuckin hell are you doin?' he demanded. 'Wasting time shootin fuckin roos and then buggerin up the floor of the woolshed.'

'Well,' I said hesitantly, 'I only shoot when I'm on a mill round or in the evening when I bring in the cow.'

Pottsy glared at me through his thick glasses. 'Listen to me. I don't like it. You're buggerin up the woolshed floor.'

'Where else am I goin to peg em out?'

'Peg em out on the ground outside.'

'That's no good. They'll shrivel up in the sun.'

'Not if you peg em out properly.'

I was trembling. I shook my head. 'They're better pegged out inside.'

I knew he knew that – and I was pushing my luck. Pottsy tried to stare me down and we had a silent tussle for a few seconds. Then he stalked off, muttering, 'Somebody ought to teach you a lesson, you young bastard.'

As he went out the door and headed to his Land Rover, I took a deep breath and sat on a bench. Phew, I thought. I got out of that by the skin of my teeth. I'd had another telling off, but he didn't tell me I had to stop. Was that a win? Whoopee! Just be careful, I thought.

Some people do get cranky as they get older. The Pottsy I knew was more than grumpy: he disliked being corrected or reminded that something needed doing; and he reacted fiercely towards people who considered themselves to be above his authority. For me, it was never a major issue; it was easy to just ride it out. He had been the kingpin at Mount Augustus for thirty-two years, and he had been very successful in all aspects of running a cattle and sheep station. But sometimes his need to be contrary and remind you that he was the boss overrode his knowledge and common sense.

There was a time when we had two mustering teams cleaning up adjoining paddocks and we all met at the same windmill for lunch camp. The horses were hitched in a line along the fence. The Yamatjis were sitting quietly with their damper and quart pots of tea in the miserable shade of a few scraggly mulgas. Four white stockmen sprawled under different trees, avoiding the ants and trying to avoid the sun. The fire flared with the unfriendliness that fires have in the middle of a blisteringly hot day.

Mr Potts, on another of his tours of inspection around the property, arrived at our windmill. He stopped a hundred yards away from us. He walked up to the tank and filled his black quart pot. He walked back to his Land Rover and lit his own fire. He ate his lunch and smoked a cigarette. When that was done, he strolled over to talk to us. Actually, he talked at us. He abused everyone, collectively and individually. Our saddles were not properly greased. Our saddle blankets were not clean enough. The horses were not well-enough shod. We were spending too much time sitting on our arses. Then he strolled back to the Land Rover, where he fished under his seat and drew out a handful of sweets and threw one to each of us. He smiled to himself and drove away humming.

Another time, Gilbert and I were taking a mob of horses from the woolshed out to a paddock to spell. It was late in the afternoon and Pottsy turned up to make sure that what we were doing met with his approval. When we let the horses out of the yards and into the Killers paddock, I rode quickly to the head of the mob to block them from tearing off. Gilbert brought up the rear. This kind of formation was standard practice. Before we'd gone a hundred yards, Pottsy raced around the mob in his Land Rover and drove up level with me and stopped. He got out and yelled at me to get to the back of the mob. 'You don't move horses like that. Get behind them with Gilbert,' he shouted.

Pottsy then moved out of the way, and I did as I was told and joined Gilbert at the back. Gilbert wanted to know what was going on and I told him. 'Silly old bugger,' said Gilbert as we kicked our horses into a fast canter to catch up with the mob that was now careering away down to the bottom gate. Once we were through the gate and out of sight in Deep Well paddock, Gilbert and I reverted to normal procedure. Some two months later, when another mob of horses was to be moved and Pottsy was in attendance at the yards, he made a point of instructing us to have a rider in front, the better to control the mob. Nobody said a word.

One Saturday morning when I was at the homestead to collect the mail and pick up bits and pieces from the store, Pottsy was standing in his office, with his right foot up on his desk. He was bent over, engrossed in trimming his toenails with his pocket knife. I was fascinated. Cutting one's toenails with a knife is not an easy thing to do. There was an old saying, 'You only cut yourself with a blunt knife.' Pottsy's blade was clearly very sharp. His office was long and narrow and led through to the veranda of the homestead. Pottsy barely acknowledged me. As I was about to leave, Mrs Potts came out onto the veranda and said, 'Ernest, don't forget that tin of kerosene in the corner. That has to go down to the woolshed.'

'No it bloody doesn't,' said Pottsy, without looking up from his toenails. Mrs Potts didn't argue. She turned and went back inside the homestead.

The following Saturday, when I was putting stores on the back of the truck, Pottsy said, 'That four-gallon drum of kero. Take that to the woolshed.' I smiled to myself as I put the drum on the truck.

During shearing, the shearers went on strike because they didn't like the water from the bore. The wool classer was in charge of the team but he was obliged to bow to the shearers' wishes in matters like this. All work stopped while the issue was discussed with my father. Shearers and rouseabouts were standing around or sitting, smoking and listening. The wool classer pointed in a northeasterly direction and said, 'We've been told there's good water at a well about eight miles from here. The shearers want you to get a supply of water from there.'

A mile north of the woolshed, at the junction of the Cow paddock, the Killers paddock and Deep Well paddock, there was a well called Fry Well. About seven miles due east, along the fence line, there was a well called Bowes Well, near the bank of the

Frederick River. There was a discussion to ensure that this was the well the shearers had in mind. When that was resolved, I was sent off in the Commer, with five empty 44-gallon steel drums on the back and a length of hose to use as a siphon. As I drove along, I wondered how the shearers' local knowledge was so good that they knew about the 'better' water at Bowes. I never did find out.

When I arrived at Bowes Well, Pottsy and Snowball were there, having a dinner camp. The fire was going and the billy was on. I drove up to the tank and Pottsy came over and demanded to know what I was doing. I explained. 'Well,' he said, 'you can bugger off outa here.'

'But Mr Potts, I have to get water for the shearers.'

'No you bloody don't. Go back and tell the shearers they can go to buggery.'

I hesitated. Pottsy said, 'Go on. Get going.'

I put the truck in gear, turned it around and started back the way I'd come. Driving slowly, I considered the consequences of arriving back at the woolshed with no water. As I got closer to Fry Well, I changed down into second gear and crawled along to avoid raising a dust cloud. Then I stopped on the north side of the tank so that anyone with a sharp eye would not see me from the woolshed. The head of the windmill was clearly visible from the woolshed and, even though there was a bit of scrub in between, it was possible to see the general shape of the tank – so there was a chance that someone could see activity down there. I filled the drums. To my taste there was no difference between the water from Fry Well and the water from the woolshed bore. But I had to try my luck. Or my bluff, if you like.

With the drums full, I drove back to the woolshed and pulled up outside the shearers' kitchen. Four of the shearers and the wool classer sauntered out. My father came over and stood with the wool classer as the shearers siphoned water from a drum and did the formal tasting. Standing in the background, watching, I was so fearful I could hardly breathe. The sipping and tasting went on for at least two minutes, until the wool classer said, 'Well, what do you reckon?'

The shearers looked at each other. No-one wanted to be the first to say something. It was agonising. 'Well?' my father said.

One of the shearers said, 'Yeah . . . well . . . it's not bad.' And turning to me, he said, 'You got it from that well we told you to, eh?'

'Yeah mate,' I said. 'Course.'

Another of the shearers said, 'That's it then, eh. Let's get back to work and shear some fuckin sheep and make some fuckin money.'

Leaning against the side of the truck, I tried to stop my knees from shaking. I went with my father to the homestead and sat in the men's dining room with a cup of tea and told him my story. 'You're bloody lucky,' he said. 'If the shearers knew where you'd got the water there would've been hell to pay. For God's sake, don't breathe a word of this to anyone – even after they're gone. You can't let the word get around. If the same shearers come back next year, and they've heard about this little sham, there'll be a blue for sure.'

In 1953, the governor of Western Australia did a tour of the station country in the Norwest. Mount Augustus was on the itinerary. Sir Charles Gairdner and his wife stayed overnight, and the next day Pottsy set up a special lunch before the visitors moved on to their next destination. My mother and father and I were invited, as were others from the area, including Laurie and Barbara Bain from Woodlands Station. Barbara, known as Bubbie, was Pottsy's younger daughter.

As the governor was saying his farewells at the car, he went to the boot and took out a bottle of high-quality Scotch whisky and offered it to Pottsy as he thanked him. Pottsy, never one to be beholden to anyone, declined the gift. 'I don't need that,' said Pottsy. 'I've got plenty of Scotch whisky.'

Sir Charles, urbane as ever, turned to Laurie Bain, who was standing nearby. 'May I offer it to you then, Laurie?'

Laurie didn't hesitate. 'Yes, sir. Thank you, sir.'

Sir Charles presented the bottle to Laurie.

If Pottsy was renowned for being cantankerous, there was another side to him that was not well known. He knew when to allow the Yamatjis to dictate terms. One could argue that he didn't have much choice. People outside the pastoral industry didn't see and could not believe that Yamatjis had minds of their own. There is a prevailing stereotype of blackfellas under the heel of the white-man boss. The blackfellas I knew exercised a high degree of choice in what they did and how they lived. Pottsy respected their right to choose and didn't fight it. He compromised. White stockmen and station hands never had the latitude that the Yamatjis did.

At Mount Augustus homestead, quarters had been built for the white station hands, who were invariably single and usually young. The buildings were standard throughout the station country: bare concrete floors, unlined corrugated-iron walls, corrugated-iron roofs with no ceilings. The men's rooms were usually side by side in a row, with the doors opening onto a veranda running the full length of the building. A communal building for showering and washing was nearby. Open-hole toilets were a further, discreet distance away. In summer the buildings were cruelly hot, which led to the men sleeping on the veranda, or further out away from the building, to try to catch any stray breeze. In winter, the buildings were freezing. The temperature in the Murchison and the Gascoyne dropped to two or three degrees in the early hours of the morning. The only escape from the cold was more blankets and heavier clothing. It did not occur to us to complain. We accepted the conditions. There was no alternative. It was the same wherever you went.

And it was the same for the Yamatjis – but different. A building of the same type had been set up for them, but they did not accept it. They had an alternative: to camp out on the ground, under a bush, alongside a fire, the way their parents and forebears had lived. That was their choice. I talked with them about why they did not use the quarters built for them. They were very patient with me. They had been asked the same question by others, many times. They explained softly and carefully. They did not like the building: they felt it was an imposition on them. To insist that they use the building was taking away their right to sit on the ground and to sleep on the ground. Those that had a woman slept with her in a swag, with their dogs beside them and with the fire only inches away. Three Yamatjis each 'borrowed' a sheet of corrugated iron and propped that against a low branch of a bush and got a modicum of shelter from the sun. Rain was rare, and when it was wet it was drenching wet, and then they decamped to the veranda of the building built for them.

The Yamatji population at The Mount fluctuated. It ranged from very old to very young, men and women and children. Some women worked in the kitchen and around the homestead. One or two women did stock work. About seven or eight men worked as stockmen and station hands. Everyone was fed and clothed by the station. Everyone who actually worked got a wage, which was more like an allowance than a proper wage. Some of the younger men were quite casual about their relationship with the management: they felt they were entitled to go elsewhere for a few weeks or months and come back whenever they liked. And they did.

The same kind of casual attitude prevailed when the Yamatjis went on pinkeye camp each year. Elsewhere in Australia this was called 'going walkabout'. The terms *going on pinkeye* and *pinkeye camp* were widespread in the Murchison, the Gascoyne and the Pilbara. I didn't know the origins, or what *pinkeye* meant, but years later I heard that it may have been because they often returned with conjunctivitis.

When I was at The Mount, the Yamatjis chose to camp at Cattle Pool for pinkeye. They made camp well away from the beaten track from the main road in to the pool, and I got the impression it was upriver and on the other side. They settled in for several weeks. As Gilbert and Mitchell explained to me, that was their time for blackfella business. They sat around the fires and drank tea and ate damper and beef – no-one would ever notice the disappearance of a young steer in that country because no-one ever knew exactly how many there were. They talked – and they made decisions.

It was at the annual pinkeye camp that the young men were initiated. The way they were described to me, the 'young men' were really older boys, in their mid- to late teens. Part of the initiation process was circumcision. This was done at a secret location where no women, or the uninitiated, could see – or hear. The edge of a stone, split for the purpose, was used for the cutting. The bruised and bleeding penis was then covered in a thick mixture of ashes and heavy earth, clay for preference. Each youth was left alone at an isolated spot well away from the main camp. The men visited each of them regularly with food and water. After about two weeks, they were allowed to return to the main camp, their rites of passage almost completed.

Gilbert also told me about the practice of whistle cocking, a harsh method of birth control. This involved cutting a hole in the urethra close to the base of the penis so that ejaculations came out there instead of from the head of the penis. In some cases, the urethra was split open along most of the length of the penis. The inconvenient side effect of either method meant that a whistle-cocked man had to squat to urinate – like a woman. Gilbert and Mitchell were very matter-of-fact about all this. Maybe they could afford to be indifferent because neither of them had been whistle cocked. The whole concept made me wince.

Early in 1953, after the Yamatjis had been some weeks at Cattle Pool, Pottsy instructed me to find out when they would be coming back to work. 'Go and find your mate Gilbert and ask him how much longer they're going to be. I've got work I need them for.'

I drove to Cattle Pool in the truck. The scrub along the banks of the Lyons River was thicker than out on the flats and I drove in along the well-worn track to a roughly cleared area for sightseers. I got out of the truck and slammed the door shut with a loud clang.

The noise was a totally alien sound in the quiet stillness. As I was making my way through the bush in the direction I thought would take me to their camp, I saw Gilbert approaching. He was wearing nothing but a sort of loincloth – and a hat. Gone were the khaki shirt and trousers. Gone were the elastic-sided boots. In his near-nakedness, his big belly seemed all the bigger.

'Gidday,' he said. 'We stop ere, eh. I heard you comin so I come out to meet yer.'

'OK,' I said. 'How are you, you black bastard?'

'Better than you, you skinny whitefella. You look as though you need a good feed.'

We had some fun taking the piss out of each other for a while, until I had to ask the question: 'Pottsy wants to know when you blokes are coming back to work. What'll I tell him?'

From the moment he heard the truck coming in to Cattle Pool, Gilbert knew the reason for my visit, but he still dawdled over giving me an answer. Eventually he said, 'Maybe a coupla weeks . . . bout that . . . depends . . . maybe a day or so earlier . . . maybe a day or so later . . . depends.'

'So I'll tell Pottsy you'll be back in about a coupla weeks, OK?'

'OK,' he said.

We lingered for a while so we could exchange whatever news we had and pay each other a few more derogatory compliments.

On the drive back to the homestead to report to Pottsy, knowing he had work that needed doing, I was nervous about how he would react. He surprised me. 'OK,' he said. 'Well, there's nothin we can do about it, is there? The work'll just have to wait.'

And with that, he gave me a few instructions about things he wanted done at the woolshed – and sent me on my way.

10

The outcamp man
and the dogger

The ebb and flow of life at Mount Augustus brought odd people into our midst. They arrived, they paused and they went on their way. Some we didn't see again, some we did. At the main homestead there was frequent traffic.

A few times, someone turned off the Cobra road and drove past the woolshed to Elliott Creek or elsewhere, but only people who knew the track and the country. Our most frequent visitors were individual contractors with jobs to do for Mount Augustus or the government. They were all characters, curious people, mostly misfits who hated living in a town and preferred working alone, miles from anywhere, for months on end, with no way of communicating if anything went bad. Bluey the new outcamp man and Clarrie the dogger were two of those.

It was late at night when my father returned from a trip to Meekatharra and brought back the new outcamp man. The dogs and I heard them coming from the Lyons River crossing. In the outback you can hear a vehicle long before it arrives. Usually you know who it is by the sound of the engine, especially when it's changing gears through watercourses. I got the fire in the stove going and put a light outside. I knew my father would be tired and in need of a mug of tea, and when he walked into the kitchen, it was plain to see that he was irritable too. 'Have a good trip?' I asked.

'All right, except this new joker never stopped talking. He'd talk the leg off an iron pot. Reckons he's about the best stockman to come to this country. Reckons we've got no horses he can't ride. Reckons he's faster and cleaner than any gun shearer we've ever seen. And I'm blowed if he doesn't reckon he can hold more liquor than anyone between Meekatharra and Carnarvon.'

'Well, sounds like he can talk better than anyone else,' I said.

'Talk!' my father said. 'Talk!' And he flung a bundle of mail on the table.

'Oh, and by the way, this bloke's name is Bluey and he's been boozing in Meekatharra for two weeks – and he's broke. He's also still hung-over.' And he stamped off to see my mother.

By and by, Bluey came up from the men's quarters for a mug of tea. I expected to see some lanky, cheerful-looking chap – I don't know why. So I was surprised when in stomped a short, bow-legged figure with a face that was serious and stern. He was in his mid-twenties. He had reddish hair and a thin moustache, and he wore faded and patched jeans and brand new elastic-sided boots that were too tight. He had a vacant, sad look in his eyes. I wondered what he would look like with a big false nose, greasepaint and baggy trousers. I'd never seen anyone look so comical without trying.

The next day, I had to take six horses out to a paddock to spell and bring in five others. Bluey was to help, because two of the new horses were for the outcamp, which was called Query Outcamp. No-one could ever explain how it acquired such a curious name. The morning had that pleasant coolness that you know will soon disappear. It gives you the feeling of wanting to savour every minute of it while it lasts. I saddled a horse called Mulberry and then began to saddle a big brown gelding for Bluey. The new man was squatting in the shade, resting his head on his hand and complaining about his hangover. As I pulled the surcingle tight, the old brown horse put his head down, humped his back and gave two pig-roots across the yard. We were all taken aback because that old horse was always so quiet, so slow, so placid and so un-temperamental that only my father would ride him. Bluey jumped to his feet. 'I'm not ridin that bloody horse,' he shouted. Though we jeered and cajoled, Bluey refused to budge unless we gave him another horse to ride.

Well, there was another horse – an aged grey gelding, a favourite of the seventy-year-old outcamp man we once had. We saddled him, and Bluey eased aboard while I let the horses out and headed them the way we had to go. Once we were out of the Cow paddock, they realised where they were going and they poked along a track that cut across country. Bluey and I followed and we yarned the way blokes do when they first meet. He had tales of his life on cattle stations in Queensland and South Australia. He told of the titles he'd won at rodeos and about the horses he'd broken in. He boasted about how he could fight – how he was so tough that the only time he'd been beaten was when three blokes took to him when he was too drunk to stand up. While he talked, cocky and sure of himself, I sized him up and saw that he had a very poor seat on his horse.

Far off, we could see the green line of gumtrees that edged Koorabooka Creek, and beyond that, the hills that marked the boundary with Elliott Creek Station. Around us the country was parched, flat and treeless. Occasionally a willy-willy sluggishly lifted, and then, as though the effort was too great, it fell back and the dust settled. It was getting hotter and the hills were beginning to dance upside down. The horses were far in front, nearly to the river. I thought we ought to catch up. I said as much to Bluey and we urged our horses to canter. From the corner of my eye, I saw the old grey horse duck his head and prop with his four legs set straight and stiff. I was dumbfounded. Bluey tumbled off and fell on the back of his neck and lay spread-eagled on the ground with the dust rising around his body like an unearthly vapour.

The old grey horse trotted away and then cantered, with flapping reins and stirrups, and joined the horses ahead. Bluey sat up, so I figured he was OK and I galloped after his horse. We raced across the crabhole flats, and the old grey horse, rebellious for the first time in his life, flew as though he was determined to evade mankind forever. He clattered down the bank of the creek and up the other side and burst into the midst of the mob and carried them on with him.

They were at the windmill when I caught up with them, milling around the trough as though nothing had happened. The old grey was easily captured and, keeping him well in hand, I let the other horses into the big paddock beyond. Then I rode back to Bluey. When I crossed the creek, I saw his diminutive figure shuffling along the sheep pad leading to the windmill. His awkward, pigeon-toed gait in his too-tight boots was comical. He had a crushed, dejected air. He refused to ride the grey again. Instead, he stumbled along the pad leading the now-resigned old horse. There was nothing for it but to leave him, so I went after the fresh horses.

We knew they were watering at this mill because we'd often seen their tracks when we were doing a mill round. Trotting and cantering, I followed the freshest tracks out to where they were feeding. I soon saw them, headed them and brought them back to the mill. Bluey was there by now, pouring water over his head and gulping from his quart pot. When I told him we had to take the horses to another mill, four miles away, where there were yards, where we could separate the ones we wanted from the mob, he groaned and complained.

This time he mounted the old grey but wouldn't go out of a walk. About half an hour later, we were tripping and stumbling on the top of a high, stony hill that looked down on the mill and the yards. Bluey was incapable of doing anything useful. He rode down to the mill, swaying in the saddle as though he were still drunk. By the time he got there, I had the horses in the yards and I had let mine go and was saddling another. Bluey looked exhausted. 'Cripes,' he said, 'it's fuckin hot. Can't we lay up here for a few hours until it's cooler?'

'Not on your bloody life,' I said. 'We'll keep moving. We're behind time now.'

Although I felt mildly sorry for him, I also wanted to laugh at his crestfallen, beaten expression. He seemed to subside even more, as if under an impossible burden.

We headed for home, driving the five fresh horses ahead of us. The sky was immense. It was dazzling. It was an empty, vacant blue. Each gust of wind was oven hot and dry and scorched our bodies through our clothes. Bluey slumped, his body jerking with his horse's jolting steps. He complained about a sore backside. He complained about the sun and the glare. He was suffering an ordeal that seemed to him to be never-ending. 'How far to go now?' he pleaded.

'Oh, about nine miles,' I lied.

'Oh Christ,' he wailed. 'I'm not gunna make it.'

'Yes, you bloody will,' I said.

And just then we made the top of a rise and saw the shining, stark-white corrugated iron of the woolshed and its cluster of buildings 300 yards away. When he realised where he was, Bluey kicked his horse and galloped straight down to the men's quarters. He leaped off, gasping, 'Water, water.' He grabbed a fat-bellied water bag and started gulping. Bill van Rijn and Albie Zilko gaped in astonishment. Pieter opened the gate into the yards to let the new horses in, and he grabbed Bluey's horse and put it away for him. Bluey slumped in a chair, legs stretched out in front, not that they went very far.

Sometimes when you were talking to Bluey, you had the feeling he was cross-eyed. I'd always assumed that when a man is cross-eyed he is cross-eyed – and that's all there is to it. Bluey was different. Sometimes he was and sometimes he wasn't. It made you feel uneasy. And Bluey being garrulous, it was ironic he was going to live alone at Query Outcamp. Query was a place that could also make you feel uneasy. It was away off in one of the back paddocks where Koorabooka Creek began. The corrugated-iron humpy rested lightly on the edge of an iron-stone flat. No trees gave it any protection. It was at the mercy of the east winds, which blew cold in winter and scorching hot in summer. Storm-tossed rains rattled on its roof and walls, making so much noise you couldn't hear yourself think. When the sky was sullen and black, it was eerie to stand on the small veranda and watch the wind kick up leaves and sticks and toss them high in the air. Bluey rode down to this back yard of the world on an airless, cloudless day when the heat was searing. He rode a hollow-backed mare that was blind in one eye. She was a good sort of horse, except she tripped and nearly fell now and then. He led his spare horse.

As I drove past with Bluey's swag and gear on the truck, I thought Bluey and the mare looked a well-suited pair. The mare stepped along with her unhurried stride, and Bluey's short legs stuck out in front, straight and stiff, like two rifle barrels. He was about as much at home in the saddle as a camel at sea. He waved vigorously to me as he bounced up and down – and I thought, well, we've had some pretty queer outcamp men and this bird surely fits the bill.

When I arrived at Query, I threw his swag onto the back veranda of his new home. As I waited for him, I looked around. The smoke-blackened kitchen was formed by closing off one end of the veranda. The two dark rooms smelled of dead socks and rancid air. The tap at the edge of the veranda supplied water from a tank a hundred yards away. I put his box of tucker on the table. It's really not such a bad place to live, I thought; I wouldn't mind it – for a while.

Bluey's range consisted of three paddocks and his responsibility was to see that the windmills that supplied them with water kept functioning. If there was a problem he couldn't fix himself, he was to phone the woolshed homestead and tell us what he thought was amiss. We'd then come with tools and manpower to fix it. In riding on his mill round, he was supposed to take notice of where the sheep were feeding and on which mills they were watering. He had to check the fences and close the gaps made by kangaroos. It was necessary for him to phone every second night to let us know he was still operating – that he was alive. Nearly every Saturday, I drove down with fresh supplies, and sometimes we brought him back to the woolshed homestead for a short break.

Bluey provided much amusement. He was so serious, so ready to believe whatever he was told. We invented the most amazing lies – and at times we misled him quite cruelly. We deceived him and gloated over our pathetic triumphs. If our jokes were clumsy and Bluey saw through our lies, he would merely look a little startled – and then forget about it without a trace of rancour or resentment. In turn, Bluey often had a wild tale to tell. 'Last night,' he told me on one occasion, 'you shoulda heard them dogs in the hills down there past the mill. Dinkum. The hair would stand up on the back of your head because' – and here he paused and gave me a look of great intensity – 'because I know them dogs is some poor jokers come back from the dead to another life.'

As he spoke, his mouth twisted a little to one side and his eyes took on that cross-eyed look. 'And they know how us humans think – and they're waitin for their opportunity. But the bastards won't get me. I'm too shit cunnin for em.'

There were times when the two of us sat on the concrete floor with our backs against the wall and Bluey told me what he thought of himself. He pointed to the scar slanting across his cheek and said in a low voice, as if he didn't want anyone else to hear, 'I got this in a fight in Port Pirie when I was working the merchant ships. Oh yes, I've been a sailor all right. I was a cook. That's how come I can look after meself pretty good now.'

Not long after Bluey went to Query, it rained heavily and the whole country became a sticky morass. Water holes were filled, and for two or three weeks the sheep would drink from wide, shallow claypans and muddy water holes. When the country dried out sufficiently, Bluey was brought up to the homestead to spend a few days, partly because we were setting up a big poker night. There is no knowing whether or not he enjoyed himself. Although he never stopped talking, no-one listened. And he was the butt of everyone's jokes. Whereas he was credulous of the most fantastic lies, he was mistrustful of the most obvious and simple facts.

Bluey watched Bill van Rijn mix a spoonful of Faulding's Lemon Saline in a mug of water and then drink it with relish. Bill offered some to Bluey, saying in a kindly way, 'Put a spoonful of this in your water and it'll improve the taste no end.'

Bluey tried it. 'Shit, you're bloody right,' he said. 'What is it?'

'Just a fizzy drink, dummy,' Bill said.

And Bluey drank another pannikin of water with the saline.

Next day we drove him back to Query Outcamp. Included in his stores, at his request, were three jars of the fizzy powder. He settled in at the two-room hut and we left him to it. What would happen to that fountain of talk, with no-one to listen to him?

After a week my father and I went to check on him. He was waiting impatiently, expecting us. Before we could ask anything about his work, he told us about the events of his first day back on the job.

'You know that lemon fizzy stuff you give me?' he asked rhetorically. 'Well,' he said, 'the next day, I drank half a jar of the stuff and in the afternoon I got the horse and went out to check on two of the windmills.'

'Well, I got a little way down the track and I had to jump off me horse as quick as I could cos I was about to shit me pants. I got a bit further down the track and I had to go again and I only just made it in time. I said to meself, "Bluey," I said, "time to get smart." So instead of putting me undies and trousers back on, I tied em up behind the saddle and I spent the rest of the day riding with a bare bum. And then me bum got sunburnt. And you know what? I drank the rest of the bottle whenever I had a drink at a windmill.'

Bluey was oblivious to our laughter. Before either of us could say anything, he continued the story. 'I'm telling yer,' he said, 'I had to keep gettin off until there was nothing left to shit. I'm not stupid, you know. I worked out that it probably had something to do with that bloody fizzy powder stuff. When I got back to the camp I had a good look at the label and sure enough it's supposed to make you shit. And none of you bastards told me.'

My father said, 'It's OK if you drink it in small doses. One or two a day.' We continued to laugh and Bluey laughed too. He was a good-natured bloke.

At dinner that night at the woolshed, we told everyone the story. Everyone laughed till they cried. The old bloke working on the plumbing said, 'He wouldn't know if you were up him unless you breathed down his neck.'

'He's as useless as tits on a bull,' Albie said.

Someone else said, 'Wish I coulda seen it.'

When the cackling and the smart comments died down, Bill van Rijn said, 'I knew that would happen. I saw from the way he was drinking it, the day before he went to Query. He didn't realise what it could do – so I didn't tell him.'

In the mood of the moment, the laughter was rekindled. But Bill didn't join in this time. He studied the tea dregs in his mug. When I looked at him, I stopped laughing.

There is a wild cluster of steep hills called the Godfrey, the Kenneth, the Barlee and the Minnierra ranges, and they separate the Upper Gascoyne region from the Ashburton region. Most of this area is unleased. No roads slice through this wilderness. The country is too rough, too harsh. Steep gullies littered with stones, tough spindly scrub and massive rocky outcrops make much of it impenetrable to vehicles. This is a haven for dingoes. When small marsupials are in short supply, the dogs drift into the pastoral country, where they can get easier pickings, such as lambs or calves. Sheep tend to cluster together when they see or sense danger, and that can be their undoing. A pack of dogs can pull down a fully grown sheep without too much trouble when sheep are bunched up, getting in each other's way.

The local government maintained a programme of paying scalp money to keep the dingo numbers down. No-one was ever optimistic enough to imagine that the dingoes could be wiped out. The men who scratch a living from dingo bounty money are called doggers: doggers by occupation and dogged by nature. The first time I met Clarrie, I was alone at the woolshed homestead. I heard the sound of an unfamiliar engine and I went outside to wait. A utility trailing the usual cloud of dust came into sight and drove slowly round the woolshed and past the shearers' quarters and the kitchen and dining shed, down to where I was waiting. The ute was battered, and when its driver got out to walk the ten yards to the homestead, he looked much the same. The dogs barked at him and he ignored them. They sniffed his trouser legs and they lost interest.

'Gidday,' I said.

The driver said nothing, just walked slowly towards me. He gave me a quick look up and down, then said, 'Gidday.'

'I'm Ian,' I said, 'Ian Parkes.'

The driver looked down at his boots and took the few steps past me towards the homestead. He squatted down on his heels, with his back against the wall. He pulled out the makings and slowly rolled a cigarette. He licked one edge of the paper and wrapped the tobacco and rolled it between his forefinger and thumb. He brought it up to his lips and let it hang there while he dug out a tin of wax matches from a trouser pocket. This was an awkward task, because he was squatting and his trouser pockets were hard to get to. All through this, he did not look at me. But when the cigarette was alight and he'd drawn in a lungful of smoke, he screwed his eyes up, raised his head, glanced at me and said, 'I'm Clarrie . . . the dogger.'

Clarrie was in no rush to say more. The silence didn't seem to bother him, but it bothered me.

'Where are you heading?' I asked.

It was as if Clarrie needed to think about this. I had to wait for his answer. He spoke ponderously. 'To the ranges . . . other side of the Koorabooka . . . east of Elliott Creek.'

'Why? Why there?'

'Because that's where the dogs hang out and breed . . . the dogs that knock off your sheep.'

I felt as if I had been admonished.

'You got a camp there, a shed or anything?'

A long delay, then, with a sigh, 'No, mate. I camp in the open.'

'All the time?'

'Mostly. If the weather's crook . . . I'll put me tent up.'

'What about water?'

'Ohhh . . . I know where the permanent water holes are . . . and I carry plenty with me.'

I looked over to the ute and saw three 44-gallon drums roped up behind the cab. 'Those three drums?' I asked.

'No, mate. Two of em are fuel.' He flicked a quick look at me.

'How long will you be there?' I asked.

'Ohhh . . . dunno . . . coupla months . . . maybe.'

I remembered my manners and asked if he wanted anything.

'Cuppa tea'll do.'

'You want to come inside?'

'Nah, mate. I'm OK here.'

I made the tea and brought out two mugs. I found a stool and sat near him. 'How do you catch the dogs?' I asked. I got the feeling I was trying his patience. He finished off his mug of tea.

'Mostly I trap the bastards.'

'Do you ever shoot them?'

'Ar, sometimes. It's hard to get sight of em . . . let alone get them in the sights.'

I grinned. I wasn't sure whether or not to laugh. He didn't look like the kind of man who made jokes. So I didn't laugh. He kept on looking down at the ground. There was another long silence while he rolled another smoke.

'Where do you live?' I asked. 'I mean, where's your home?'

'Cue, mate . . . got a house in Cue . . . the missus and the kids live there.'

More silence.

'I better be goin. Wanna find a new place to camp.'

Clarrie unfolded himself from where he was squatting and walked slowly over to his ute. He checked the load, checked the tyres. While he was doing this, I checked him. I suppose he would

have been in his late forties. He was a bit above average height –
and lean, lean as a kangaroo dog. His arms and hands and face
were leathery brown. Don't ask me what colour his hair was. I don't
know. He never took his hat off.

He seated himself in the ute and started the engine. I stood near
the driver's door. 'See you later,' I said.

'Yeah, mate . . . see ya.'

I walked over to the gate into the Cow paddock and opened
it for him. He drove through and headed off down the track. I
thought, by the time he gets to the gate into Deep Well, he'll have
forgotten I exist.

Over the next year, we saw Clarrie three more times, either coming
or going, never staying. Except for the night we organised the big
card game. He turned up right on dinner time and he allowed himself
to be persuaded to eat with us. He was as taciturn as ever, but at the
mention of the big game, he lifted his head a fraction, and I'm sure I
saw his eyes brighten and his head give the flicker of a nod.

A table was set up with a blanket covering, outside the men's
quarters. It was too hot and humid to play inside. There was no
wind. There were moths and insects by the thousand and we hung
two hissing Tilley pressure lamps just beyond each end of the
oblong table. The players were Bill, Pieter, Bluey, Albie, Clarrie and
me, and my father for a short while. We played pontoon and after
a couple of hours we switched to poker. We played classic draw
poker, with jackpots. In between hands, when the cards were being
shuffled, we filled in the time telling dirty jokes. By midnight we'd
run out of jokes, and we continued with anecdotes. Clarrie didn't
tell jokes or stories. He listened. If something appealed to him, his
lips would shut tight and twist in what I assumed was a kind of
grin. At two o'clock we stopped and went to bed. Next morning,
when we gathered for breakfast, there was no Clarrie. We went
looking. His ute was gone. We didn't see him again for another
three months.

11

Top dogs and great horses

Not long after I arrived at Mount Augustus, a black kelpie bitch gave birth to five pups. The father was a black-and-white Border collie. After they were weaned, four of the pups were given away, leaving one male, fluffy and black and round. Nobody wanted him. My father persuaded me to take him on. So he came to live with us at the woolshed homestead and had to be adopted by Smokey and by Peter, my mother's grey cocker spaniel. They played with him and bowled him over and over in the dust. As I trained him, he accepted that he was my dog. For a long time I couldn't decide on a name, so it was, 'Here, boy. Good dog.' After a while, he probably thought his name was Boy. Then one day, when we were leaving for a day's muster, I had to stop and wait for him while he cocked his leg. He must have had a very full bladder because it took two goes. Each occasion was followed by the ritual scratching in the dirt and the kicking of dust over his waste. My father and the others were riding on. 'Hang on a jiffy,' I called, 'I'm waiting for my dog.'

They turned, saw me some way behind and stopped. The next day, the same thing happened. Again I had to call, 'Hang on a jiffy.' And that's how Jiffy got his name, although it was frequently abbreviated to Jiff.

Jiff grew into a strong, medium-sized dog. He was a bit bigger than his father and Smokey, and twice the size of his mother. Like Smokey, he became a one-and-a-half-man dog. By that I mean he worked wholeheartedly for me, a bit grudgingly for my father and not at all for anyone else. Smokey was the other way round: my father's dog through and through, half mine, and no-one else's. This is not something we taught them. It just happened that way. Mind you, we never did lend our dogs to anyone – under any circumstances.

When I worked in South Australia, I was told that a sheepdog is a sheepdog – and not a pet. On Winnininnie, the dogs were kept chained to their kennels when not working. I was discouraged from being too friendly with them. Make a pet of a sheepdog, they said, and it'll be no good as a working dog. My father and I disagreed with that. We felt that, with our dogs, one role enhanced the other and they were inseparable. It seemed to us that our dogs worked better for receiving recognition and affection. Like horses, dogs will give and give until they have nothing left to give. They will work from sunup to sundown, even until the pads on their paws are worn and bleeding and they can't take another step because of the pain. Because of this, we bought leather dog boots and tied them onto each paw when we had many successive days of mustering in hard country. Dog boots were very necessary where the ground was infested with prickles. The boots were cleverly made to allow the independent movement of each toe. Sometimes a boot would come off and be lost, but mostly they were used until the leather wore out.

To have a good dog at your beck and call, day and night, imposes on you a responsibility, and that includes giving it the reassurance that you belong to each other.

We were mustering for shearing and had picked up a large mob of wethers, maybe 500 or so, before lunch camp. There were four of us: my father, Mitchell, Gilbert and me. We settled the mob and set Smokey to watch them, not that we were not watching too. We boiled our quart pots and made tea. We chose the mulga trees that offered the most shade, Mitchell and Gilbert under one tree, my father and I under another. We sat on the ground to eat our crib and drink our tea. When that was done, we lay down, our heads propped on our saddlebags, our hats over our eyes. For fifteen minutes or so we dozed, leaving Smokey in sole charge of the mob. It was always so pleasant, wisps of smoke from the fire sometimes drifting in our direction, combined with the smell of the mulgas and the earth. Lying on one's back on the ground to sleep is a good feeling. When you wake and look up, you can almost feel the earth turning in pale blue space.

We had learned to stave off sleep to keep an eye on Smokey. If he thought we were not watching, he would play a game. If he felt we were watching, he would not. So we peered out from under the brims of our down-turned hats and lay quietly and waited. Smokey was on his stomach, front paws out before him, struggling to keep his eyes open, head nodding. Then he stood and stretched and yawned. He glanced at us and then walked closer to the mob, one very deliberate, slow step after another. He chose a particularly large wether just inside the mob, and he stalked it. The wether soon knew it had been chosen and it never took its eyes off him. The rest of the mob ignored him, except for those closest to the one he was after – they moved aside. As Smokey stepped closer and closer, building pressure on the chosen one, it arched its neck and stamped its front hooves until, suddenly, it broke out. That was the normal reaction. Previous sheep usually went a few yards before pausing and having a confrontation with Smokey and then returning to the security of the mob. This wether bolted into the scrub, with Smokey on its heels. They raced out for forty yards. Then Smokey ran up alongside the sheep's shoulder and turned it in a wide arc, like a horseman camp-drafting, and brought it back to the mob, on the opposite side to where it had been originally. The sheep slammed right in and buried itself. The mob stirred a little. Some that were lying down stood up and others became restless. Smokey deterred them from moving away and patrolled at a suitable distance until he was satisfied they were settled. Then he lay down again where he had been before and dozed. We felt like clapping and cheering.

He was the only dog I have ever seen who engaged in that kind of game. He did it with great skill and control, but only if we deceived him into thinking we were asleep. On this particular day he took it to a new level of mastery.

Mount Augustus was the place where I really began to learn about horse relationships. The crowning pleasure was riding them, but all horse relationships start on the ground. You watch their behaviour and how they relate to you. Every horse has its own character and personality. Every horse has its own temperament. There are similarities and common traits, but there are subtle differences. The qualities of each horse are to be respected. Once they understand what's expected of them, most horses are willing and cooperative. Some more than others want to please you, and they are the ones that get your attention and capture your affection. I rode many horses at Mount Augustus and there wasn't one that I did not enjoy. Some, like Spitfire and Bunty, have a permanent place in my heart.

When we were mustering, we each had two horses, which we rode alternately. The working week was six days. The work span of each horse was six weeks and then it was turned out in the paddock; it was brought back in to work again later. When they were in work they were hard fed, meaning they were fed chaff and oats. This was long before the days of processed feed cubes and additives.

The horse yards were about 150 yards to the north of the woolshed. Six feet in front of the yards, to the west, there was a large shed that housed the truck, the feed room and the tack room. Further west were the men's quarters and, further still, the homestead.

At changeover time, we rode out to the paddock where the mob of about twenty horses was running and brought in the whole lot. That was an event that stirred up everyone – horses and riders. The feeling of riding a top horse behind a mob of equally top horses was exhilarating. Horses love to run, and it was necessary to have one rider in front of the mob, with a stockwhip to crack to check the leaders. But close to the yards, the lead rider turned aside, and the mob, relieved of the constraint, galloped into the yards, pig-rooting and swirling around, the dust rising high in a red cloud. Apart from the odd squeal and scuffle, they settled down and milled around. We picked out the fresh horses we wanted, put them in another yard and let our old horses into the mob. Then three of us each took one of our fresh horses and drove the mob back to their paddock. While we were doing that, the remaining couple of stockmen started shoeing the new horses. When the riders returned from the paddock, they too set about shoeing. Most of the horses usually had enough hoof to handle one day's mustering – in that country hooves wear away quickly.

To begin with, Pottsy told us which new horses to bring in to work, but he left it to us to decide who rode which horse. After about three months, Pottsy started being specific about the horses he wanted me to ride. The first was Spitfire, a small black mare with a full belly and a short girth.

Spitfire was anything but a spitfire. Naturally, her name was abbreviated to Spitty. She was the first horse I really bonded with. At every opportunity, she demanded to have her head rubbed. She had a beautiful eye. Large, soft, lustrous, attentive eyes are indicative of a cooperative horse. Spitty was always willing and always responded quickly. Pottsy eventually told me that he wanted me to ride her at the Landor Races gymkhana. Maybe he had that in mind when he first told me to ride her. She was the perfect gymkhana pony.

At dinner camp out in the paddock, I didn't tie her up. I just looped the reins over the pommel and she'd stick around. Usually, she'd stand right behind me as I sat in the threadbare shade of a wilted mulga. Mostly she played with my hat. Sometimes she removed it and let it flop to the ground.

Out in the paddock she worked willingly. She anticipated my thoughts and she'd catch me off guard. She'd sight stock as soon as I did, and she'd be up on her toes, head high, ears pricked, tail swishing, glancing back over her shoulder at me as if asking me why we weren't getting going.

There were only two problems with Spitty. The first was a weakness in her back, which showed up the first time I rode her and if I let anyone else ride her. Other riders invariably sat back in the saddle, and when they halted and asked her to stand, she buckled in the hindquarters. When I rode her, I sat as far forward as possible and leaned on the pommel with both hands so that my weight was almost over her withers. It's an unnatural position for a rider, but, somehow, with Spitty I could balance there quite comfortably. And she didn't buckle in the hindquarters when we stopped and stood.

The second problem was girth galling. Not all horses are prone to this, but Spitty was. The skin was rubbed raw in a patch where the girth came up from under her belly. The standard treatment on stations was to urinate on girth galls. But that didn't fix Spitty's problem. Nor did a pad of wool. The solution was to ride with a loose girth. I just had to be careful when I mounted and to watch out if we had any hard riding, because the saddle would slip to one side when we turned. There were some near misses when I almost fell off, but, because I was aware, I used my weight in the stirrups to compensate to keep the saddle more or less balanced in the middle. It never slipped back, because the curve of her belly prevented that.

At the far northern end of Deep Well paddock, running from east to west, was Koorabooka Creek. The plains to the south drained into this creek and the terrain was unusual. Trying to head a mob of wethers one day, Spitty and I were flying at a flat-out gallop when a front hoof plunged deep into the ground. Spitty went down headfirst and catapulted me far out in front. I hit the ground and rolled over and over. When I stopped and looked up, I saw Spitty finish her last roll and then get to her feet. In that situation, most horses would take the opportunity to clear out. Not Spitty. She stood there, reins dangling, dust swirling, looking at me. I too got to my feet, none the worse for the tumble. I was worried about Spitty, though, and I checked her over from head to tail, side to side, all four legs. I led her around to see if she was lame and, thankfully, she was unharmed. I put my left arm around her nose and hugged her head. When I remounted, we continued on our way more cautiously.

Spitty enjoyed having fun – her way. This took the form of dropping her head when we were cantering and indulging in a flying pig-root. That was how she let me know she was feeling well and wanted to fool around. I enjoyed it, and I let her have her head and just sat there and rode it out until she'd had enough – which was never very long. She was always controllable and she always pig-rooted in the direction I wanted to go. Then it was back to business. But one evening I was bringing a small mob of very lively killer wethers into the yards at the woolshed. When they started to break away, we accelerated to head them off, and Spitty felt it was time for her favourite game. The next thing I knew I was flat on my back in the dust and Spitty was standing still, the saddle hanging under her belly. She looked at me with her ears pricked, as if to say, what the hell are you doing down there? Well, the girth had been really loose, the saddle had slipped right under Spitty and I went with it. I jumped up, replaced the saddle, tightened the girth a couple of holes and away we went. From that time on, Spitty never indulged in her game again. No amount of encouragement from me could ever get her to drop her head and pig-root. It seemed she had decided that if I was silly enough to fall off she didn't want to play the game any more.

The highlight of my relationship with Spitty was preparing her for a novelty race at the Landor Races gymkhana. It was called the Leading the Horse Race. The race started with the rider on foot, leading his horse for fifty yards; then, within a distance of ten yards, the rider mounted the horse and galloped to the finish line, one hundred yards further on. Pottsy told me to teach Spitty to trot beside me while I ran alongside, with the reins up over her neck. Then, when I was ready, I grabbed hold of the pommel and vaulted up. I gathered the reins, leaned forward and Spitty took off as fast as she could go. There was a dirt road running through the Cow paddock and out through the set of double wooden gates into Deep Well paddock, a mile from the woolshed. Spitty and I practised up and down this track. We ran together, and I vaulted on; we galloped flat out for twenty yards, stopped and did it all over again. Even when we had the routine down pat, we still kept doing it, because it is fun doing something you're good at. I thought, look out Landor, here we come. It was well known that Laurie Bain and his brother Alan were the stars at the Landor gymkhana every year, and I thought, this year I'm going to give you a run for your money – in this event at least.

Early in my time at The Mount, Pottsy sent my father and me to Query Outcamp, where I was to find the horse called Mulberry and ride him back to the woolshed and use him for stock work. This was before Bluey's time and there was an old man at the outcamp who told me that Mulberry was a helluva buckjumper. He showed me a depression in the ground and said it had come from the last bloke who tried to ride him. I half-believed him, and I thought, that's nice, Pottsy didn't tell me that. Mulberry was a mottled black and brown, with a purplish tinge, which is how he got his name. I caught the horse easily. I saddled him with no problem; I led him a little way along the track, tightened the girth and surcingle and gingerly put my foot in the stirrup and swung into the saddle. Keeping the reins tight, I asked him to go forward, nudging him with my heels. I was ready for the explosion. But it didn't happen. Mulberry was as quiet as a lamb. For one thing, he had the flattest hooves I'd ever seen and they were worn right down and he was sore. We settled into a slow walk and tiptoed along the bush track until, four hours later, we arrived at the woolshed.

The next day I had to shoe him and it was the trickiest shoeing I ever had to do. His front hooves sloped right out instead of being upright, which made it impossible to get the nails as high up in the wall of the hoof as they should have been. Time changed all that. By shoeing him more frequently than usual and rasping the hooves right down, I managed to get his hooves reasonably straight.

While I was engrossed in shoeing him that first time, Pottsy came around the side of the shed and leaned on the rail to watch. The feed bins for the horses were half 44-gallon drums, quite common on stations. But Pottsy didn't like them as they can have rough, sometimes sharp, edges. He had told us to use what he called 'proper feed bins' made from galvanised sheet metal. Pottsy kicked the feed bin in Mulberry's stall and said, 'What are you using these fuckin bins for? They're no good. You should be using the proper feed bins.'

I had always been nervous and tentative when I was within range of Pottsy, but this day I was tired from struggling with Mulberry's shoeing and, before I could think what I was saying, I said, with a bit of bite, 'We're using these because we don't have any proper fuckin feed bins.'

Pottsy stared at me, expressionlessly. He didn't say a word. He turned around and went back along the side of the shed. I've done it now, I thought. Shit, I'm really in trouble. Pottsy's gunna kill me.

I carried on with shoeing Mulberry, anxiously waiting. A few minutes later Pottsy returned – and I was quaking. He came right up to the stall and said, 'You're right. There aren't any proper feed bins in the shed. Get some next time you come into the homestead.' With that he went to his Land Rover and drove home. Not a word was ever mentioned about my cheeky outburst. And I didn't apologise. From that point on, I had more confidence when I was with him. He still had the upper hand, which is the way it should have been, but I was much less intimidated.

As the weeks rolled by, Mulberry became strong and fit. Then one morning, to my surprise, he put his head down and bucked when I mounted. It was nothing that couldn't be handled easily. After three or four bucks, I pulled his head up and reined him in, and we were on our way. There was no more frivolity for the rest of the day. And that became a pattern with him: first thing in the morning, a few bucks to let me know he was well and truly alive.

A few months later Pottsy gave me a horse called Perkin. He was a dark-brown-cum-black gelding, about 15.2 hands. He had won at Landor in 1952 and he was in the racing string again for 1953. Although he was a good horse and I liked him a lot and we got on well, he didn't have that extra dimension of wanting to really connect with me the way Spitfire had.

Then Pottsy told me there was another horse he wanted me to ride for stock work in the three months leading up to the Landor Races. This time, I got a strong sensation he was actually giving the horse to me. He wasn't giving him to me, of course, but there was a tone in the way he said, 'As well as Perkin, I'm giving you a horse called Bunty to ride.' At face value, there was no particular change of tone, just Pottsy's usual gruffness. Perhaps it was in the way he looked at me, eyeball to eyeball, studying me. I soon came to feel that Bunty was truly mine.

At Pottsy's suggestion, I went down to the stables to meet him. The stables were bush-timber yards, with the stalls along one side, shaded by a brush roof and with a brush wall at the back. There were a few horses moping in the yards. The big bay gelding was easy to identify. He had a high head carriage and alert, soft eyes. As I looked him over, he looked at me with a calm steadiness that seemed to say, I know who I am. Who are you? At that moment, I wondered if Bunty was being given to me, or I was being given to him.

Four days later, I returned with my saddle and bridle to ride Bunty back to the woolshed homestead. Pottsy instructed me to walk and trot the horse in his work, only rising to a canter if it was really necessary. Under no circumstances was I to gallop. And that was that. No further information. It was left to my imagination to consider the consequences if Bunty was injured in any way through my careless riding.

Bunty was a four-year-old. He had a splash of white on his forehead; he was about 15.3 hands, not that long broken in. So I was quite wary as I led him out of the stables, across the soft red dirt, through the wide bushes to a relatively open area where I would mount up. I tightened the girth. He turned his head a touch. His near-side big brown eye watched me. I shortened the reins, eased up and gently came to rest in the seat of the saddle, my eyes on his head, watching his ears. I was ready. Bunty stood. I thought, what now, you bugger? I was waiting for his reaction. Would he buck? Would he protest in some other way? Pig-root? Hump his back? The seconds seemed like minutes. 'Time to go, Bunty,' I said. I loosened the pressure on the reins and eased my weight back. He shook his head once, he made his decision and we moved off. It was that easy.

As we walked along the side of the dirt road that connected Mount Augustus with Cobra Station and beyond, going ultimately all the way to Carnarvon, stride by stride I relaxed. Bunty was already totally relaxed. I picked up his rhythm, his beautiful, flowing, graceful stride. His head was up. No hesitation. No questioning. I was heading him into new territory, yet he seemed to be quite sure of himself. His confidence gave me confidence. Two young bucks starting out on a new partnership!

He bowled along on a loose rein and four hours later we arrived at the woolshed stables. I hosed the sweat off his back and neck and legs and let him loose in the big yard, where he could roll. I stood inside and leaned back against the rails. I watched the big boy go down in the middle. He rolled from side to side, throwing up the dust. When he was finished, he did what all horses do. He raised himself on his front legs, looked around, sighed, and heaved himself up on all fours and shook himself. Then he did something other horses don't do. He walked slowly over and stood four feet away from me and looked me in the eye, with his ears pricked.

Feeding the horses every morning and evening was a job rostered among the stockmen, and I had to do my share like everyone else.

But I drew the line at Bunty. No-one else fed Bunty. As soon as he saw me, he let me know he was pleased to see me – and the feed bucket. I let him know I was thrilled to see him: I groomed him and talked to him. I knew every square inch of his hide. I knew what his reaction would be to anything that might happen at any time. Bunty was a joy to work with and to ride. A day of mustering was never a chore when I had Bunty. He took to stock work like a well-bred sheepdog instinctively understands sheep. To say he was the calmest horse I had ever ridden might make him seem lacking in personality. He was well and truly alive and ready to leap into action in an instant. And when the action was over, he would revert to his calm, relaxed self – but always, he was alert.

In 1953, the Landor race meeting was on 31 August. A month before, I rode Bunty and led Perkin in to the homestead to join the other five horses that made up the racing string. There they were all fed and lightly worked before the two-day trek to Landor.

Mount Augustus always had two thoroughbred stallions, each with his own mob of mares. For a while, we had one of them in a sheep station paddock. His name was John Tresillian. He sired very fast horses and that reputation was widespread. He also had a reputation for being dangerous. He was feared and disliked by most stockmen. In spite of that, Pottsy was still mighty fond of the horse because he bred beautiful hacks and racehorses.

Stockmen carried stones in their saddlebags when they went to fetch him and his mares, or to muster in his paddock. He scared the living daylights out of one bloke by racing up behind him and rearing in the air and striking at him with his front hooves.

He attacked Albie and another stockman one day when they were riding to a windmill. He flew at them like a fury, ears laid back flat on his neck. Albie fled. The other beat John Tresillian round the head with the handle of his stockwhip. That made the stallion more determined than ever. He clamped his jaws on the rider's thigh and pulled him clean out of the saddle and dropped him on the ground. Having achieved that, John Tresillian seemed satisfied and trotted away and joined his mares. Albie sat under a big mulga some distance away, laughing. But Albie then had to catch the other bloke's horse and bring it to him. When he had to help the bloke get back on, the stockman was in so much pain he could stand on only one leg. With Albie on the ground trying to lift the other bloke up, the horse was fractious and started to snort and kept backing away. At the same time, Albie's horse caught the mood and was pulling back. Albie had to control the two horses, get his mate into the saddle and keep an eye on John Tresillian in case he came back for another go. But he succeeded and they got back to the homestead, from where the injured stockman was later taken to Meekatharra Hospital.

Two days after the incident, Pottsy gave instructions for Albie and someone else to muster the stallion and the mares and take them to the main homestead. Albie agreed, but the other said he wouldn't do it. My father warned him that he couldn't just refuse. They argued, and others joined in. Most agreed that he had every right to refuse this order. John Tresillian was John Tresillian and no-one would have a bar of him.

'I'll have to tell Pottsy you won't do it,' my father said.

Go ahead, was the reply. We were all hanging around the phone when my father rang Pottsy.

'Well, sir, he refuses to muster the stallion. No, sir. Yeah. Reckons he doesn't want to get savaged.'

Then there was a long response from Pottsy. We heard my father. 'Yes, sir. All right. I'll tell him to roll his swag. Yes, sir. I'll bring him in to catch the next mail truck.'

When he put down the phone, my father said to us, 'He wants Albie and Ian to go out with Snowball. OK?'

The next morning we were armed with stockwhips with freshly plaited crackers, and had plenty of spare crackers in our pockets. A stockwhip has four parts: a handle; a long, tapered body of plaited leather, at the end of which there is a two-foot-long leather thong;

and, finally, a cracker made from plaited cotton, tied to the end of the thong. It's the cracker that makes the noise – and crackers wear out. Hence the pocket full of spares.

When we got to the paddock, which was in the direction of the main homestead, Snowball said, 'Keep im in the mob. We spread out. Right out. Crack your whips. Keep cracking. We get the mob moving, he won' leave the mob.'

Snowball was right. I didn't know about Albie, but my heart was pounding so hard I thought it would burst my chest. To begin with, the stallion threatened us from a distance, but the mares gathered into a mob and started moving in the direction we wanted. It was more important to John Tresillian to stay in touch with his mares than have a confrontation with us. Once we were through the first gate and into the next paddock, Snowball went to the lead, and both John Tresillian and the mares settled down. By the time we'd covered the fifteen miles into the homestead yards, it was a docile bunch of horses. All we had to do then was ride the twenty miles back to the woolshed. Snowball was too tired and stayed for the night. Albie and I arrived back feeling more than a little pleased with ourselves. At dinner that night, everyone wanted to know how we did it. We had great pleasure in telling them, giving nearly all the credit to Snowball.

Moving cattle or sheep is one thing. Moving a mob of horses is quite another. Apart from their beauty, horses have so much character, so much emotion. They can be warm and affectionate – and they can be volatile. They look you in the eye and they communicate with you. You have a relationship with each and every one. And, oh, what grand horses the Mount Augustus horses were.

12

Landor Races

Halfway through August 1953, Pottsy moved me in to the main homestead for a few days before we rode the horses to Landor for the races. Landor racecourse was about fifty miles from The Mount and we were to arrive a week before the races began. This gave the horses time to recover from the fifty-mile walk and to settle in. The days at the homestead were spent practising for the gymkhana events with Albie, with occasional coaching from Pottsy. We concentrated on the Bending Race; the Flag and Barrel Race; the Leading the Horse Race – and with jumping into a quick start, especially for the Two Furlong Flutter. We cleaned our gear and oiled it. We polished our saddlebags and quart-pot carriers for the Best Dressed Stockman event, even though we knew we'd do it all over again early in the morning of the day of the gymkhana. Idle time was an opportunity to yarn with the Yamatjis and learn more about them.

One was an old man called Nail, who was sort of married to a woman called Sally. He was never without a grin and a laugh – and he loved to chew a rock-like tobacco that he mixed with the fine white ash from burning the leaves of a particular bush.

Nail was reputed to be a rainmaker, so I said to him one day, 'Nail. What about some rain? Don't you think it's time you cooled the place off a bit?'

Nail chuckled, tilted his head and said, 'Might be later on, you know.'

'Yes, but what about now, Nail?'

'Oh, no more,' he said. 'Can't do nuthin now. Might be later on I'll fix im up.'

Knowing the station's average rainfall was seven inches, I told him he wasn't doing a very good job. As if to signal that that was the end of the matter for the time being, Nail turned his head and spat out a long squirt of masticated tobacco.

When I watched Mitchell and Gilbert with the other Yamatjis at the homestead, it dawned on me that they stood slightly apart. They definitely belonged to the clan, but they did not totally accept all the laws laid down by the elders. For one thing, they were resisting having a woman imposed on them rather than having one of their own choosing. Time was on their side, because in the 1950s the strictest disciplines of their tribal forebears were steadily losing force among station Aboriginals. The authority of the elders was waning.

The 'marital' arrangements were becoming looser; the strength of the commitment depended on the intensity of feeling of one or the other, or both. We referred to Aboriginals' partners as wives and husbands – it was natural and respectful. They followed suit – but the terms were not to be taken literally.

What did prevail in the Upper Gascoyne and the Murchison was that a young man's first partner was often an older woman whose man had passed on. Similarly, a young woman's first partner was often an older man whose woman had passed on. That way, inexperienced young people were teamed up with older people, who could teach them. And, as I was told with grins, the older people got the benefit of young partners in their later life.

The morning of the big day of our departure to Landor was clear and crisp. Apart from Albie and me, there were five Yamatji stockmen – Old Fred, Tommyhawk, Pincher, Nail and Willy – and one Yamatji stockwoman, Sally, to drove the seven racehorses. We all came together in an open space outside the yards, where the ground was sandy and red. Everyone at the homestead gathered there. They straggled in, a handful at a time, sometimes singly or in pairs. They filtered between the thick bushes that obscured the stables from the homestead. All came to watch the departure of the Mount Augustus mob. Some of them perched on the top rails of the yards. Even though we were going only fifty miles down the road and even though we would be back in two weeks, it was a special moment, a special departure – because we were going to the Landor Races. The pride of Mount Augustus, the beautiful horses, was entrusted to us. The mood was happy, carefree and cheeky. There was much giggling among the Yamatji women, with their hands held up to cover their mouths. 'Them other fellas from other stations are goin to find out about Mount Augustus horses,' I heard someone say.

Standing in the midst of the milling horses and their riders, with Spitty beside me, I felt I was part of the Mount Augustus mob. This was an excitement I had never felt before – a strange trembling inside. The feeling was intensely enjoyable. It was all new. Spitty danced around me, jerking her head up, turning it this way and that, and every now and then nearly yanking the reins out of my hand. She was excited but she didn't try to run away. She wanted to see everything that was happening. She was alert to every sound, every movement. I'm sure she too enjoyed the feeling of the moment.

Finally, all the riders were up and mounted, and Pottsy ordered someone to open the gate and let the racehorses out of the yards. Two of the riders took the lead and the rest of us hemmed the loose horses into a bunch. We headed off south, travelling beside the main road. Albie and I rode our gymkhana horses but none of the seven racehorses was ridden. The racehorses were Bunty, Perkin, Pretty Maid, Roy, Corrillie, Rex and White Eye. The blackfella called Old Fred was in charge of everything and everyone. He had done this trip many times. Old Fred knew Pottsy well – and Pottsy knew him.

To walk the racehorses in a mob to the racecourse was normal practice. That was how it had always been done. It did not occur to me that there could be any other way. When we got to Landor, I found that a handful of stations had trucked their horses. Today, everyone trucks them.

So, we walked, two in front of the mob and six behind and to the side. To begin with, the racehorses had to be checked and blocked. They soon settled down and followed the two riders in the lead. Horses are herd animals and all these horses knew each other. There was no likelihood of any horse wanting to leave the mob. They stepped lightly around fallen branches and outcrops of stone. Sometimes they paused and snatched mouthfuls of feed. As for me, I thought I'd died and gone to heaven.

The Mount Augustus truck overtook us and carried on down the road. It was loaded with feed for the horses, our swags and gear, and everything we needed to camp overnight and the week ahead. The truck was at the Pink Hills Bore, the halfway mark, when we arrived. Everyone except Albie and I knew what to do. But Old Fred gave us gentle instructions in his soft voice.

As the night closed in, the temperature dropped and we all huddled around the fire, hands thrust deep into our coat pockets. With the truck driver, there were now nine of us. The Yamatjis sat on the ground but Albie and I sat on upturned buckets – we reckoned we got more of the heat of the fire that way. We drank black tea and we talked. And while we talked, Nail's woman, Sally, cooked dinner. She was a good cook and we relished the flavour of the dampers she cooked in the ashes.

Sally had an enormous bottom lip. When she pointed in a direction, she used her lip and extended it until it looked like a great thick saucer. She had a high-pitched whinnying giggle that was quite incongruous considering the size of her. She planted her huge bulk on the ground by the fire, almost in it, and prepared the food there.

With all of us sitting by the fire, there were no arguments, just quiet chat. Some had little or nothing to say. There were a few games of pickety. This was played with a double-bladed pocket knife, both blades opening out from the same end, not opposite ends. One blade was long, the other short. The long blade was opened out fully, but the short blade was set at right angles to the long blade and the handle. Lightly resting the tip of the long blade on one forefinger and holding the base of the handle in the other hand, with a finger underneath, the knife was rested on the player's boot on the tip of the short blade. With a deft flick, the knife was launched, spinning, straight up. The object was to land the knife in the dirt, on the point of either blade, or on the back of the knife with the blades pointing in the air. Points were awarded relative to difficulty, a system that varied from camp to camp.

Reluctantly, we drifted off to our swags, falling asleep to the occasional sounds of the fire crackling and hobbled horses shuffling in the dust. For a while, I lay on my back and gazed up at the sky. It was so clear, so pure. Sleep did not come quickly. The tingling of excitement would not go away.

Mid-afternoon the following day, we arrived at the racecourse and took our pick of the horse yards along the bank of Aurillia Creek. The yards were several hundred yards from the racecourse and the station camps. All the stations in the area had permanent camps right on the edge of the creek. What an array of structures! All shapes and sizes. Corrugated-iron roofs and walls, sometimes brush walls. There were tents of various kinds. Most of the camps had an open fire to cook on, usually just back from the steep drop down to the dry, sandy bed of the creek. First-time visitors from big cities could be forgiven for thinking they'd arrived at a shanty town for refugees. In a sense, it was: people were seeking refuge from the solitude of living on an isolated sheep or cattle station. Here they caught up with friends and relatives for several days of socialising. The hospitality was free flowing and generous.

Big, heavy, thick-trunked river gums stood like white sentinels along the bank. Between the creek and the racecourse grandstand and the bar and other buildings, the ground was hard and stony. Within minutes of arriving, the red dust found its way into your clothes and into the pores of your skin. The solution to that was the line of hot showers inside open-topped corrugated-iron structures. These gave privacy and protection from the wind. Such luxury out in the middle of nowhere amazed newcomers.

The Mount Augustus mob was one of the first to arrive. I filled in my time grooming the horses, especially Bunty, Perkin and Spitty, and helping with chores at the racecourse. People arrived in dribs and drabs from other stations, and a handful of committee men made sure the water supply was OK at all points. The racetrack was graded, the grandstand was swept clean and the bar was hosed out.

By Saturday, nearly everyone had arrived, including my parents. They were at the Mount Augustus camp, but I kept my swag and gear at the horse yards. Everyone settled in and got organised for the Calcutta on the Sunday night. A Calcutta is a form of gambling in which all the horses entered in a big race are 'auctioned'. Ownership does not actually change hands. All the money from the auction goes into a pool and is divided between those who 'bought' the horses that came first, second and third in the race. It is quite common for syndicates to be formed in order to have more funds to invest. But at bush race meetings such as at Landor, racehorse owners liked to buy their own horse in the Calcutta – if they could.

Race day turned out to be a long day. I was up at five in the morning to feed and care for the horses and watch some of the owner-trainers give their prospective winners a pipe-opener over two or three furlongs on the racetrack. Pottsy scorned those who did that. One of the rules at Landor at that time was that the horses had to be grass fed until just before the race meeting. In Pottsy's view, grass-fed horses had only one good gallop in them and he wasn't going to waste it on a pointless blowout in the morning. He was quite scathing in his disdain for the methods of other trainers, even when they were successful. As far as he was concerned, he was right and the Mount Augustus record at Landor spoke for itself.

Well, race day brought its rewards – and its disappointments. Bunty won the first race, the Maiden, by seven lengths. Watching him charging down the straight and past the winning post, my heart was pounding. It was the most exciting experience of my life. That, however, was to be the highlight of Landor for me: no success after that was as personal or as sweet.

The second race was the Ladies Bracelet, the second-most important race on the card. It was won by Mr and Mrs D.M. Scott's Moonoogee, a five-year-old brown gelding. Rex, our four-year-old, who was carrying the bottom weight, came nowhere. The Mount Augustus mob was sombre. But we were in the winner's circle again when old White Eye won the Belele Plate. Perkin won the fourth race, the Mount Augustus Stakes.

Then the Landor Cup, the big race. Moonoogee was too good for Roy, so the Scotts took out the big double. The sixth race was the Natives' Race and Perkin did it again. The seventh race was a consolation for horses that had not run a place in any of the previous races. This was the Mount James Plate, and Rex won and Pretty Maid came second. The eighth and final race was won by White Eye. The final tally for the Mount Augustus team was six wins from eight races. I too had a good day: I backed all the Mount Augustus horses, except in the Ladies Bracelet. Although I had six winning bets, my proceeds were not a lot because the odds were so low. Bunty was even money, for example.

In the course of this, I became well acquainted with the legendary Harry Finlay. He was known far and wide as The Silver Fox because of his mane of silver-grey hair. Harry was a shearing contractor, who doubled as a bookmaker at Landor race meetings and at the Eastern Goldfields round. I bet with him at Meekatharra and Mount Magnet, but I didn't go to any race meetings at Cue or Yalgoo. Each of these places usually had two race meetings every year. Harry was so well regarded that, in 1968, together with another bookmaker, Ted Farrell, he was made a life member of Landor, officially the East Gascoyne Race Club. It is hard to imagine any other race club awarding life memberships to bookmakers.

With the last race over, the bar was the place to be. All around it people were packed ten deep. The beer flowed fast and the talk was loud and enthusiastic. Then, one by one, people drifted away to shower and get changed for the barbecue and the dance. Some of the women wore long dresses and the men looked uncomfortable wearing ties and jackets. The dance floor was concrete and out in the open. By eleven o'clock everyone had had enough and dispersed in two general directions. The wives and girlfriends and children made their way back to the station camps, and many of the men headed for the two-up school behind the bar.

Two-up was illegal, but the police turned a blind eye at Landor and at the race meetings at places like Meekatharra. Traditionally, it was played with two pennies, but at Landor and other places in the Norwest, three head-and-tail dice were used. The gamblers crowded around the table, sometimes three or four deep, under the light of a pressure lamp.

My basic system was to double up when I lost. It's doubtful that it was the best method of wagering, but it served me quite well. It was a method that was frowned on because some bettors felt it put them under pressure if the same person wanted to keep doubling up every time they lost. To be discreet, I masked what I was doing by placing bets with different people. That way I could be methodical instead of haphazard.

During the night, a well-known station man came to watch the game, standing beside one of the players. When the dice came his way, he was asked if he wanted to toss. He was reluctant. 'I've only got five quid with me,' he said.

Someone said, 'Go on, Doug. Give it a go.'

Doug hesitated and finally said, 'Bugger it. Gimme the dice.'

He then tossed six heads in a row. He had a fistful of cash, but he couldn't leave straightaway. That would have been frowned on. It was one of those protocols that help keep society civilised. So he stayed for another hour – and then he left with nearly 200 quid in his pocket.

If the race day was a big day, for me the next day was even bigger. That was the day of the gymkhana and my opportunity to ride and strut my stuff. Spitty was as toey as a cat on hot bricks. We did our best and suffered disappointment after disappointment. The Bains were as good as their reputation. They came first and second in all the important events, like the Bending Race and the Flag and Barrel Race. In the Best Dressed Stockman event they looked like aristocrats of the outback. Like most of us, they wore the traditional white moleskin trousers, blue shirt, brown Akubra hat and tan elastic-sided boots with Cuban heels. The difference was their total package: beautifully groomed horses with flowing manes and tails; polished saddles, bridles, girths, saddlebags, quart-pot carriers – and even breastplates, which I had never seen before; and blackened hooves. It was too much. There was never a moment's doubt that they would be awarded first and second – no doubt in Laurie's and Alan's minds and no doubt in the minds of the rest of us as we paraded for the judges. Laurie and Alan accepted the judges' decision with an equanimity that seemed to say, 'Well, of course. Who else would you dare give first and second to?' The rest of us had to agree. Laurie and Alan were in a class of their own compared to us. Sitting quietly on Spitty, I thought, you blokes just wait until the Leading the Horse Race.

The disappointments of coming nowhere in all the preceding events were put behind me, and I steadied myself for the race for which I had prepared so hard. This event was run on the racecourse. It started just around the bend into the straight, with the finish line in front of the grandstand. There were so many entries that there were three heats and then a final. I observed the first heat and the struggles of the competitors to run and lead reluctant horses – and the chaos at the point where they had to mount. Horses were pulling back, swinging around, overexcited by all the activity. Some were pig-rooting. Not the Bains' horses: they led perfectly at a trot and were calm and well behaved when it came time to mount.

Then it was my turn at the starting line. The starter shouted 'Go!' and Spitty and I took off; I was running, with Spitty trotting fast beside me, the reins already over her neck. We hit the line beyond which I could mount but we didn't stop – we kept going. We were side by side. Stride for stride. I gripped her neck with my left hand and took hold of the pommel with my right and said, 'Go, Spitty, go!' She jumped straight into a canter, and I vaulted up and landed in the saddle and gathered up the reins and leaned forward over her neck and let her have her head. We were going flat out as we raced over the finish line. I looked back and saw all my competitors, bar one, still struggling to mount. The only one who was up was still way behind. It took another hundred yards to slow Spitty down and stop and turn around and canter back.

While the third heat was being prepared and then run, I stood with Spitty over near the rails of the straight. Harry Finlay came over and said, 'We've got you at four to one on for the final, Parksie. You'll shit it in.' I was only vaguely aware that people were betting on the gymkhana events and I was awed at being the short-priced favourite for the final.

After the third heat was decided, all the finalists walked back to the starting line and lined up again. Within seconds, it seemed, the race was on and Spitty and I were running for the mounting line. This time we were running faster than we did in the heat. I don't know why. We had so much margin in the heat we could have strolled along and still won. But no, we upped the tempo and Spitty was already cantering instead of trotting as we went over the line. I had hold of her neck and the pommel, but she was going so fast she dragged me along and I couldn't find my feet in order to spring up. I tried desperately. I jumped but I didn't have enough momentum to get my right leg over her back. My body fell across the seat of the saddle. I had no control over the reins. Spitty accelerated. I fell off and rolled over and over in the powdery red dust of the straight, finishing up under the rail in front of the grandstand. Spitty galloped to the end of the straight. Spectators were laughing. My ignominy was unbearable. All that preparation was down the drain. My one opportunity to find glory and defy the Bains was gone. And it was my own fault. I blew it.

Spitty and I competed in the remaining events. We tried. Spitty gave me everything she had, but we weren't good enough. Or, rather, I wasn't good enough. As I nursed the pain of my disaster over the coming weeks and months, I consoled myself that we had had a great triumph in our heat of our special event. We had shown what we were capable of. We had demonstrated what a man and a horse could achieve together – providing both were under control.

That evening, when we were at the barbecue, my father told me that Pottsy had sold Bunty to Allan McDonald from Mangaroon Station. I felt as if I'd been kicked in the stomach. Bunty would not be returning to The Mount with all the other horses. We would say our farewells the next day and McDonald would take him and race him. I thought, I don't know who this McDonald bloke is, but I hate him. Later that night I went to the horse yards, wrapped my arms around Bunty's neck and cried. I buried my face in his mane and wept quietly so no-one would hear. I loved that horse so much. I couldn't believe that I'd ever have another horse like him.

Next day I busied myself with packing up to leave, and I tried to think of anything and everything but Bunty. But Allan McDonald came and took him away and left me with an aching pain that would not go away.

When we left Landor to ride back, Sally wasn't with us. 'Where's Sally?' I asked Nail.

'I chuck it away,' he said.

That gave me a shock. Nail was such a mild old man, I couldn't believe it. 'What do you mean, you "chuck it away"?'

'Ohhh – I get sick of im. Always talkin, talkin, talkin. Yockai, yockai, yockai.'

'But you can't just throw your wife away like that.'

'Why not? He silly one that one. Talk too much. Drive me mad, you know.'

'But Nail, what have you done with her?'

'Ohhh – I send im away to nother station. Might be I'll git im back later on.'

And he did get her back. They seemed to be quite fond of each other and when they got on each other's nerves they simply split up for a few months. Sometimes they even took on new partners. But they were always back together again at pinkeye-camp time.

13

Watershed

You get to meet nearly everyone at Landor Races and, apart from casual visitors, those you don't meet you get to know by sight. It was at Landor that I met Tom Steadman, the owner of Errabiddy, a small station south of Landor.

Tom was an identity no-one could ignore. He was tall and solidly built and carried himself with authority. He spoke with a faint leftover touch of an English accent, provincial rather than highly educated. He was prominent in the district and was a leading light at Landor, being a committee member, the handicapper and a successful racehorse owner. In 1948, he won the Bracelet with a horse called Digger, which then won the Landor Cup in record time.

The day after the gymkhana, as we were packing, Tom Steadman came to the Mount Augustus stalls, leaned on a rail and beckoned me over. He said he'd heard good things about me and he'd observed me working with the Mount Augustus horses. He invited me to work for him, but not immediately. He explained that he was negotiating to lease more land and he expected to finalise the deal in a month or so. Like everywhere else at that time, Errabiddy was drought stricken and he needed the extra country to help him get through. Drought or no drought, it did not deter the local pastoralists from putting in several days at the races. They had unshakeable faith that the seasons would change for the better.

His timing was good because I was starting to chafe at the bit, ready to get out from under the protective arm of my father. There is an old saying that you can't train a sheepdog with its mother, and I agreed with that. I told Tom I'd talk it over with my parents when we were all back at The Mount and I'd write to him with my answer.

Over the following weeks, I struggled to come to terms with my emerging identity. Who was I? What was I? Friction with my father was becoming more frequent, fuelled by my growing ego. When he sent me out with Albie to bring in 600 head of sheep from the 1,400 in a holding paddock, I did. But I didn't physically count them. I was pretty good at looking at a mob of sheep and estimating their number fairly accurately. When the sheep were delivered to the woolshed yards, my father counted them and came up with the precise number, 642. He turned to me and paused for a couple of seconds. 'Did you actually count these sheep in the paddock?' he asked.

'Well, not exactly.'

'What does that mean?'

'Well, I can look at a bunch of sheep and I can tell how many there are just by looking at them. You wanted six hundred, and we brought in six hundred and forty-two. That's near enough.'

'Near enough's not good enough,' he said. 'What if you'd brought in less than we need? Next time you bloody count them.'

To my immature mind, he was splitting hairs. There was no imperative about 600. We needed about that number for drenching the following morning. A few more or less made no difference. But what if my estimate was out by a hundred one way or the other? That would have made a difference. I resented being told off, but I followed his instruction about counting from then on.

More and more, the tension between us was growing. Even though the fault lay with me, in my mind, a move to Errabiddy seemed like a good solution. So my parents and I talked through the pros and cons of leaving an iconic station like Mount Augustus and going to a much smaller, less highly regarded property like Errabiddy. Reluctantly, my parents agreed, and I wrote to Tom Steadman.

Communication with Tom had to be surreptitious. If I was seen communicating with him, it would raise Pottsy's suspicions – and hackles. There was a telephone system on Mount Augustus, but the woolshed and the outcamp could not phone past the main homestead. I had to give my letter to the mail-truck driver on the quiet and ask him to give me Tom's reply personally – whenever it might come.

In my musings, I thought about what it meant to be known as a Norwester. For years, I had been conscious of the term.

As a boy I had heard the term used often in our household. My father's father, having been a pioneer of Onslow and having lived there for fifty years, was considered a Norwester. My mother's father, who managed Peedamulla Station, on the outskirts of Onslow, was not a Norwester, because he spent most of his working life in South Australia and didn't ever stop thinking of himself as a South Australian. Jack Henderson, my mother's brother, thought of himself as a Norwester, and he was accepted as that.

The term cropped up frequently among station people, especially at Landor, and I began to see that it was not just inclusive, it was exclusive. There was an element of class distinction about it, and I sensed that my parents and I were excluded. I wanted to be a part of the world of sheep stations, part of the hierarchy, but I could feel a barrier. It was a barrier that might dissolve with time, a long time.

Geographically, Norwesters occupy a region that starts roughly south of the Kimberleys and goes all the way down to just north of Geraldton. It extends from the coast as far east as Wiluna. It seemed to me that a really genuine Norwester was one who had put down roots for a lifetime, or who was second or third generation. Norwesters had the kind of kinship that was the natural outcome of being a distinct group of people. The reality is that birds of a feather will flock together – and that's good.

My experience at Landor made me aware that my parents and I were not perceived as Norwesters. Did I want to be part of a world in which I was not fully accepted? That distancing inculcated in me a sense of being an outsider. Striking out on my own, being independent, was part of my being defiant.

In the meantime, life at Mount Augustus continued and we waited for Tom Steadman's reply.

A new storage shed was being built at the woolshed and I was sent in to the main homestead to pick up a truckload of corrugated iron. I drove round to the back of the main shed where building materials were laid out in stacks. There were three different kinds of corrugated iron. One stack was brand new; the other two stacks were used, one more so than the other. I went to the homestead to see Pottsy about which iron I should take. He wasn't there. I asked Doris, one of the Yamatji women, if she knew where he was. 'He gone to Geraldton – with Mrs Potts,' she said.

'When did he go? I didn't know he was going to Geraldton.'

'He gone two days ago. Big meeting. The boss was on the phone – yellin. Then they're goin to Perth.'

'When will he be back?'

'Coupla weeks.'

'Bugger. I need to know which corrugated iron I should take to the woolshed.'

'You better speak Mr Hickey. He from Jimba Jimba. He come up to look after things while the boss away.'

'Well, where is this Hickey bloke?'

'He down the stables.'

I zigzagged through the bushes to the stables and called out, 'Mr Hickey. Mr Hickey.'

There was no answer. The place was silent, not a person in sight. I wandered through the main yards. There was no sign of him. I thought, now's my opportunity to have a look at Pottsy's legendary saddle, hand made by Syd Hill in Queensland. Some of the blokes used to talk about what a beautiful saddle it was – and no backside but Pottsy's ever sat in it. I opened the tack-room door. It was dark inside and the light from the open door fell across the floor, where I saw a white man on top of a blackfella, with his hands on the blackfella's shoulders, and they appeared to be struggling. I could see his face beneath the brim of his hat. He was someone I'd never seen before. His expression was grim. My first thought was, Christ, he's having a fight. Then, in a flash, I realised. The blackfella was a black woman, lying on a carefully laid out chaff bag. They were having a njeem. I backed out as quickly as I could. I shut the door quietly, hoping he was so engrossed he didn't get a good look at me. My heart was pounding. I hurried back towards the homestead, dodging from one bush to another, trying to hide my escape. I'd gone about fifty yards when I was brought to a sudden stop by Hickey yelling, 'Hoy. What the bloody hell do you want?'

It was hard to speak without stammering. 'Um – um – I need to take corrugated iron back to the woolshed and – and . . . I need to know . . . which corrugated iron I should take back – take back. Do you know?'

Hickey was trying to roll a cigarette and his fingers were shaking and tobacco was falling off the cigarette paper. Without looking at me, he said, 'Take any fuckin iron you want.' With that he rolled the cigarette and licked the paper and sealed it.

'Right. Right,' I said. And I scurried off. If I had had a tail, it would've been between my legs. My heart was still pounding as I loaded the sheets of iron onto the truck. I drove back to the woolshed, my mind churning with confusion.

'Everything all right?' my father asked when I got back.

'Yeah, yeah, everything's sweet,' I said, avoiding looking him in the eye. 'Pottsy's gone to Geraldton and a fella called Hickey is standing in for him while he's away. Hickey comes from Jimba Jimba.'

We were both aware that Jimba Jimba was owned by the Viveashes, who were part-owners of Mount Augustus.

By late September, the weather was warming up. There had been no rain through the winter and the paddocks were threadbare. Clarrie did not appear to be making any impact on the wild dogs. There was plenty of evidence that the dingoes were killing sheep. Not huge numbers, but enough to cause concern and stimulate some kind of action. In all the time I was there I didn't set eyes on one wild dog, but I saw plenty of paw prints in the powdery sheep pads that led to water.

Pottsy decided that I should devote a few days to dropping baits, using either strychnine tablets or crystals. I rode out early in the morning, with a crib for my lunch in one saddlebag and with another saddlebag full of raw meat. The meat was cut into inch cubes, and I sliced a little pocket in each and inserted a strychnine tablet. These morsels were dropped beside the sheep pads about five to ten yards apart. Dingoes, with the sharp sense of smell of all dogs, would pick up the scent, find the meat and swallow it. Over several days, I threw out hundreds of baits, but I didn't see dead dingoes as a result. Who knows? Strychnine doesn't kill instantly, but I believe it doesn't take a lot of time. Maybe dingoes could cover some ground before the poison stopped them.

Despite the grim task of dispensing poison, it was very pleasant riding a good thoroughbred horse at an easy walk for six or seven hours through that widespread landscape. The horse I rode was called Brownlock. He was a favourite of my father's, steady, reliable and comfortable. My rifle was slung across my back, and when we sighted kangaroos, I stood Brownlock and shot from up on his back. He was always steady as a rock. When I made a kill, I baited the carcass with strychnine crystals.

Looking at the ground, reading it, was enjoyable. Studying the prints made by animals and birds, I recalled what Snowball taught me and gauged the age of the tracks, not just by days but by hours.

Mitchell and Gilbert had also been my tutors; the difference between them and Snowball was that Snowball's lessons were master classes.

Every patch of ground was a picture. The colours of the earth, the shapes and colours of the stones, the dead plants and the living plants, leaves and sticks scattered at random – all starkly beautiful. Every small piece of the earth, no more than a few inches wide, was an intricate, highly detailed miniature, with a myriad of subtle variations of tone. Sometimes I dismounted and walked very slowly, Brownlock patiently following, occasionally nudging my back or my arm with his nose. It was rewarding to pause and kneel down and look closely at a patch of earth.

In the shade of a mulga after a lunch camp, I lay flat on my back, arms outstretched, feeling the earth heavy beneath me, feeling it slowly turning, searching as far as I could into the blue above. I liked doing that. I always felt good afterwards. Then I lay on one side, the better to see what the ground right beside me had to offer. And over all was the silence, broken only by the sounds of birds and by the creak of the windmill and the water overflowing from the tank if the shut-off mechanism was not working properly. Silence. And stillness. Every day the same. Year after year. It was soothingly sublime. I could understand how some men were addicted to living alone in the bush.

On the eastern end of the sheep country there were windmills on fence lines that separated the cattle country from the sheep country, with water troughs on each side. These mills were tended to by Bris Ford, the windmill man based at the main homestead. To make it to one of these mills for lunch camp was something to anticipate. Bris planted watermelon seeds if the mill was in wanderrie country, with its low-lying red sandbanks. He scattered seeds in the soft red earth alongside the tank, where the overflow gently watered the plants, and the plants grew dense and wide, spreading the flow of water. It was like finding treasure to arrive at one of these mills and lift the leaves and uncover big, ripe, cool watermelons. I thought of Bris as Australia's answer to America's Johnny Appleseed.

The season worsened and Pottsy decided to move all the breeding stock of horses to Jimba Jimba Station, where there was ample feed. This meant droving a mob of 154 horses 160 miles, more or less, depending on whether the drovers followed the roads or cut across country. The horses would graze as they went, spread out, shepherded by nine Yamatjis under the charge of Old Fred. The trip would take more than two weeks, and every two or three days Pottsy would drive out in his Land Rover with Snowball and catch up with them to see how they were travelling.

The breeding horses were mustered from somewhere east of the sheep country. When the mob arrived at the sheep country, as instructed by Pottsy, I was to ride with them until they went through the boundary into Cobra Station. After leaving the homestead at Mount Augustus, the mob camped the first night at Wilson Bore, on the Lyons River. I joined them the following morning just as they were leaving. We followed the river to McEwen Well, where we had lunch camp. We continued on along the river until we came to a windmill called Marden, in the bottom southwest of the sheep country. Here there were brush yards made from rough timber, wide at the bottom, with long branches stacked one on top of another until there was sufficient height to deter the stock. In the late afternoon my father dropped off my swag. I was to camp the night and ride with them the next day until they crossed the boundary.

I don't know why it was necessary for me to travel with the mob for a day or so, and camp one night with them when I was only an hour's ride from the woolshed. There were nine experienced blackfellas to manage the mob. One young whitefella wasn't going to make a scrap of difference. Perhaps Pottsy thought it would be good for my education. Perhaps he wanted to find out more about me: Old Fred would tell him. Maybe he was grooming me. Whatever his reason, I was to be forever grateful.

Think of this: a stripling of eighteen, madly in love with horses, droving a very big mob of the best-bred horses in the country. Bays, browns, chestnuts, a few blacks, a few greys – they showed their class with every step they took, with every swing of their heads, with every elegant movement. If I had thought I was in heaven when I was in the team that drove the racehorses to Landor, this was something that surpassed even that.

In the gathering night, I sat by the fire with the Yamatjis and ate bungarra baked in ashes and embers. We also had our regular tucker, but the bungarra was a treat. One of the Yamatjis had found it that afternoon. I sat beside Old Fred while he used a long stick to whack the ash-covered mound that was the baking lizard. From the sound of the whack, he decided it was ready to eat. Two fellas lifted it out away from the fire and placed it in front of him. Old Fred leaned over and took hold of a rear leg, which fell away from the body, steaming. In a soft, ceremonial kind of way, he handed it to me. 'You eat im,' he said. 'This real good tucker.'

I did eat it – and it was good tucker. 'What about the tail?' I asked. 'That's supposed to be pretty good.'

'Yeah. Righto,' said Old Fred. He was not going to get up from where he sat. He gestured to one of the younger fellas to separate the tail from the body and break it into sections. A piece from the base of the tail was given to me. The flesh was moist and full of flavour, firm but tender. I licked my greasy fingers and grinned at Old Fred. Old Fred put his black hand on my white arm and said, 'Go on. Eat more. Eat what you want.' I ate a few more mouthfuls, and with everyone else tearing at the carcass, it was quickly finished.

Forty yards away, 154 horses were milling around in the brush yards. In the bright moonlight I could see them moving, seething in a thick cloud of dust. There were occasional squeals and grunts. I stood up, brushed the dirt off the back of my moleskins and walked over. I stood just outside the yards and watched. Never had I seen a sight like it. So many horses in one mob concentrated in one huge yard, a writhing conglomeration swimming silkily in the dusty moonlight. I thought, I may never see anything like this again, ever. I tried to capture and absorb every sound, every sight and every smell. I wanted to keep that picture, that vision, in my mind forever. I walked part of the way around the yards and then dawdled slowly back towards the fire, not wanting to lose the moment, stopping every few strides to drink it all in, over and over. Old Fred was still sitting there, watching me. He said, 'Come ere an have a drinka tea. Les talk a little bit.'

Again, I sat down in the dirt with him, and we drank tea and we talked; mostly I listened. The firelight flickered on the overhanging leaves of nearby trees; their white trunks shone out of the dark. There was no other light, no bright light. Just the moonlight casting deep shadows. The way Old Fred talked about Pottsy made me think that Pottsy was more than the boss of the station – I think Old Fred and most of the Yamatjis saw him as a leader, their leader. They respected his authority and his judgement. Then it came time to climb into our swags, and I stood up and bent over to help Old Fred to his feet. Poor old bugger. He could ride a horse all right, but he wasn't too good at walking on his own legs. He straightened up. He wasn't a tall man and he was carrying some weight. He leaned on my arm and gave a few instructions to the Yamatjis about watching the horses through the night. Then he shuffled off by himself to his swag.

Many times I've wondered how Pottsy would have managed without the likes of Old Fred and Snowball and the other old blackfellas he relied on. It was a big responsibility to drove 154 valuable thoroughbred horses 160 miles. But Old Fred knew the country and he knew horses and he knew the Yamatjis he had around him – and Pottsy knew him and they were loyal to each other.

The next morning we moved the mob through Bangemall paddock to the boundary and into Cobra. I dearly wanted to go on with the mob. For an hour or so I rode with them, and then I said my farewells to Old Fred and the others. I stood my horse and watched until the mob was almost out of sight. Finally, I neck-reined my horse around and rode back to the woolshed. It felt as though I had just lost something precious.

In mid-October we heard from Tom Steadman. He wanted me to start on 24 November 1953. So I told Pottsy I was leaving to work at Errabiddy. Pottsy gave me that stare of his and said, 'Are yer sure?'

Yes, I was sure – and I said so. Pottsy looked at me and didn't say another word. When I reflect on our relationship, I wonder what was in the back of his mind. Maybe something. Maybe nothing. I'll never know.

At the end of 1953, Pottsy wrote in the station journal, 'The season was a drought, all stock very poor all over the run. We sold cattle that could hardly walk – sent them away by truck. We sent some of the horses down to Jimba Jimba.'

For 1953, Mount Augustus Station's income was cattle: £15,683 and sheep: £40,174 16s 10d.

The sheep may have been just as lean as the cattle, but they still grew wool.

PART THREE

STATION HAND

Employed for routine work on a
station, which may include stock work

14

Tom Steadman

As I was aware, 1953 was one of several drought years in succession. At Mount Augustus, the rainfall was a mere 379 points. Given that the average was around seven inches and that there were 100 points to an inch, 379 points was useless. Depending on when it fell, even seven inches did not guarantee a good season: for that the rainfall had to be better than average. There was consolation and encouragement in the continuing good prices for wool. Offsetting that, sheep were dying like flies in the Gascoyne and the Murchison. Fortunately, station owners such as Tom Steadman had benefited from several good years. He had husbanded his resources and could carry on and survive until the rains came and the feed could grow and the sheep could breed. Everyone spoke of the good times to come. But the big wool clips from this part of the Norwest would be a long time coming.

Until I went to Errabiddy, I had been employed on company-owned or family-owned long-established properties with salaried managers. Now I was in the employ of an owner-manager who had literally started from scratch. Tom Steadman was born in 1906 and he came to Australia with his brother in 1926. He had a letter of introduction from Mr R.E. Bush, of Bristol, England. Mr Bush owned several stations in the Upper Gascoyne, including Landor.

To start with, Tom and his brother worked at clearing land for farming at Popanyinning in the wheat belt, just north of Narrogin. His brother soon found the heat and the flies too daunting and he returned to England. Tom was undeterred and decided to use his letter of introduction and find out what life would be like on a sheep station in the outback.

In August 1926, he took the train to Meekatharra and then the mail truck to Landor, where he was given work. Tom was made for station life. He worked at Landor for seven years and was given management roles, which included running Mount James Station, also owned by Mr Bush, and, ultimately, Landor itself. By 1933, he was straining at the leash to own property himself. He was granted the lease of some country adjoining Landor. As a thank you for his long commitment to the Bush family, they granted him a block of Landor's land, along with some sheep and cattle.

That was the start of Errabiddy. For a young immigrant from England, it was a dream come true. But what a tough dream! To begin with, Tom lived in a bough shed and sank wells and built fences. Not only was the country hard, times were tough as well: in 1932 unemployment in Australia hit a record 29 per cent; 1933 was the height of the Great Depression. From then on, Australia slowly recovered. As if Tom Steadman and his fellow pastoralists did not have enough to contend with, they were hit with a debilitating drought, which lasted from 1936 to 1942. It is hard to comprehend how they survived.

Errabiddy homestead and its buildings were spread beside the road that linked Meekatharra and Mount Augustus and beyond. Travellers were obliged to slow down and drive more sedately through the collection of buildings, most of them erected by Tom and an offsider.

When the gold mines at Wiluna closed in 1947, the town all but shut down and Tom bought the Union Bank building. He broke it into sections and transported it all the way to Errabiddy, about 230 miles. Re-erected, it was an imposing building. The high-ceilinged main office became the living room. The back rooms were converted into bedrooms and an office. The kitchen was in what remained of the old homestead. A few yards away he built a bough shed for really hot days. A bough shed acts like an oversize Coolgardie safe, with water pipes around the sides at the top to trickle water down through the brush walls. With any breeze through the walls, the inside was refreshingly cool.

Not many men could have done what Tom did. Whatever it was – dedication, determination – he made himself into a successful pastoralist and became a hard man in doing so. Struggling to survive can do that to people. In Tom's case, at the core of his hardness was self-discipline, bloody-minded self-discipline. How else do you cope, year after year, with extreme heat, flies, never-ending dust, windmills breaking down, stroppy shearers, fluctuating wool prices, and second-hand vehicles and machinery requiring constant maintenance? And distance, the mind-numbing miles of corrugated dirt roads that separate you from human company. Tom was hard – and he could be intolerant. Anyone who wasn't tough enough was intimidated by the hardness in his eyes and the scornful edge in his voice. Those traits are typical of many outback people. Was he vulnerable? Indeed he was. His two sons were the centre of his life and if anything happened to them he would have been devastated. He was determined that they would have an easier life than he had experienced and he gave them the kind of education he never had. In that way, he was a classic father.

Around the house, Tom and his wife, Kay, created a gleaming, lush garden, in brilliant contrast to the drab bush. The men's quarters were the usual corrugated-iron walls and roof, with a concrete floor. Jiff and I had a small room to ourselves and the room next to us was occupied by a young man four or five years older than I. His name was Gerry Smith and his family owned a sheep station called Mooloogool, northeast of Meekatharra. His elder brother, Brian, was managing the family property and Gerry had started out on the road to independence. Gerry was married and had a child, but there was no place for his wife at Errabiddy. She was a teacher, so she lived and worked in Meekatharra.

Gerry and I strode straight into friendship. It was just as well. Due to the drought and the uncertainty of the times, it was natural that the mood in the homestead tended to be sombre. Being young and unaffected, we were happy to be left to amuse ourselves in the men's quarters after dinner each evening.

To start with, our work was to check the many windmills around the station, fix those that needed fixing and feed horses and stock at the homestead. On our rounds, we collected sheep that were so starved they could no longer stand. We brought them back to the homestead and put them in a large enclosure behind the house. There they were fed and watered individually and, from time to time, carefully helped to their feet to see if they could recover the use of their legs. Most of them died.

Then we learned why Tom really wanted us. He packed us up in a 1936 Chevrolet ute and we followed him to country he had purchased from Milly Milly Station. As the crow flies, it would have been about fifteen miles from the Errabiddy homestead; it was more like twenty-five miles by the route we had to take. Apart from ten miles along the main road, the route went along bush tracks, up and down hills, through gullies and across stony watercourses. We bounced around in the ute, slowing right down to first gear in place after place. We were told this land had not been used since 1938 and I could understand why. Through neglect, the windmills weren't pumping and the fences were mostly flat on the ground. The job for Gerry and me was to get the windmills working and then fix the fences.

Our primary concern was the ten miles of fence that would become the new boundary with Milly Milly Station. Along this fence there were three bores with windmills and tanks, and troughs for the stock to water. One of the windmills was pumping and that's where we set up camp. It was the middle one of the three.

It was December 1953. The temperature never seemed to be less than 110 degrees in the shade. It was probably 130 to 140 degrees in the sun, where we worked. The heat radiated up from the stony ground. If one of us made the mistake of leaving a crowbar or a Stillson lying flat anywhere, it quickly became too hot to handle. And the flies. Where did they come from? They materialised out of nowhere. No, we did not have corks dangling from our hats. No, we did not have fly nets to drape over our heads. Still, we couldn't complain. We had the luxury of a water bag each.

Our first day on the job, we were to fix the first windmill, the one we passed on our way in to where we were camped. We were up before sunrise. The relative coolness of an early morning in summer is an invitation. A few deep breaths of bush air fill you with a compulsion to get going. So we did. We made our way at a slow pace along the rough track, where we could find it. It teased us by disappearing, and we had to get out and see where it emerged again. The terrain was too rough for the track to run alongside the fence line all the way. It ducked off into the bush to avoid outcrops of rock and heavy thickets of mulga and to find a better passage through creek beds. Fortunately, we had our tracks from the day before, but they were hard to see on the stony ground while we were driving.

We set up to fix the windmill. This meant pulling the column to get to the pump. The column consisted of lengths of two-inch-diameter galvanised-iron piping, and the pump was screwed to the bottom length; all of this was inside the bore casing. Inside the column, lengths of small-diameter rod connected the leather buckets in the pump at the bottom to the gears at the head of the windmill. That enabled it to suck the water up from deep underground. Pulling the column meant using a block and tackle to raise each length of pipe up within the framework of the windmill tower. Then it could be disconnected from the one below and stacked out of the way. The one below was clamped, and the clamp rested on the top of the bore casing while the rod inside was disconnected from the section of rod below. Sounds simple – and it is. What we did not know was the depth of the bore or the length of each pipe. The fact that the windmill stand was unusually high should have warned us.

Our initial shock was that each length of pipe was twenty-one feet six inches. Why that particular length, no-one has ever been able to tell me. As we were pulling on the ropes of the block and tackle, we thought we would never get to where the first length was coupled to the second. And when we did uncouple the two, we were shocked by the weight. Twenty-plus feet of galvanised-iron pipe weighs a hell of a lot. We settled in to the work and eventually we had four lengths of pipe and rod stacked inside the windmill frame. Lengthwise there was only just enough room. I eventually found that the bore was near enough to 120 feet deep.

Gerry and I worked together as though we'd been partners for years. At this point in pulling the column, there was a pattern to how we worked, a tacit understanding. Then Gerry did something different. When we had the fifth length up and out, Gerry guided the bottom end to where it would rest on the rim of the bore casing, instead of on the ground. I don't know why he did that. The bore casing stood up about eighteen inches from its concrete collar. Normally we lowered the pipe all the way to the ground. With the pipe sitting on the rim of the bore, Gerry said, 'Undo the block and tackle.' I did and then I heard an almighty scream, and I turned to see Gerry clutching his right foot, and the end of the pipe now on the ground. I yelled, 'What's happened?'

Gerry was incoherent. He moaned; he swore; he was gasping. I helped him out from inside the windmill frame to where he could sit on the ground. What I saw then took my breath away.

The pipe had slipped off the rim of the bore casing; Gerry's right foot had been on the concrete collar, and the pipe had dropped the eighteen inches, with who knows how much weight behind it, like a giant leather punch, and sliced clean through the top of his hobnailed boot and his big toe and the one beside it. I undid his boot and gingerly removed it, which may or may not have been a good idea. His two toes were not completely severed but they were hanging on by a meagre strip of skin and flesh.

I brought the ute over as close as I could and helped him into the passenger seat. Gerry sat with his foot and toes wrapped in a towel. He clutched the bundle with both hands while I picked our way across country until we hit the main road. Judging by Gerry's moans and swearing, the pain was excruciating. It was the drive of my life. Each bump jerked and jarred Gerry's foot and brought a new outburst of outrage. Considering the whole trip across country was nothing but bumps, the vocal onslaught beside me was nonstop.

Errabiddy homestead at last showed up. Mrs Steadman, who had been a nurse, did her best to relieve Gerry's distress, while Tom got on the pedal wireless to the Flying Doctor. I hung around not knowing what to do with myself.

It was late in the afternoon before we heard the Flying Doctor's plane. He buzzed the homestead and Tom jumped in a ute and sped off to the landing strip, about three miles away. The doctor wanted to see Gerry before putting him on the plane. Maybe it was just to make sure that taking him to hospital in Meekatharra was really necessary. The inspection confirmed that. Then there was a needle jab for the pain and Gerry was gently transferred to the plane and waved on his way. We didn't see each other again until about eight months later, when I went to work at Belele Station, where my uncle Jack was the manager. Gerry and his wife were living and working there at the outcamp called Buttah. He was not much the worse for his accident at Errabiddy.

Grumbling about the inconvenience, Tom worked with me to finish off what Gerry and I had started at the first mill. We drove down to the new country each morning and drove back to the homestead in the late afternoon. He wouldn't settle for anything less than the comfort of the homestead, where he could also have a cold beer. You couldn't blame him. He'd earned the right to take it easier. But reactivating the windmills was as far as he would go. The fencing had to wait until he could hire another pair of hands. This didn't take long. When the next mail truck arrived from Meekatharra it delivered a very stout, middle-aged Italian called Luigi, who preferred the abbreviation Lui. He was probably in his mid-forties and to me that was getting old. Lui, to Tom's dismay, was not fluent in English. The best he could do was a convoluted pidgin version, even though he'd been in Australia for twenty-five years.

Tom could be impatient and he had a temper. Lui showed he also had a temper, and I thought, here we go, there could be a nice old blue here. I couldn't speak a word of Italian but I could, with a bit of thought, unravel what Lui tried to say in English. That's when I became an interpreter, much like I'd been with Snowball. Tom quickly gave up talking directly to Lui and, instead, spoke to me. I simplified what Tom said and explained it to Lui. Lui, in turn, responded in his own way and – when Tom stopped repeating 'What the bloody hell is he saying?' – I translated for him. After a while, I wasn't sure whether I was an interpreter or a referee. There were times when I would have enjoyed using a whistle to get the two of them to shut up. Eventually I learned that Lui had arrived in Australia from Italy in 1928.

Later on the day he arrived at Errabiddy, Tom sent me off with Lui in the Chev ute to the new country. The remnants of a bough shed were standing forlornly a short distance from the first windmill, now working, and we set up our camp gear in the meagre shade of what was left of the roof. We placed our swags on opposite sides of the relic. Tom had followed us and we unloaded a tuckerbox and bags of potatoes and onions. Included was a pound of butter. I was amazed. I thought, how long is a pound of butter going to last in this weather? I soon found out. That evening, Lui used half the butter to cook onions and meat in a frying pan. When I started to wash the dishes, he jumped up in great alarm and rushed at me, yelling, 'No. No. No.' I thought he was going to hit me.

'No what?' I asked.

'You noa wash.'

'You're bloody joking.'

'What joke? Leava pan. Leava my plate. Noa wash.'

'OK. OK. Calm down.'

Next morning, Lui took the frying pan, which overnight had acquired a thick film of red dust across the whole surface, and plonked a chunk of the remaining half-melted butter in it. I shuddered. I declined his offer to cook breakfast for me. By the time we got back to the camp that afternoon, it was no surprise that what remained of the butter had totally melted.

If Gerry had been a real mate to work with, Lui was the opposite. Trying to work with him on the fence was nonstop conflict. He had his way of doing things and that was the only way he would do them. Fencing is not a complicated task. In this case, we were not starting from scratch. The old fence was still largely usable. Many posts had rotted at ground level, which resulted in sections of the fence having fallen over. We cut new fence posts and placed one alongside an old post and twitched the two together. It's called dummying. It was still necessary to dig holes for the new posts and that is a story in itself in this country. But you don't dummy a strainer. Strainers are heavy posts to which the long lines of fencing wire are attached and then pulled tight. Broken-off strainers are replaced.

As the old posts are lifted and twitched to the new posts, the old wire fence comes up with them. It's then a matter of tightening the wires or replacing those that are too rusted and broken. How you could have an argument about the sequence of any of this was beyond me, but we did. By the end of the second day we weren't talking to each other. This was not a good situation for two blokes working together, an hour's drive from anywhere.

Thankfully, Tom came out for an inspection on the third day, and Lui and I put our situation to him. With the wisdom of Solomon, Tom split us up. Because Lui couldn't drive, Tom let me take the ute. My camp was further down the fence line, and I worked westwards and then up the west side. This left Lui with the east end. It didn't bother him that I had the only vehicle. He was happy to see the back of me. One of the benefits of having the ute was that I could prospect for good mulga fence posts, and if they were well away from the fence line I had the transport to take them where I needed them. Poor old Lui had to carry his on his shoulder, although I did quite a bit of that too. And poor old Tom had to learn to communicate with Lui without an interpreter. I smiled to myself at that thought.

In the days that followed, I began growing into a new self. For a start, I discovered that I liked being alone for days on end. Let me rephrase that. I enjoyed being alone with Jiff. A good dog can be good company. The sharp edge of loneliness is blunted. A relationship between a man and an animal is a curious thing. At its best there is a subtle and sensitive level of communication. There is a bond and, true, part of that bond is forged in the man's ownership of the dog. The dog has no doubt whom it belongs to. It's a bond that's quite unlike a bond between two people, or between two dogs. In our case, it was indissoluble, which was not unusual for a man and a dog in the outback. Fifty years later, I still miss him.

For the next two weeks, each day fell into the same pattern. I was out of the swag at first light and kicking the coals of the previous night's fire and throwing small sticks on top. Then I put the billy on the coals and built up the fire. I walked twenty yards away and relieved myself. Next, a wash and a shave. Wearing stubble never appealed to me. By this time the sun was up over the horizon and flooding the landscape with light. Toasted damper came next, with whatever may have been left over from the previous night's dinner. After that, there was no point in hanging around. I tidied the camp if I was going to be there for another night or I packed everything onto the back of the ute.

My bed was a standard outback steel stretcher with foldout legs. It was permanently up on the left-hand side of the back of the ute, with the camping gear, the tuckerbox, the water drum and the small toolbox on the other side. The crowbar, the shovel and the axe were kept under the stretcher. When I cut fence posts, that's where they went too. With my swag tied down on top of the stretcher, it was all compact and neat.

Then it was on with the job. The time? No later than six o'clock. I picked up from where I'd left off the day before and worked until twelve. That's when I boiled the billy and ate lunch and had a spell for half an hour. Sitting around for any longer was bad. It was too easy to dwell on the discomforts of the heat, the flies and the work. The heat was so unremitting and oppressive that the only way I coped was by working. That way I stopped thinking about it.

Each day had the same routine: swinging the axe to cut mulga fence posts, digging post holes and straining wires with a hand auger. Digging holes required driving the crowbar into ground that was like concrete and then scooping the dirt out with an old bully-beef tin – a post-hole shovel was a waste of effort and time: the hole was always too big. By using a small hand-held container, I could restrict the hole to the thickness of the post.

Where there were too many rocks to dig a hole, the post was anchored. Mulga rails were laid on each side of the post, at right angles to the fence line. Big stones were placed on top of the rails to weigh them down. Then, double lengths of wire connected the ends of the rails to somewhere near the top of the post, and the wires were twitched. Thus the post was braced on each side and stayed that way until the mulga rails on the ground rotted, which took many years.

The constant work with steel tools in the heat and dust produced calluses like strips of hard black rubber on the pads of my fingers and on my hands. No amount of washing could remove the blackness. The calluses were valuable because the alternative was blisters. No-one used gloves. No-one was aware of the possibility that gloves might be available – and useful. For all I knew at that time, work gloves were yet to be invented.

The physical exertion and the effort of using all my strength to get something in place was something I relished. It was rewarding to see the professionalism of my wire straining and the way the wires were wrapped around the post and twisted back on themselves. I was fanatical about digging the holes for strainer posts the regulation three feet deep or as close to that as the terrain would allow. The loose soil was rammed in around the posts until they were so tight they might have grown there. Drilling holes through fifteen-inch strainer posts with a hand drill was as tough as any part of the job. With both hands on the drill, I couldn't wipe the sweat out of my eyes or brush the damned flies away. And while I was working on one task my mind was planning the next.

My pride in the fence I was rebuilding was intense. In my mind, no-one should ever be able to point a finger of criticism at my work. You may think that I was becoming mad or, at the very least, obsessed. Maybe, though I think I was focused, not obsessed. Committed, not mad. After each lunch camp, when I thought I couldn't continue, boredom and my determination to finish the job drove me out into the sun again.

There was only one occasion when my isolation gave me cause for serious concern. I was on my hands and knees scooping dirt from a post hole when I felt a sting on the left side of my testicles. 'Bloody bull ant!' I said. Without standing up, I tried to crush it in the folds of my trousers. That failed, because I then felt a really sharp stab of pain. I jumped up, hastily undid my trousers and dropped them to see what was happening. And there was a black-and-green centipede clamped on my flesh. It was about five inches long and had a body about half an inch wide. I pulled it off, threw it to the ground and used the heel of my right boot to grind it into the dust. What do I do now, I asked myself? The pain was increasing. Can you die from a centipede bite, I wondered? I decided to carry on and see what would happen. As the afternoon progressed, a lump started swelling beside my left testicle. By early evening, the lump was as big as an egg – and hard. Well, well, I thought, now I've got three balls. The pain was just tolerable, so I thought I'd review the situation in the morning. When I woke, I found that the lump had reduced in size and was softer. Over the next three days it subsided completely.

At five each afternoon, with enough daylight to set up and prepare dinner, I looked for somewhere suitable. I scanned the landscape for a place for a night camp that I would enjoy.

It was always a place that had a presence, the status of being some kind of landmark; nearly always on rising ground with a prospect; usually with at least one tall tree with a character that engendered respect; always with a clear area for the ute and plenty of clear space around the fire. No matter how hot the day, the first thing I did was build the all-purpose fire – the billy-boiling fire, the cooking fire, the talkative fire, the living fire, the firelight. I kept the fire going until late into the night, always aware of the dancing flames and the variegated oranges and reds and the brittle, crackling noises that were a living presence in the silent, greying emptiness all around. Bird life was scarce if I was camped far from a windmill. Kangaroos were somewhere else too. The only wildlife was the occasional small lizard and the ubiquitous ants. One of the reasons I kept my stretcher up on the ute was because ants will go up steel frames but they won't go up rubber tyres. Ants in a swag are very unpleasant.

As night took possession of my world and me, the heat lost its bite, the sky demanded my attention and I sought my swag, where it was raised up above the earth. The swag was unrolled and spread out. I gave my pillow a shake and lay down. Mostly, there was no wind. If there was any movement of air, it was intermittent and soft. Jiff jumped up and lay under the stretcher. Having strung the aerial through the branches of a tree, I turned on my STC portable radio, the most powerful available at the time, and tuned in to the ABC's 6WN, their classical music station. Lying on my back, gazing up at the stars, I welcomed the wonder of classical music into my realm. Beethoven, so insistent, forceful, inspiring at times, yet so soothing at others; Wagner, inducing that pleasurable feeling of sombre melancholy; Mozart, captivating and exhilarating. In the silence and the stillness of the bush, they elevated me with a feeling of exultation.

The music gave me joy. The sky gave me joy. The night gave me joy. That I was alive made me euphoric. Gratitude filled me. I could not believe I was the same person who in the middle of the day wanted to give up, stop, walk away. Now I was being replenished, restored. I wanted to cry out, 'Hey, I'm here! I may be only a pinprick in this endless, deserted landscape and this endless universe above me, but I am here, right here.' The stimulation kept me awake, not wanting to end the experience. Sometimes I fell asleep with the music still playing. Every night was the same. Every night was to be treasured. Every night was a reward. Every night affected me and moved me along an emotional path I could not define or describe – or understand. All I knew and felt was that, within myself, I liked wherever it was I was heading.

That was how I entered 1954. Through the last hours of 1953, I listened to 6WN until it closed down for the night and for the year. Then I trawled the dial until I found a station, I don't know where, that was playing jazz. My New Year started with the new sounds of Lionel Hampton, Stan Kenton, Gerry Mulligan, Dave Brubeck. Elsewhere in Western Australia, people were partying – singing, dancing, hugging, kissing. In my vast space I was at peace with my world and with myself and my dog.

After three weeks, the fencing was completed. The windmills were pumping and the troughs were brimming with cool, clean water. Lui caught the mail truck to Meekatharra and I returned to the homestead. My principal new task was to transfer stock from the eaten-out paddocks to the almost-virginal new country. My day started with feeding horses, chooks and invalid sheep at the homestead, and it ended the same way. When that was done, there was the wood to chop for the kitchen stove. In between, I rode with Jiff to where sheep had been trapped. Trapping was a simple matter of turning off the water at a windmill. The sheep numbers varied from day to day, but there were never more than a hundred. They came in to drink and, finding no water, they stood around, or lay down, and waited. They had no motivation to go anywhere. But when I arrived, they had to go, and go where I directed them. This was always south, towards Tom's new country, along a fence line to a corner, where I let them through to the next paddock.

Every morning I rode out at 7.30 and it was often 9.30 before I was where the sheep were waiting. Before starting out with the mob, I released the water into the trough and let the sheep drink. It was always ten o'clock before I re-gathered the mob and started them on their way. With rare exceptions, the stock could travel no more than four miles in a full day. The pattern each day was the same. A handful of reasonably strong sheep took the lead and had to be continually restrained. At the back, the stragglers had to be physically pushed and nudged along, and helped to their feet when they folded their legs and sank to the stony ground. While I was doing that, except for the leaders, the mob stopped until I got the stragglers up with them. Then they lethargically moved on.

As soon as a mob was gathered and moving down the fence line, I dismounted and walked. A horse would not, or could not, walk at a slow enough pace when ridden. Mostly I led the horse; sometimes I tied it up under a shady mulga and left it while I inched the mob along another two or three hundred yards.

My workmate, Jiff, was good at running around the mob and heading off the leaders, but that usually stopped the whole mob. Sometimes it was more effective for me to walk or run around to the front and throw stones in front of the leaders to make them slow down. But then the stragglers lay down and I had to hurry back to get them going before the leaders were too far ahead. Later in the morning, the leaders were content to plod along with the rest of the mob and I only had to concentrate on the stragglers. At midday I let the mob flop down while I took a break under a mulga in the scant shade. I wondered if I would be able to get the whole lot to their destination. They were all heartbreakingly frail, just skin and bone, indifferent to my urgings. To lift one up in order to put it on its feet was easy: they were weightless, empty woollen bags. By mid-afternoon, Jiff was bored and sick of the whole business and I had to urge him to take an interest. The horse was the one who had the least work to do.

Six hours after we set out, we reached the end of our tediously slow journey. Released into their new territory, some sheep immediately subsided. Others spread out, seeking anything they could eat. Jiff, my horse and I each took a long drink and headed back to the homestead, with the pathetic intermittent bleating of the sheep fading in the distance.

Freed from the constraints of the sheep, I let my horse slip into his easy, striding walk and, from time to time, a steady, measured trot. There was no hard riding. This horse had to work again the following day, and the succeeding days. On the two-hour ride in to the homestead, I contemplated life at Errabiddy. This was not the kind of station life I wanted. Errabiddy was too small. The country was too hard. I hankered after the softer country out from Carnarvon and one of the big, well-established stations in that area. Riding back in to the homestead, with the setting sun and a northwesterly wind full in my face, I pulled my scarf up over my chin and nose to prevent my fair skin from being cooked.

It was disheartening to salvage sadly weakened sheep and bring them back to the homestead and the convalescent yard at the back. There was only ever a handful of sheep in this yard and it hardly seemed worth the effort to save a few dozen when they were dying in their hundreds out in the desolate scrub. At best, it was a token effort. The enormity of the situation was made worse by the diabolical crows. At Winnininnie I had seen crows hopping beside newborn lambs, trying to peck their eyes out – and succeeding all too often. Here, at Errabiddy, they stood on the backs of sheep that were too weak to stand and they drilled down through the wool and ate the kidneys. Seeing that happen infuriated me. Whenever

I had a free moment I patrolled with my gun, but it was virtually impossible to get a shot at a crow. With their extraordinary eyesight, they saw the weapon the instant I appeared. If I had no gun, they took their time. I hated them with a vengeance.

Of the sheep we nursed, most of them died and then it was my job to take the carcasses and dump them out in the bush well away from the homestead. In spite of that, we kept at it. The futility of it all never overrode the need to do something. For Tom, it must have been heartbreaking to continue to maintain the station with his principal resource, the sheep, rapidly dwindling. The ever-present questions, to which there were no immediate answers, were when would the rains come; when would there be feed; when would the stock regain their strength; would there be enough sheep left to justify bringing in a shearing team to produce a wool clip? The future for the Steadman family looked dark.

Tom divided his time between driving around the station to check on the waters and the stock, and working in his office. Errabiddy was about 192,000 acres. This was small compared to other stations in the Gascoyne and the Murchison, but big enough to demand several hours of driving on bush tracks to get from windmill to windmill. Tom spent much of his time in his office. He was coming to terms with the introduction of provisional tax and how he and other pastoralists could overcome its draconian effects. Tom was instrumental in preparing a submission to the taxation department to demonstrate its unfairness. After several hearings, including one in Meekatharra, the tax payments were amended to make them less onerous for pastoralists and farmers.

Every evening, after dinner, Tom disappeared into the depths of the house and I helped Mrs Steadman do the dishes. It was then that she talked to me and I listened. With just the two of us, I was able to look at her openly and see her for the lady she was. She was not conventionally beautiful, but I could see that she would have been an attractive young woman. She was well educated, she spoke well and she cared about personal standards. She showed often that she was genuinely concerned about the welfare of others, and this was reflected in the respect that other station people had for her. Maybe that was why she became a nurse and rose to being a nursing sister. Or perhaps her profession taught her the importance of caring. Perhaps both. To me she was a lady of dignity and quality.

When she married Tom, the uncertainty she faced was daunting. She went to live in a place she had never seen, a place that was 120 miles from Meekatharra, the nearest town. She had no conception of what hard and desolate country it would be. She couldn't have imagined the heat and the dust. She had no comprehension of what it would be like to live in isolation most of the time, with only her husband for company at the end of the day. But she did know she was fearful of the unknown. A certain amount of fear is no bad thing – it can keep you alert for the unexpected.

Quite often I was grateful to find she had done some of my chores for me before I had arrived back at the homestead. She made me promise never to tell Tom. In his view, my chores were my chores, regardless of how long my day had been.

At that time, with the drought and the problem of provisional tax, I think her two sons, David and Ainslie, were a great consolation. Without them, her life would have had much less meaning, and satisfaction. Tom provided her with a comfortable homestead and, in spite of droughts and fluctuating wool prices, financial security most of the time. Other than a handful of station people, not many who met this woman, with her quiet and dignified authority, would have been aware of the challenges she had to overcome to be her own person and to make her place in that world.

After two weeks of moving sheep, seven days a week, the black calluses peeled off my fingers and hands in strips to reveal clean fingerprints and handprints. After three weeks, I had transferred about 1,500 sheep to the new country. How many of them survived, Tom would find out many months later.

Tom continued to spend capital on new fencing and he brought in a team of three to do the work. They were led by a young man whose name was Mark. He was tall, slim and good looking and had a roguish way about him. He was cagey about his background, except to say that he had originated in the eastern states. There was a rumour that he was on the run from Sydney crims. Out in the bush, he and his men often worked without shirts and we could see thick scars and welts on Mark's torso. When asked about them, he laughed and said, 'That's a long story.' On the quiet, Mark's offsiders hinted at gang warfare in Sydney. It was not unusual to come across runaway men in the station country. A man could disappear into the outback, using an assumed name, and nobody asked too many questions.

Tom had me camped out to work with them for a week and then moved me back to the homestead to take care of the place while he and Mrs Steadman drove to Perth for a few days.

Shortly after Tom returned, the pump in the bore at the homestead gave way, and fixing it was a weird experience. Originally, Tom had sunk a well, but it had not produced enough water. So about six feet away from the well, he had a bore drilled to a much greater depth, where there was a good supply. He then shifted the windmill above the well over to the bore.

To fix a pump in a well you don't have to pull the column totally out. You go down the well and stand on a narrow platform and do the work from there. All of which means the windmill can be relatively small – and cheaper to buy and easier to erect. Not so with a bore: the whole column must be removed. That's why the windmill frames over bores are so high – to accommodate the long lengths of pipe. This windmill was much too small to handle piping inside the frame.

Tom's solution was to cut a passageway, called a drive, from the well through to the bore where he had positioned the pump. This was fifty-six feet from the surface. To get to the pump, I had to go down the well and along the drive. But the well made enough water for the water level to be above the drive, so the well had to be pumped out with a petrol-powered pump.

The underground passage was about five feet high. Having to work in that confined space, half bent over, with chain tongs and Stillsons, by the light of a torch, was difficult enough, but the well kept making water and it kept rising. If it was waist high before I'd removed the pump, I had to evacuate to the surface and empty the well again. The weird and unpleasant experience was being deep underground, bent over in a narrow drive, with water rising up my legs and body, battling to disconnect or reconnect the pump and the column. When that happened, there was a feeling of such urgency it bordered on panic. It was a unique setup, one I had never heard of before – or after.

All through my time at Mount Augustus, and again at Errabiddy, Ian Bridson and I stayed in touch by letter and through my infrequent visits to Perth. His stint with his uncle being completed, he was teaching English at Hale School. In early February 1954, the Bridson family invited me to the wedding of Ian's elder brother, Bevis. That was too good an opportunity to miss, not only to catch up with Ian, but also to see my cousin Pamela during the few days I was in Perth.

Pamela was my father's niece, eight years older than me. She and her sister, Gay, were very beautiful young women. In my eyes, they were charismatic. Pamela was tall and shapely and blonde. Gay was tall and willowy and red haired. They were as glamorous as film stars. It was exciting to be in their company. They both married soon after the war, but Pamela's marriage didn't last, which left her unattached and available to mentor a young cousin. Gay was more remote – and busy with her married life.

My first real contact with Pamela was when I went to Perth from Mount Augustus. We got on well together and we shared interests that I could not share with many others. Cousin Pamela was a serious woman. I mean she was seriously female – and she had a serious outlook. She was training to be a kindergarten teacher. She was also studying psychology, not in relation to understanding children, more to do with understanding human nature – and herself. She was listening to classical music and reading good literature. We talked for hours. At eighteen, I was ripe for someone else to lead me further down the track that the maiden aunts and Ian Bridson and Bill van Rijn had shown me.

In the station country, women were few and far between – and they were the wives of station owners or managers. If they had daughters, they were invariably away at boarding school. The only time I met women around my own age was at Landor Races – and they were visitors from Perth. A handful of intelligent, interesting older women stood out like beacons. Peg Campbell at Mount Gould Station was one. Mount Gould was on the Meekatharra to Mount Augustus mail run and I met Peg several times passing through. Kay Steadman was another and, later at Koonmarra Station, Connie Lee-Steere influenced my thinking. But Pamela was in another category altogether.

Her intensity made it difficult for her to come to terms with herself and with other people. She spent too much time alone in her flat, reading, thinking. I was aware of this, but it didn't bother me. My youthful energy and various enthusiasms lifted her out of her melancholy. She assumed the role of a big sister and enjoyed having a younger male sibling to guide.

She introduced me to foreign films: Italian and French, with subtitles. *La Strada* and *The Seven Deadly Sins* gave us a lot to discuss. The films were perceived to be terribly avant-garde, dangerously risqué and maybe not the sort of films that nice people went to see. They were usually shown in small cinemas that were upstairs or downstairs, almost out of sight. Many became classics of world cinema.

Then there was dining in good restaurants. It was not fine dining as we know it today, but there were a few dishes that were slightly adventurous: chicken Maryland was pretty exotic then. We sat for hours over dinner and we talked. Afterwards I walked her back to her flat – and we talked.

We talked often about personal relationships, about love and about sex. She advised me strongly not to waste myself having sex with anyone I did not really care about. 'Wait until you meet the right person,' she said.

'How will I know when I've met the right person?'

'You'll know. When your toes curl up when you're making love to her, you'll know she's the right one.'

That was food for thought. How was I to know in advance what was going to happen to my toes? She was dead against trial and error. 'Wait,' she insisted. 'Wait until the right one comes along.' I thought she was giving me good advice, but it left me in a quandary. So where was I going to meet young women so I could find the 'right one'?

There was nothing in station life that was equivalent to the combination of Ian Bridson and Pamela. This does not mean I was unsettled, but it does mean that the attractions of Perth were beckoning. I was going to miss the kinds of discussions I was having there when I went back to the bush.

Returning by air was a practical option in those days, as MMA (MacRoberston Miller Airlines) serviced stations throughout the Norwest, using an eight-seater Dove plane.

After about an hour in the air on my way back after the Bridson wedding visit, I asked the hostess what time we would be landing at Errabiddy. She replied that the plane was not going to Errabiddy. 'What do you mean?' I asked. 'I'm going to Errabiddy.'

'No,' she said, 'you're going to Edmund.'

'Edmund be buggered. I am going to Errabiddy.'

She went to the cockpit and returned with the manifest and showed me. Errabiddy was there as my destination, but it had been crossed out and Edmund had been written above it. It was a palimpsest rather than a manifest. Edmund was more than a hundred miles further north. Back she went to the pilot, and the plane banked to one side, swung around, straightened up and headed in a different direction. She sat on the armrest of the seat on the other side of the aisle and we chatted with the only other passenger. Then the pilot called to her again. When she returned, she said, 'The pilot wants to know if you're familiar with the country around here, because he doesn't know where we are. Would you please go into the cockpit and tell him where to go?'

As I made my way forward I thought, this is a lot of fun. I sat in the seat beside the pilot in the nose of the plane. The pilot pointed to a station homestead below. 'Is that Errabiddy?'

'No, that's Landor.'

'Well, where the bloody hell is Errabiddy?'

'You've come too far. Turn round and go back.'

'OK. Now you sit there and guide me.'

'See that road down there. Follow that and it'll take you straight back to Errabiddy.'

We flew low over the homestead and Tom came out. He waved and jumped in his ute. We landed on the dirt airstrip as Tom arrived in a cloud of dust. Like a bolt out of the blue sky, I was back at Errabiddy, on the ground, in the heat and the dust and the flies – with the outback landscape shimmering into the distance.

In March 1954, I decided to move on. My parents had left Mount Augustus a couple of months after me, when my father was invited to take over much of the management of Koonmarra Station so that the owner, Herbert Lee-Steere, could take a step or two back.

They wanted me to join them and, because I was at a loose end, I agreed. On 20 March 1954, I left Errabiddy after having been there for only four months, although it felt like a year. The experience was valuable and memorable. Most importantly, it took me to a new level of confidence.

15

Herbert Lee-Steere

Koonmarra is about seventy miles south of Errabiddy, and Meekatharra is about fifty miles further on. On the Meekatharra side of Koonmarra lay Belele Station, where my uncle Jack was manager. With my mother and father and me at Koonmarra and my uncle Jack and his wife, Lindsay, at Belele, we were in unusually close proximity, within a half hour's drive of each other. Visits to Belele were frequent.

Herbert Lee-Steere was a nephew of the first Sir Ernest Lee-Steere, who owned Belele Station. In 1924, Sir Ernest gave Herbert a parcel of shares in Mount Augustus, which he was helping to fund. He sent him up to get experience with Pottsy. That included working out in the bush with a Yamatji and his wife, putting up fifty-two miles of boundary fencing for a sheep section. Later, Pottsy sent him up to Yanrey Station, near Onslow, to help muster 700 cattle. Enie Bain, the father of Alan and Laurie of Landor fame, drove the mob down to Mount Augustus. At the same time, Pottsy bought 2,500 ewes from Yanrey, and Herbert was responsible for droving them to Mount Augustus. The route was across several hundred miles of rugged country with very few watering points. The sheep arrived at Mount Augustus on New Year's Day 1926.

Herbert then left Mount Augustus and, after a stint down south, he took up the land that became Koonmarra. Sir Ernest made some Belele land available to him and helped him with finance. He lived at Koonmarra from 1927 to 1980. He and his wife, Connie, built Koonmarra from scratch. They lived in bough sheds in the bush, building fences and sinking wells. By the time the Parkes family arrived, they had established a good homestead with well-maintained gardens, and the usual collection of station buildings for men's quarters, machinery sheds, stables and stockyards, and a woolshed. In the period after the war and into the fifties, they reaped the reward of the high prices for wool. They had achieved much. Both Herbert and Connie were respected far and wide. They were generous with their hospitality and Herbert gave people his time and advice. Tom Steadman's sons, David and Ainslie, were two young men who enjoyed the benefit of Herbert's hard-won knowledge.

The year 1954 was a time when Herbert and Connie should have been able to look forward to taking it easier. What we quickly learned was that their relationship was on its last legs, and it wasn't long afterwards that Connie left and bought a property in the hills outside Perth. During the three months I was at Koonmarra, I witnessed the steady disintegration of their marriage. As I had with Tom and Kay Steadman, from the Lee-Steeres I learned how much work and commitment and dedication goes into building and running a successful sheep station. My admiration for both Herbert and Connie was unaffected by their personal differences.

The Herbert Lee-Steere that I knew was tall, strongly built, handsome, personable and very approachable. Connie was a good-looking woman, very intelligent, with a mind of her own, and very aware of other people. There was never enough detail in anything that was said to shed light on their situation, just an undercurrent of animosity on her part.

Herbert had three station hands working at Koonmarra. Two were young blokes and the third was in his late thirties or early forties.

The two younger ones were like so many others: lazy, slow, always whingeing. The four of us shared the men's quarters. It was there one night that I had my first political argument.

The young blokes were complaining about their conditions and how unfair it was that Herbert and his wife had such a nice homestead. 'It's just not right,' one of them said. 'Why should we be camped in a dump like this while they've got what they've got?'

'Gives me the shits,' the other said. 'We're just as good as they are. Problem is the unions just aren't bloody strong enough.'

I had been trying to read my book through this, but after ten minutes, I couldn't stand it. I waded in.

'The reason Herbert's got money and you haven't is because you piss your wages up against the bars in the pubs in Meekatharra. Herbert and his missus have slogged their guts out for years, living in bush camps with the flies and the dust and the heat.'

'Arghh. What a lot of bullshit,' one of them said.

'Bullshit, nothing. They're entitled to what they've got because they've worked seven days a week and you blokes are too dumb and too slack to get off your arses.'

And the other said, 'Whether they own the fuckin station or not, we work here too and we're entitled to an equal share in all the money it makes.'

And so it went – for half an hour. The argument became more and more heated. If it keeps going like this, I thought, there's going to be a punch-up. I backed off. I tried to sleep, but I was simmering. It was a long time before I settled down.

And where was the fourth bloke while all this was going on? He was sitting outside on the veranda, smoking and talking to himself. His name was Paddy and he talked to himself from the time he woke in the morning until he fell asleep at night. It was Paddy this and Pat that. He yarned and gossiped – and argued – with himself. 'Hey, Pat,' he'd say. 'What time is it?'

'How the fuck would I know what time it is? You bloody well know I haven't got a watch.'

'Well' – pointing at me – 'why don't you bloody ask this young joker here?'

'All right, Paddy. I will. For Christ's sake – get orf me back.'

Then Paddy or Pat, I never knew which was which, would say, 'Hey, smart arse with the flash watch. What time is it?'

It was a bit strange at first, but after a while it didn't bother me. In fact, sometimes the 'conversations' were quite amusing. Sometimes they were heated. Sometimes Paddy and Pat were best mates. Sometimes they were at loggerheads. Fortunately they never came to blows. I don't know how they would have managed that.

In the Upper Gascoyne and the Murchison, the best seasons were at the start of the year, if rains fell in January or February, or across both months. The rains were brought by cyclones off the northwest coast. When that happened, the country was transformed within days. Rich, deep-green grasses grew abundantly. Shrubs and bushes sprouted new leaves. Creepers emerged from nowhere and climbed all over dead trees. And the earth steamed. Most days were around the 105-degree mark, and where the ground was soaked, pale thin clouds of steam wafted up. The atmosphere was so humid and heavy you could hardly breathe and your clothes were soaked with sweat just from riding around. When the grasses dried out, they were still good feed for the stock for months after.

Winter rains, in June and July, had a different result. What grew was called herbage. It rose to a bit above ankle height. It produced flowers and blossoms. And it died off more quickly than summer grasses. As stock feed it was OK, but not as good as the grasses.

The Upper Gascoyne and the Murchison had been dry for two years. No summer rains, no winter rains worth speaking about, from June 1952 through to April 1954. Mount Augustus and Errabiddy had felt the effects, and both Pottsy and Tom Steadman had taken defensive action.

None of the people I met, including Herbert Lee-Steere, ever lost heart. Basically, they remained confident and optimistic that the rains would eventually come. They all kept meticulous weather records, and history showed that droughts were never permanent. The challenge was to survive.

Herbert decided to move his small herd of cattle to another property that could support them. This was a station called Kalli, about sixty miles southwest of Koonmarra. The task of moving the 180 head was given to Paddy and me.

Why me? I thought. I don't want to spend two weeks droving cattle to Kalli and then riding back to Koonmarra with this mad joker.

We set off, with me on horseback driving the mob and Paddy driving the horse and cart with all our camping gear and fodder for our three horses. Paddy's horse was tied with a lead rope to the cart. We were to take it in turns to drive the mob and the cart. Two days down the track, the unridden horse was allowed to run free and follow the cattle.

Droving stock on a long trip over many days is a slow business. With sheep in good condition you might do five miles a day; with cattle you might do ten. You let them spread out and feed as they go. You have to strike the right balance between making distance and letting them get a bellyful. But our stages were really dictated by the wells and bores along the way. Herbert gave us directions before we left and while we were en route. Like Pottsy, he spent a lot of time in his Land Rover. He drove at the same speed too. I thought, maybe that was bullshit when Pottsy said his slow speed was about minimising oil changes. Maybe it was because they were never in a hurry. What was the point of driving like the clappers? It was probably a good state of mind.

It became very boring droving the cattle, especially when it was my turn to drive the cart. It became extremely tiring too, because we weren't getting much sleep. During the day, whoever was driving the cart plodded along behind the mob, stopping and just sitting and waiting for the cattle to move on a few yards. Whoever was on horseback rode from one flank of the mob to the other, holding

James Porter Henderson, my grandfather. In his eighties, he still took on the task of burning off and he was still ready to give his grandson a cheeky grin. More than anyone, he stoked the fires of my imagination about a life on sheep stations.

Jack Henderson astride his horse, Bosun, at Elliott Creek Station, in 1941. Bosun was reputed to be a 'one-man horse' and, for me, that added immensely to my uncle's aura as my hero. The camels in the yards were used to pull a large dray.

Cousin Penny, aged nine, Uncle Jack and me, aged fourteen, on the Harley Davidson at Moorarie Station, 1948, during school holidays. Sometimes, he'd take us out on a windmill run and sometimes, on the spur of the moment we'd visit neighbours fifteen miles away.

My mate Bill Moxham at Winnininnie Station in his Citroën. In this car we hooned around at speeds up to forty-five miles an hour! And it took us to Marrabel, nearly 300 miles there and back, to see our first rodeo.

Right The beautiful stone-built men's quarters at Winnininnie, with the old police station in the distance – and me, the raw jackeroo, after a long day on the job.

Looking south to Winnininnie homestead and the outbuildings from the ranges less than a mile away. These hills were steep and were like a barrier to the north end of the station and the great saltbush plains of central South Australia.

Great Aunt Mary, on the left, and Great Aunt Maggie, in their garden at Poltoonga in St Peters, Adelaide. Together with Great Aunt Dorothy, who passed away while I was in South Australia, they gave me a collection of classic works of literature to treasure, and insights into our family history in Ireland and Scotland.

Opposite This strapping young lad of seventeen was at the mercy of the great aunts when it came to long games of rummy in the afternoon. They also made me keep my wits about me when it came to their subtle teasing.

Ian Bridson operating a boring plant out in the middle of nowhere at
Towrana Station, south of Gascoyne Junction. I worked with him for two
months to learn about drilling for water, but I learned a lot more about
literature. Ian was a University of Western Australia graduate and went
on to teach English at Hale School.

The boring plant camp at Towrana. At night, by the light of a pressure lamp, we sat at the table in the tent, reading Shakespeare's sonnets and Browning to each other, with Ian explaining what was meant by lines I didn't understand.

Ian Bridson's blitz wagon 4 x 4 going nowhere. Even after a modest rain, that country could be treacherously slippery and boggy. The four-wheel drive couldn't cope and we had to wait until the ground dried before we could go anywhere.

Mount Augustus rises abruptly, 715 metres above the stony, red sandplain and it commands your attention from the moment you first see it. From then on, it mesmerises you with the intricacy of its gullies and folds and the variety of its vegetation. It is a landmark in the Upper Gascoyne and it was a landmark for me in my youth – and will be forever.

The legendary Ernest Potts seated on the left, with the Fitzgeralds from Cobra Station, just west of Mount Augustus, May 1941.

Back row (L to R): Elsie Fitzgerald, Lindsay Thomson (who married my uncle Jack), my mother (whose name was Margaret but she was always known as Madge), Eric Fitzgerald, Madeline Potts (Ernest's wife), Patty Darcy, Barbara Potts (the Potts' younger daughter).
Middle row: Ernest Potts, Percy Fitzgerald, Jack Henderson.
Front row: me, aged seven, and another young visitor.

Mount Augustus woolshed, as it was in 1953. The high price of wool at that time enabled the station to survive the drought. But when prices went down, and stayed down, sheep grazing was abandoned and, sadly, this building was demolished.

The sheep yards at the woolshed and the horse yards beyond. The shed housed the Commer truck and tools and, at one end, it was partitioned off to store feed for the horses and tack: saddles, bridles, halters and other horse paraphernalia.

Andy Johansen (from Norway) and Bill van Rijn (from the Netherlands). Old Andy was a fencing contractor and Bill was a migrant, working as a station hand. Bill introduced me to Dostoevsky's *Crime and Punishment*, and that stretched my thinking about literature.

My very special friend Gilbert Dooler, who taught me a lot about being a stockman – and, more importantly, taught me about Yamatji culture.

Gilbert, holding my horse and waiting for me to get on with the job. He was the classic professional stockman, always properly kitted out. His concertina leggings were all the go at the time; I had the same.

Mitchell Dooler, brother of Gilbert, and another good friend. Among the three of us there was much horseplay, but many evenings we sat and just talked. What they told me was surprisingly open and frank, considering I was a young whitefella.

Opposite My relationship with Gilbert was a highlight of my time in the outback. We worked well together and we enjoyed each other's company. With Gilbert, it was always easy, nothing was a problem, there was always time for a joke.

Snowball, who by example taught all of us about working with stock – and about dignity. He never acted in haste, he never raised his voice in anger, and he was always quietly effective in whatever he did.

Albie Zilko, a young stockman at Mount Augustus, who had a frightening encounter with a savage stallion. This horse terrorised all stockmen if he thought his herd of mares was being threatened, until Snowball showed Albie and me how we could get the better of him.

Maurice Parkes, my father, with a steady, favourite old horse. Often, the personality of the rider matched the personality of the chosen horse, or maybe it was the other way round. Unlike some horses, this one was not bothered by having a waterbag hanging round its neck throughout the day's mustering.

Dinner camp for my father and his inseparable dog, Smokey, in the only decent shade for miles.

Jiff, part kelpie, part Border collie. Like most good sheep dogs, he was typically loyal. But Jiff was much more than a workmate: he was my soul mate when I needed him.

This is Smokey, the dog who belonged totally to my father and a little bit to me. He was the cleverest dog I have ever known. They say animals can't reason, but I'm not so sure about that.

My dear little mare, Spitfire, a great stock horse and a great gymkhana horse. We had a relationship that was a lot like that of a man and a dog. She liked to stay close to me at dinner camp, which was unusual. But she was always quickly on her toes and ready to go when it was time for action.

Bunty, a once-in-a-lifetime horse for me, as a stock horse, and for Allan McDonald, as a racehorse. Bunty thrilled me from the moment I set eyes on him, from the instant I slipped into the saddle, with every day of working together.

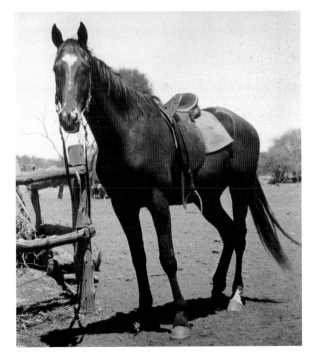

Over page High summer at Mount Augustus, yet these sheep are in good condition, living off the leaves of shrubs and bushes.

Gerry Smith, my first workmate at Errabiddy Station. We got on well, which was fortunate considering we had to camp way out in the bush – just the two of us. He left us after an accident and I missed him.

Jackie Stevens, my first big challenge when I took over the mustering camp at Belele as head stockman. Twice my age, ten times as much experience – and he had to put up with me as the boss. He let me know he was not impressed.

Doug Fraser keeps an eye on a bungarra seeking safety up a dead mulga.
But the bungarra was mistaken; it was in a much more vulnerable
position there. This one was close to five feet long, a similar length
to another I carried by the tail for half an hour as I rode back to the
mustering camp one afternoon.

My grandfather in his going-to-town clothes: a three-piece suit, with a touch
of dash – a small handkerchief in the top pocket. He had a pocket watch
that he placed in his waistcoat and secured with a gold chain.

Opposite Ready for another nine-hour day in the saddle. The brand on the
horse's near side shoulder was called a 'flying U' and it was well recognised
throughout the Norwest because it was the Mount Augustus brand.

In its own way, this tree is as majestic and awesome as Mount Augustus.
On the bank of the Gascoyne River, on Mount Clere Station, this tree has
commanded Teamarra Pool for hundreds of years. Every time I go north,
I return to this place and camp – to savour the night and the company of
this ancestor river gum.

them in a manageable bunch while gently moving them along. Occasionally, one or more separated from the mob and had to be brought back. Mid-afternoon, the driver of the cart picked up speed and drove straight through the mob, out the front and on to the next watering place to make camp. Then the cart driver saddled his horse and rode back out to help the lone drover.

Mostly, the windmills were on a fence line, and if we were lucky, they were in a corner. It made life easier at night for two lone stockmen to keep the mob settled. With two fences forming a right angle, we made camp in a strategic position that restricted the mob. Once the cattle had watered, we stopped them from wandering off looking for more feed. Eventually, they settled for the night, dropping down on their front knees before lowering their hindquarters to the ground. There they lay on their stomachs and chewed their cuds. At times, some of them were restless and stood up and started to walk out. They had to be dissuaded and turned back. The trick was to do that without disturbing the whole mob. These were not really wild cattle, but neither were they quiet and domesticated. They had to be handled with care. Sudden movements and loud noises would have them on their feet and itching to move.

The main reason our little cattle drive was so tiring was because Paddy, or Pat, and I had to walk the mob all night. When they were fully settled, one bloke could do it alone while the other slept for two hours. Then we changed over. We walked. Perhaps I should say, we crept. Fortunately, we had bright moonlight. We moved as silently as possible through the thin scrub. Sometimes I stood still and let the minutes slide by. When I saw movement, a beast getting to its feet and starting to move out from the mob, I walked smoothly across to where the beast could see me and, without a sound, took a step towards it. It stopped and paused. I took a step closer, watching the rest of the mob at the same time. It took one step back. I advanced another step. This slow dance continued until the beast slowly and ponderously turned and went back into the fringe of the mob and settled down.

Kangaroos coming in to drink at the trough, seeing the mob of cattle blocking their way, stopped to look and think about what to do. There were times, when I was standing still, that roos coming in didn't notice me and stopped a few feet away. They leaned their bodies to one side and then to the other. They raised their heads or bent forward and pointed their noses to decipher the smell. They knew what cattle smelled like. It was the concentration of smell and the spread of bodies so close to the water trough that puzzled them. It deterred them from hopping all the way in. The slightest movement from me and they turned and were off. They never disturbed the cattle.

Even when he was walking the cattle at night, Paddy continued talking to himself – in a whisper so soft you could hear him only if you were right beside him. He must have had a fertile imagination. He never ran out of things to talk about.

Early in the morning, well before first light, some of the mob had had enough of lying down and were restless. That's when both of us had to be on the job.

After six days on the track with the cattle, it was a relief to get to the paddock at Kalli where we could let them go. It was a lovely sight to see their backsides disappear into the scrub. It was a luxury to make camp and have a good meal and eat in peace and roll out the swag and sleep the night through without interruption. Then we had the almost two-day trip back to Koonmarra, plodding along with the horse and cart.

When Herbert sent my father to Meekatharra to pick up pipe fittings, my father asked if I could go with him to get my driver's licence. Herbert readily agreed.

My father left me at the police station with the Land Rover while he went over the road to Elders to pick out the fittings. The constable gave me a form to fill in. He quickly did the eye test and said, 'Let's go.'

Nervously I slid in behind the wheel, and the constable settled in to the passenger's seat, with a clipboard on his knees. I started the engine, put the Land Rover into first gear and moved away from the kerb – no problem. Slipping into second gear was no problem. Twenty yards down the main street, changing up to third gear was no problem. Then the constable heaved a great sigh and said, 'Bloody hell, you've been drivin these bloody things for years. Turn round and go back and I'll give yer yer licence.'

Back in the police station, he asked, 'I spose yer can drive a bloody truck too, can yer?'

'Yeah,' I said.

And that's how I got my licence to drive both cars and trucks.

In May, nearly two inches of rain drowned the country and the roads and tracks were unusable. For a week, we were pinned down at the homestead and Herbert had us all working on the maintenance and repairs that were always being deferred. After that, he sent five of us out to his northern paddocks to start mustering for shearing. This camp was very high class. We were provided with an old caravan that was very much the worse for wear. My father and I slept in the caravan; Paddy and the other two slept outside on stretchers.

This area of Koonmarra was wild country. There were many breakaway hills that glared red and white in the sunlight – layers of red sandstone and white limestone. These flat-topped hills had sheer sides. Edges were broken away, and large chunks and rubble littered the base. To get up to the top meant riding around the base until there was a slope a horse could climb. Once on top, it was glorious. With the cold wind tugging at my leather jacket, my horse heaving from the climb and Jiff panting alongside, I scanned the valleys below and the hills on the other side. From up high, I could absorb the details of the thickets of mulga, the patterns of watercourses, and the open spaces dotted with shrubs. The herbage was starting to show. The country was changing colour. The red was disappearing beneath a covering of fresh green growth. I savoured my reveries. But they had to stop: there was a job to do.

Many times I was still out in the paddock beyond nightfall. One vivid memory is of a wide valley falling away below in the moonlight. The hills in the distance were black, with the rising moon beyond. A mob of sheep, bleating, picked their way down the side of the crumbling breakaway. My horse threw me from side to side as she stumbled down through the stones. Far away, I saw the small red dot of the campfire where the others were probably waiting, especially my father, concerned about my late arrival. In that country, it was quite common for musterers to be sent in different directions, returning independently to the camp with whatever sheep they had found. The promise of hot food and fresh tea competed with the pleasure of riding through the cold outback night.

Across the flat floodplains of a creek, the dust rolled lazily, as I worked the mob along the fence line. Jiff was doing his job on the flanks. On the flats, the moonlight was less bright and the night blacker. Two hundred yards from the campfire, Smokey materialised from the shadows beside me. Once I spoke to him, he was satisfied it was me and disappeared around the mob and made contact with Jiff. Then my father loomed up on foot and we put the sheep through the gate into the holding paddock. I dismounted and, leading my horse, we walked together back to the camp, while we brought each other up to date with the doings of the day.

The chinking of hobble chains and the knocking of hooves against feed bins were the only noises in the night.

There was another inch and a half of rain in June. This gave the herbage a boost. The country was revitalised and the sheep were in good condition. Being back with my parents again, living and working with them, revived the feelings I'd had at Mount Augustus. I wanted independence. My parents were good parents but they always had their eye on me. That was natural, but it was constraining. The feelings I had at Mount Augustus resurfaced.

There was still something about the Lower Gascoyne country that appealed to me more than the Upper Gascoyne and the Murchison.

As I'd experienced at Doorawarrah, the Lower Gascoyne was softer, with many long, red sand hills, with wide claypans in some places. Besides, Carnarvon was a bigger town than Meekatharra, and, with the banana plantations and the market gardens along the banks of the Gascoyne, it was more interesting. I'd had good times there, especially when I was working for Ian Bridson. It had become a place I felt I knew. Meekatharra was harder and tougher, not a place where I wanted to linger. I decided to leave and head back to Carnarvon to find work there.

When Jack Henderson, my uncle, heard that I was leaving Koonmarra, he asked me to help him out with the shearing at Belele. There was no urgency about going to Carnarvon and I had nothing to lose, so I agreed.

PART FOUR

HEAD STOCKMAN

In charge of all the stockmen
and the stock work; one step
down from overseer

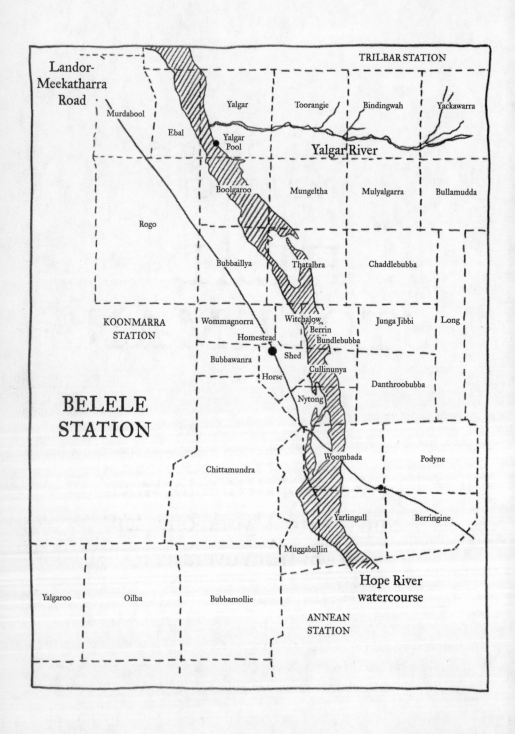

16

Jackie Stevens

The road from Meekatharra to Mount Augustus ran right past the homestead at Belele Station. Apart from the shearing shed, which was off to the right, all the homestead buildings were on the left as you drove north.

A station homestead is often like a small village set in the middle of nowhere. In Belele's case, as a village, it was quite substantial. More or less in a straight line, running east to west, there was the manager's house and garden; then the kitchen and the men's dining room; quarters for the house staff, including the cook and the yardman; quarters for the station hands and stockmen; and a bit further on, the stables and stockyards. A second line of buildings ran parallel to the first, starting with accommodation for guests, the general storeroom and the manager's office. In front of this line of buildings there was a spacious thoroughfare, dusty and dry – constant traffic powdered the surface.

On the other side of this broad throughway, there was a line of sheds housing vehicles and machinery – and a workshop for servicing and repair work. It was while I was working in that building that my life took a sudden and quite unexpected turn. It was the first week of July 1954 and I had just arrived at Belele. The shearing team was due in six weeks and the stockmen were out at a camp about twenty miles from the homestead. They were working their way through the north eastern paddocks, mustering the sheep and pushing them into paddocks closer to the homestead and the shearing shed. Looking back at the events that unfolded, I can't help wondering if my uncle Jack had an inkling of what was to happen. I'm not saying he was prescient or that he set me up. More that he knew men and, perhaps, he read signs that there could be a problem brewing. It would have been typical of Jack if he thought it handy to be prepared. We'll never know. What I can tell you is what happened.

Being July, the day was cold. A stiff, gusty easterly was blowing, whipping up puffs of dust between the two rows of buildings. Jack was out somewhere in his big powerful International ute. With all of the stockmen out in the bush and the station hands working elsewhere, there were only a few of us at the homestead. Jack had told me to spend the morning servicing the jeep and the truck. So I was inside the big vehicle shed, with the sliding metal door closed to keep the wind at bay. Except for Jiff, I was on my own.

I was working on the jeep from down in the pit. There was a silence you could almost touch all around. There were little creaks and groans from the door as the wind pushed and shoved. This dialogue accentuated the general absence of noise inside. The click of the grease gun when I attached it to the nipples under the chassis of the jeep was a good sound, because when the clink became a clunk I knew the nozzle of the gun had bedded firmly onto the target nipple. I listened to these delicate sounds inside and the robust gusts of wind outside. Feeling calm and content, I went about my work. At four months short of being twenty years old, I was quietly confident: a combination of my experiences to date and the ingenuousness of youth.

My reverie was interrupted when one of the big full-height sliding doors was pulled back and a stockman stepped in. He had the light behind him, and all I could see was that he was tall and of average build, not too slim, not too heavy. He appeared to me to be in his middle twenties. When he walked right in, I recognised him. His name was Mark. I had met him some months before at Errabiddy. When the fencing contract at Errabiddy ran out he took on the job of head stockman at Belele. He was clearly distressed. 'Fuck, mate. Where's Jack?' he asked. I climbed out of the pit and wiped my hands on a piece of cloth.

'Out somewhere. I don't know. He'll be back about twelve.'

'Mate, look at this.' Mark swivelled round, lifted his shirt and dropped his trousers to show me two long gashes, one across his right buttock and the other diagonally across the back of his right thigh.

I asked the obvious question, 'What happened?'

'That fucking Jackie Stevens,' he said. 'I had a blue with the black bastard and when I turned my back he got stuck into me with the axe.'

The wounds were superficial: no tendons or muscles severed, but still it was a mess. I reckoned the axe must have been blunt. His trousers were soaked in blood. I'd never seen anything like it. I was awed.

'So where is he now?'

'Gone bush.'

'Gone bush?'

'That's what I bloody well said. Gone bush. I want Jack to take me to hospital and get rid of Jackie bloody Stevens.'

We walked over to the manager's house, and Jack's wife, Lindsay, had a look at the wounds and applied disinfectant. Then we settled down to wait for Jack. When he turned up, Mark gave him the story. Then Jack told me to get back to greasing the jeep while he had a word with Mark. Ten minutes later, Jack came over to the shed and said, 'I've given Mark the sack. If he can't control the mustering camp, he's no bloody use to me. I'll take him out to the camp at Yangee Bore to pick up his gear and then I'll run him in to Meekatharra. You take over the camp. I'll take your swag out with me. You can ride Mark's horse out to the camp. Come with me.'

Jack led me to the stables and out into the yards. He pointed to a big black thoroughbred mare. 'That's the horse he was riding.

Her name's Mulba. There's a black gelding out at the camp. His name's Pitch. He'll be yours too. Interchange with Mulba. That stock saddle on the rack there – that'll be yours. And that bridle on the peg. Apart from Jackie Stevens, there are two white stockmen out at the camp. Their names are Frank and Tony.'

'What about Jackie?' I inquired meekly.

'You can sort that out,' he said. 'Now listen. Yangee Bore is at Yackawarra paddock. You should finish mustering Yackawarra tomorrow night. You can then do Bindingwah next door, which you should clean up in two days. I'll come out and see how you're going and you can then move to Mungeltha Bore when you muster Toorangie. Two days there should be enough. Then move to Barro Well so you can muster Yalgar. You'll camp there till the end of the week. I'll come and see you again. You might need more time to clean up Yalgar. Anyway, I'll tell you what I want you to do then.'

With that, he turned on his heel and strode out of the stables and over to his ute. I was confused – all these Aboriginal names for the paddocks and windmills. All I could remember was Yackawarra. I thought, well, the blokes at the camp will know. I fetched my swag and a small bag with a change of clothes and took them out to the ute and tossed them in the back. Mark was already in the passenger seat. Although he turned his head slightly towards me, he didn't look me in the eye. Jack gave me directions on how to get to Yackawarra, then jerked the driver's door open, got in, slammed the door, hit the accelerator and charged off, leaving a cloud of dust that drifted fitfully away. That was the last I saw of Mark. I will never forget the look of dismayed defeat on his face.

From the homestead to Yangee Bore was about twenty miles. It was a three-hour ride if I trotted along. I'd get to Yangee around five, which would leave me enough light in the day to see what was what with the camp. Mulba submitted to the bridle and the saddle willingly, and I led her out and walked her for fifty yards and adjusted the stirrup leathers because Mark was longer in the leg than me, and then tightened the girth and the surcingle. We headed off, with Jiff running on ahead and coming back and running on again. Mulba was a good walker with a nice, easy stride. It wouldn't take much urging for her to walk at a steady four miles an hour. I thought to myself, Mulba, you and I are going to get along very well.

As I got closer to Yangee, I saw the windmill in the distance, the head poking up above the mulgas in the foreground and above the white gums along the banks of the dry Yalgar River. This was all new country for me. Not just the place – it was a new experience to be in charge of a mustering camp. And not just your average team of blokes, as one of them was violent. This felt like a good example of being pushed off into the deep end.

When Mulba and I arrived at the camp, the two whitefellas were sitting on their stretchers, warming themselves by the fire. There was a post-and-rail fence around the windmill and the tank. I unsaddled Mulba, threw the saddle over a rail, hobbled her, took off the bridle and let her go. As I walked over to the campfire, one of the men said, 'Who the fuck are you?'

I introduced myself and found out which was Tony and which was Frank. Without beating around the bush, their next question was, 'What's going on?'

'Didn't Jack tell you?' I asked.

'Not really,' Frank said. 'Just that he was taking Mark into Meekatharra to the hospital and that someone else was comin out to run the camp. So we've just been sittin here waitin.'

I asked them to give me a rundown on the stoush. Seemed it was an argument about something of no real consequence and it got out of hand when Mark gave Jackie a mouthful. Jackie waited until Mark turned his back, grabbed the axe lying close by and swung it at Mark's backside. Jackie must have been pretty quick because he got in the second blow before Mark could turn or get out of the way. Mark lunged at Jackie but Jackie dropped the axe and bolted into the scrub.

'What about Jackie?' one of them asked. It seemed to be an echo of a question I'd heard before.

'What about telling me where he is?' I replied.

'Dunno where the bastard is,' said Frank. 'He took off after he attacked Mark and we haven't seen him since. I reckon he's out there in the bush somewhere – waitin. Or he's just pissed off and won't be comin back. We're not that far from the Meekatharra–Mount Clere Road and he could probably pick up a lift in two or three days.'

'If he does come back, I'm leavin,' Tony said. 'I'm not stayin in this camp with him.'

'Me too,' said Frank.

'Oh,' I managed to say. 'So you'll both just clear out and leave me with him?'

'Fuckin oath,' said Frank. 'He's a fair dinkum arsehole. I wouldn't piss on him if he was on fire.'

'Righto,' I said. 'First of all we have to see if he's coming back because there's no sign of him at the moment. So we might as well start getting dinner on the go.'

Dinner was a roast shoulder of mutton, with roasted onions and boiled potatoes. The light faded. Evening spread itself around us and it seemed no time before it was dark. After the meat and the onions had been cooking for an hour and a half, I put the pot of potatoes on a bed of coals. Why boil the potatoes instead of roasting them? My thoughts were going in all directions and I wasn't thinking clearly. We made a billy of tea and sat and waited. The conversation revolved around the mustering they'd been doing with Mark, embellishments on the story of the stoush and, more interestingly, some background on Jackie.

He came from somewhere in the Jigalong area. There was a story that, some years before, he had shot and killed a whitefella over near Leonora. For his punishment he'd served seven years as a black tracker for the police in Perth. If that was true, Jackie was going to be a challenge for me. I also found out that Frank and

Tony were both about two years older than me and Jackie was in his early forties, as far as they could tell.

Right about when we'd arrived at the point where we didn't have much else to talk about, Jackie emerged out of the dark. He was slow moving and cautious, almost tentative. He was a bit below average height, average build. We made our introductions. He gave me a surprisingly small, soft hand. We shook and he sat down on the ground beside the fire, with his left leg bent back under his right leg, which was stretched straight out in front. He helped himself to a quart-pot mug of tea and sat there and appraised me. His face said, I've been around, I've seen it all before, you can't tell me anything I don't already know. Was it my imagination, or did his eyes also say, I know a fool when I see one? It was all very quiet. I did my best to appear relaxed. Tony and Frank sat and didn't say a word – and they would not look at Jackie. The only mention of Mark was when I told Jackie that Mark wouldn't be coming back and that I was taking over. There was some discussion about where we'd be mustering in the days ahead. They knew Jack's mustering plans and they were able to wise me up about the names of everything, drawing maps in the dirt. But they didn't know any more about the lie of the land than I did.

I decided to test the potatoes to see if they were cooked. With a fork in my right hand, I reached out to lift the lid off the pot with my left hand, but, before I could, Jackie said, 'Watch out. You'll burn your murra.'

'Shit,' I said. I reached around and picked up a stick to slide under the handle on the lid of the pot.

'Crikey,' said Jackie, 'you speak Yamatji?'

'Yeah,' I said. I let it go at that, because I knew only a handful of words. The effect was immediate and I felt Jackie straighten up. When I looked at him, he had a new air about him. Maybe it was respect. Whatever it was, some kind of nexus had been created. It was now night and it was hard to read his expression. The firelight flickered on his face and, as he studied me, even though the whites of his eyes were bloodshot, they stood out in contrast to his skin and the blackness of the night. Yes, he was a mature man. And I was a youth.

The meal over, Jackie went to his swag, forty or fifty yards away from the campfire. Frank and Tony cleaned the dishes and I watched how they went about it. When they finished we sat by the fire and talked very quietly. It made me very apprehensive to think about the two whitefellas clearing out and leaving me alone with Jackie, partly because I wasn't sure I could handle him and partly because it would leave two of us to do the work of four. Having had a glimpse of Jack's temper, I could imagine his reaction if Frank and Tony rode in to the homestead to quit. It wouldn't be the two of them he'd be angry with.

I thought I'd try a little friendly persuasion. We moved a little further out of earshot of Jackie, and I quietly let them know that I was determined to get the work done, Jackie or no Jackie, and that I would appreciate some moral support. When I'd said my piece, Tony gave me a vote of confidence, 'Well, if you're prepared to stay and carry on, I'll give it a go with you.'

A surge of confidence travelled right up from the pit of my stomach to the top of my head, but I didn't move a muscle, I didn't change my expression, I didn't alter my tone of voice. 'What about you, Frank?'

'No. Bugger it. I'll be leavin in the mornin. I'm not goin to hang around waitin for that arsehole to have a crack at me.'

On that note, we retired to our swags. It didn't help that the night was cold and the wind blew over and under our stretchers. The canvas groundsheet gave protection from the wind but the cold still penetrated. We slept in our clothes: moleskin trousers, work shirt and socks. I had a blanket, of course, but my horsehair mattress was only about an inch thick and I kept waking through the night, stiff and cold. If I was lying on my side, the ache in my hip woke me and I gave the other side a turn until that too started to ache.

The next morning, while Jackie brought the horses in and tied them up to the fence and gave them a feed, I cooked chops for breakfast, which we had with cold damper, washed down with billy tea. Nobody spoke much. Frank and Tony continued to keep their eyes down. Jackie, on the other hand, maintained his silent observation of me. He had no interest in the other two. I was his mark. He had plenty of time to make his assessment. We made up our cribs for lunch and went over to the horses. We brushed the sweat and dirt from their backs, put the saddle blankets in place, followed by the saddles and bridles. Out of the corner of my eye, I watched how the men handled the horses and the gear. The way a man slips the top of a bridle over a horse's ears and lays it down and smooths out the forelock can be eloquent. How they moved, whether smoothly or abruptly, would give me some idea of what sort of horsemen they were. We girthed up and put the cribs in our saddlebags. No-one was in a hurry to go anywhere. We walked out into the paddock. This gave the horses time to get used to the feel of the girth again and gave them the opportunity to let off any early-morning steam bottled up inside. I especially wanted to see the behaviour of these Belele horses. Frank walked with us. Frank girthed up and mounted. I looked up at him and he looked down at me.

'Well,' I said, 'what are you doing?'

'I'm comin with you,' he said.

'I thought you were leaving.'

'Changed my mind.'

'Righto,' I said. 'Well, can you muster in from the fence? Tony, can you muster in from him? And Jackie, can you muster in from Tony? And I'll take the inside. We'll all meet at the northeast corner and camp there for lunch. Let's hope the wind keeps blowing from the south.'

It was a typical day's mustering. We zigzagged our way parallel to the west fence until we hit the northern boundary and then swung round and went east. The country was mostly low hills with wide, flat watercourses running down into the Yalgar River, which was as dry as a bone. We met in the northeast corner and Jackie was the only one who'd picked up any sheep – twenty-two ewes. We were ahead of schedule so I ruled out a lunch break. Instead, we continued on to Tranter Well, where we would get water for our quart pots. We pushed the ewes south into the wind and about halfway down we started picking up more and more sheep. We didn't try to make a mob of them – just let them run away from us into the wind, which was where we wanted them to go. We stopped at the windmill and lit a fire to boil the quart pots. After we had been in the saddle for about four hours, the tension in the team had eased off a little. But only a little. Tony and Frank were still not happy with Jackie. They probably never would be. And I was still in the process of working everyone out.

Our pace slowed down in the afternoon. We had covered the ground quite quickly in the morning because we'd had no sheep. As the day wore on, we gathered up more and more until we had a mob of 900 or so. We moved them along the south fence until we got to the corner and the camp. We let them into Mulyalgarra paddock, on the southwest side. By this time we were ready for another quart pot of tea and dinner.

As I'd been riding along, scanning the scrub and the flats for sheep, I thought about how I would handle these men and the situation. I'd already got the impression that Tony and Frank wouldn't do any more than they had to. Left to their own devices, they'd sit on their backsides and smoke. Tony was quieter than Frank and was fairly uncomplicated and straightforward. He was by no means a simpleton, but he wasn't all that bright either. Frank, on the other hand, showed signs he could be on the smart side. If he got a bit too sure of himself, I figured he might be cheeky. For the time being, he was wary of Jackie, which was a restraint. Knowing that Jackie was my responsibility gave him comfort, but not so much that he could stray into overconfidence.

Jackie, of course, was a different story. Jackie was a very experienced stockman and horseman. Mustering sheep is not rocket science. The methods are universal, especially given the size of the paddocks where we were and the relatively open country. You start with the fact that sheep feed into the wind, and if the wind has been consistent from a particular quarter for a few days, you'll have a good idea of where they are not likely to be as much as where they probably will be. Regardless of the wind, some paddocks were peculiar in that sheep favoured one area or another, and it was handy to know their preferences. However, that was local knowledge and none of us had that. So, like me, Jackie was feeling his way. He spoke when he was spoken to and did not volunteer any thoughts of his own. There was nothing about him that was in any way threatening, except his history and his silent self-possession.

While I was mustering, I mulled my father's advice, 'You get a lot further with people if you ask them rather than tell them.' I knew from the little experience I'd had that he was right and I decided to make it a practice. It turned out to be useful advice because I soon learned I wasn't always right and there would be a better end result if I listened.

Len Boothby's dictum was still ringing in my ears: if a job's not worth doing properly, it's not worth doing at all. He had given me that message with the same forcefulness as he had instructed me about closing gates. Call it naiveté, if you like: I decided to lead by example. This meant finding the stragglers that everyone else had overlooked; being first one up every morning and the last to hit the swag; shoeing the horses that were too difficult and fractious for everyone else; keeping going and keeping everyone else going when they wanted to quit; never asking anyone to do anything, any task at all, unless I was prepared to do it myself. It wasn't that I wanted to be a hero. All I wanted was that they would respect me as their boss and accept my word. Simple enough, except I found out the hard way that it's never that simple.

17

Life in the mustering camp

On my second day in the camp, we cleaned up the stragglers in Yackawarra and we knocked off earlier than usual. It was time to start sharing the camp work, so I asked Tony to cook dinner. This meant roasting or boiling the meat and preparing what few vegetables we had. Tony sat on the ground with the bag of potatoes, a basin and a sharp knife and started peeling. He was nearly finished when I noticed black smudges on the white, freshly peeled potatoes.

'Did you wash your hands before you started doing that?' I asked.

He looked up at me as if I'd asked him a trick question. 'No, what for?'

'For Christ's sake. Go and wash your hands, and wash the potatoes while you're at it.'

Tony groaned, got to his feet and went over to the water trough and lightly rinsed his hands.

'That's not enough,' I said. 'Use soap and get your hands properly clean.'

More muttering from Tony and sideways looks from Frank and Jackie. Memories of Ian Bridson's admonishments flicked through my mind, especially his uncompromising insistence on immaculately clean pots, pans, dishes and cutlery. This camp's pots and pans looked as though they'd never ever had a good scrub.

The next day we turned our attention to Bindingwah. It was much the same terrain as Yackawarra, except that the hills were a little higher. Before we rode out in the morning, I asked Frank to do dinner that night and to make a fresh damper for the next day's breakfast and cribs.

When I got back to the camp in the late afternoon, Frank was already there. The fire was going and he was preparing to make the damper. I unsaddled my horse and let it go, and I walked over to the camp. Frank was gently kneading a mound of dough. As he did, he left dirty fingermarks. Here we go again, I thought. 'Cut away the dough where you've left fingerprints,' I said.

Grudgingly, he did as he was told. Seeing that I was in the right frame of mind and since the body odour of all three was on the nose, I asked him how long it had been since any of them had had a bath or a shower. 'Not since we were at the homestead,' he replied. 'What's it to you, anyway?'

'Well,' I said, 'I reckon it's like this. Everyone should have a big clean up every few days.'

'Bullshit. How do you think we can do that out in the fuckin bush in a musterin camp?'

'Pretty simple, really. We've got buckets. We've got water over at the tank. It's not hard to strip off and wash yourself all over.'

'Not in this fuckin weather, I'm not. It's too fuckin cold.'

'Well, watch me,' I said. I grabbed a metal bucket, filled it with water and put it close to the fire. I packed more wood around it. When it became hot enough, which didn't take long, I went over to the tank, found a spot where the tank broke the wind a bit, stripped off and washed myself all over. Then I filled the bucket with fresh cold water straight out of the tank and rinsed myself off before using the towel. Frank shook his head in disbelief and got on with the job of making dinner.

* * *

The next morning it was Tony's turn to fetch the horses, while I kicked the fire into life and got the chops going. The morning was brisk and fresh and my light jacket barely kept the chill at bay. As usual, the sky was clear, and the sun was just starting to show an orangey pink on the horizon. There was not much wind, just faint movements of air from time to time. Frank and Jackie were still rolled up in their swags, probably awake and stalling. 'Come on, boys!' I called. 'Wakey wakey, hands off snakey.'

They stirred, grumbled, and reluctantly emerged from their swags, pulled on their boots and shuffled over to the fire, tucking in their shirts on the way. They warmed their backsides and then strolled off to relieve themselves behind a bush. By the time the chops were cooked every morning, the horses were usually back from wherever they'd gone during the night. But not this morning.

All the horses were hobbled and one had a bell around its neck. A horse can't walk or trot properly when its two front legs are linked together by a chain connected to leather straps around the fetlocks. But it can shuffle along and it can go short distances at a truncated kind of canter. Normally horses don't go more than a half a mile or so from the camp and the horse tailer tracks them until he can hear the bell. When they're aware of his presence, sometimes they try to elude him. That is usually short lived. Hobbles are very inhibiting unless a horse is extremely determined. More often than not, the horses accept defeat quickly and will stand and wait for the horse tailer to come right up. He then catches one of his horses, never someone else's horse, puts the bridle on and removes the hobbles, tying them around the horse's neck. Then, keeping a good grip of the reins of his horse, the tailer walks over to each of the other horses and removes their hobbles. If they're close to the camp, he will chase them back on foot. If they're not close, he will jump on his horse bareback and ride. The horses know the ropes and generally head straight back to the camp, where they can expect to find a feed of chaff and oats waiting for them.

Frank and Jackie and I ate our breakfast and wondered why Tony and the horses were not back. Tony had been gone since six o'clock and it was now 7.30. We contemplated the options: was the silly bugger lost? Couldn't he find the horses? Or, having found them, did his horse drop his head and plant him and gallop off? Or had he had an accident? I was about to send out a search party to follow the tracks from the previous night when Tony walked out of the scrub and up to the fire. 'So, what's going on?' I asked.

'Fuckin horses. I hate the bastards.'

'OK. Where are the bloody horses then?'

'They're up in one of the gullies nearly up to the Trilbar boundary. I couldn't catch the bastards, could I?'

My impatience had been shifting into that zone called anger while I'd been waiting and now it suddenly approached boiling point. At this rate we wouldn't get a full day's muster, and if the situation didn't improve, we wouldn't get any at all. I felt like swearing at Tony but didn't. Instead, I glared at him. He ducked his head. 'Shit, mate, every time I went near one of my horses, the bastard kept movin out of reach. Wouldn't let me put the bridle on.'

The scene he described was a familiar one. Not all stockmen are good horsemen. They do stock work because it's a job and horses are a means to an end. Many lack patience and do not have a real interest in understanding horses.

I picked up Mulba's bridle, called Jiff, and said to the three blokes sitting around the fire, 'Wait here till I get back.'

I strode off in the general direction of where, from Tony's description, I thought I'd find the horses. After about twenty minutes, I started to simmer down, and I thought to myself, crikey, you're a dumb bastard, telling the blokes to wait at the camp for you. What else are they going to do? They're probably saying the same thing to each other and having a good laugh. They're also probably looking forward to your comeuppance if you return empty handed. Well, stuff em. I won't be coming back without the horses, no matter how long it takes.

The country was rough and my high-heeled boots were not designed for bushwalking. But walk I did, and as fast as I could. Half an hour later, I saw them before I heard the bell. Like Tony said, they were up a wide gully. Being still annoyed, I didn't bother about trying to stalk them and sneak up. I just headed straight for Mulba. As I got closer, I slowed down and took the aggression from my walk. When the horses saw me, three of them started to make an effort to get away, with varying degrees of energy. Mulba thought she'd make a move too, but into a thin stand of mulga where a few dead trees were lying at angles on the ground. She got herself into a situation where she had difficulty finding an escape route she could manage while hobbled. She paused to reflect, and I walked slowly up to her, talking softly, keeping my eyes on her near-side front leg. She was misled into thinking I was more interested in picking up her hoof than putting a bridle on her.

She let me come right up, and I bent down and stroked her leg all the way down to the leather strap of the hobble. Keeping my fingers in contact with her leg and then her shoulder, I straightened up and ran my hand down her neck and gave her a rub. I was facing her, so I turned side on and slipped my right hand and arm under her neck and chin, and placed my hand on her nose. In this position, Mulba's head was locked in place by my right hand and arm and by my body. That is, unless she decided enough was enough and cleared out. With my left hand, I brought the bridle up to my right hand and slipped it up over her nose and over her ears, and put the bit in her mouth with my left hand.

She was now mine. I tied the throat lash, undid her hobbles and then removed the hobbles on the others. I vaulted onto Mulba's back, neck-reined her around and headed them all back to the camp. If I thought I was in for a pleasant ride back, I was wrong. As we started to come out of the gully, the lead horses took off at a flat-out gallop and the rest followed. Mulba and Jiff and I brought up the rear, nearly flat out. Mulba just wanted to go. She objected to being restrained. She didn't buck or pig-root, but she reefed and bounded. She jerked me this way and that. She kept shaking her head up and down, trying to get free of my grip on the reins. It was essential that I was in control so that I could steer her where I wanted to go, not where she wanted to go. I wasn't afraid. I was too angry to be afraid. It was the idea of being swept off by a low-lying branch that didn't appeal. Then I would lose my horse – and my pride as well when I eventually trudged into the camp.

Staying on her back was my number one priority. That's not easy when you're galloping over rough ground, negotiating obstacles here, there and everywhere. The only aids I had available were the reins, of course, and, more importantly, my seat. The reins are not much use if you're bouncing around on a horse's back. To brace myself to be able to use my weight, I clamped my legs on her sides. As we got down to level ground, where the scrub was sparser, I was able to let her have more of her head. We still had to weave and turn through the scrub and over shallow watercourses, and my legs were feeling the strain. The other horses were now 200 yards or more in front and still going like the clappers, heading straight for the camp and the windmill.

When I caught up, the horses were milling around, sticking their heads in feed bins, taking up mouthfuls before pulling back to give a few pig-roots and farts. Red dust was swirling everywhere. The three men were standing around, unable to make up their minds what to do. With the mood the horses were in, the two whitefellas were wary about catching a stray kick of exuberance. Not Jackie. Jackie looked at me and I looked at him and, without a word from either of us, he silently eased over to one of his horses, a grey mare. She was sweet natured and Jackie was well aware of that. He slipped a bridle on her and led her over to the fence, where he hooked the reins to a piece of wire. If she pulled back, the leather thong joining the ends of the two reins would break and the bridle would not be damaged. He then carried a feed bin over to her.

As I slid off Mulba, my legs were trembling so much they nearly gave way. The tendons on the inside of my thighs ached and begged for relief. But there was no time for that. 'Catch the bloody horse you're going to ride today and tie it up to the fence. Then hobble the rest of them,' I said.

Anger still had a grip on me, though it was quickly being joined by a feeling of triumph. I'll show you, you bastards, I thought. Jiff finally arrived and went straight to the water trough, stepped in, lay down and drank.

That evening, after my fourth day in the camp, Jackie was given dinner duty. As I gave him the news, I reminded him that clean hands were required. He shrugged his shoulders, as much as to say, 'I think this is all bullshit, but I'll do as I'm told.'

Sitting by the fire after we'd eaten and the dishes were done, Tony said to Frank, 'D'yer want a game of draughts, mate?'

'Sure,' said Frank.

Out came the draughts set and I watched while they played. Jackie sat on the other side of the fire, looking across from time to time, but he seemed more interested in poking at the coals with a stick. Frank won the game and they played another, which Frank also won. Frank looked at me. 'D'you want a game?'

'Yep, I'll play,' I said.

I won that game and the second. Tony then wanted to play me and I won two games with him. This is too easy, I thought.

No-one said anything much after that. We made a billy of tea. We did not have much to talk about, just the odd anecdote. We drank the tea and stared into the fire. Then Jackie said, 'I'll play if someone wants.'

We all looked at Jackie. Three of us on one side of the fire, Jackie on the other. 'You know how to play?' I asked.

'Yeah,' he replied softly.

'Righto,' said Tony. 'Come over here.'

Jackie slowly rose off the ground, went around the fire and sat down opposite Tony. They were both cross-legged, with the board between them, the twenty-four black and white pieces laid out. I watched with some curiosity because I couldn't imagine that Jackie would be able to beat Tony and I wondered how he would handle it. But I was wrong yet again. Jackie took his time in thinking about his moves, and his black hand languidly moved his black pieces as he methodically took all of Tony's white pieces. Jackie's hand and arm movements were slow, deliberate, fluid and graceful. His composure was total. He looked up at Tony. 'You wanna play again?'

'Bloody oath,' said Tony. He quickly set up the board, this time giving Jackie the white pieces, as it is the custom to swap colours for every new game. Tony was anxious to regain some status, having not won a game all night. The ease with which Jackie beat Tony the second time destroyed Tony's equilibrium totally and he instantly called it quits.

I stood up, put more wood on the fire and raked the outside edges of the coals and ash towards the middle. The object was to have a deep bed of red-hot coals in the morning. It would be covered in a blanket of fine white ash, so a few twigs and small sticks thrown on top would get the fire up and running again and ready for the billy to make tea. The temperature was dropping and I put my jacket on. Tony had gone off to have a leak. Jackie and Frank were both gazing thoughtfully into the fire. 'Well,' I said. 'Are you blokes going to have a game or not?'

'Oh . . . yeah . . . all right,' said Frank. And he moved to where Tony had been sitting and started setting up the board. Jackie remained as expressionless as he had been all night. With the same slow, deliberate movements of his hand and fingers, he placed his pieces and demolished Frank without any apparent effort of mind. I could see Frank's temper starting to rise, so I said, 'I'll give you a game, Jackie.'

Frank got up and slouched off into the bush, silently passing Tony, who was on his way back. As we were setting up the pieces, I asked Jackie, 'Where did you learn to play draughts?'

'I was workin for a drover fella over to Wiluna for a while an he taught me.'

I thought, hmm, he cleaned up Tony and Frank pretty easily. But they're not much chop. I ought to be able to knock him off. Frank materialised out of the night and stood by the fire and took in the scene. Tony was sitting on his stretcher, watching. Jackie sat impassively. It was impossible to detect what he might be thinking or feeling. We started the game. Jackie never made a move in haste. Nor did he delay for too long. It was almost as if he had a set time for thinking about each move. And then that languid black hand would gently lift the chosen piece and place it equally gently in its new position. But there was nothing gentle about the thought behind the move. It was always offensive. Being on the defensive was annoying, so I tried to attack back. When I did, I found to my cost that Jackie's move had more behind it than I had imagined. He beat me easily. It rankled. I figured I had been too casual. I underestimated him. I was keen to play again and assert myself.

The next game took longer to play, and although there were times when I thought I might get the upper hand, Jackie still prevailed. He didn't say a word. Just sat. And watched me. Waiting. And we played a third game. Maybe I lost confidence. Maybe I was getting tired. Whatever it was, however hard I tried to concentrate, Jackie had no trouble winning again. He still didn't say a word. I shook his hand and said, 'Well done.'

It wasn't easy for me to get those words out, even though I readily admitted to myself that it was well done, that he did play well. Far too well for us. There was no comment from Tony or Frank. The mood in the camp was sombre. We tidied up and went to bed. That was the first and last time we played draughts. The board and the pieces stayed packed in a bag, out of sight and unavailable. No-one ever mentioned draughts again.

On the third day of mustering Bindingwah, we cleaned up the stragglers and finished by mid-afternoon. We were expecting Jack at around 3.30 and, right on schedule, he roared up in his International ute. I reported on the numbers we had mustered and how things were going. I let him know that I was not impressed with the slack attitude of the men. Jack heard me out and departed. We packed the camp wagon and harnessed the two horses. We went off along the ten-mile track to Mungeltha Bore, where we would camp while we mustered Toorangie. Those of us who were riding led our second horses. Tony was driving the wagon, and his horses just followed along behind the whole mob of us.

The two horses that pulled the wagon were something to see. One was a draught horse; the other was a carthorse. The draught horse was a beautiful, big, black 16.2-hand mare called Swanny. She had a thick mane and tail and a white blaze splashed on her face. The carthorse was a bay gelding called Reg, who was about 15 hands, nowhere near as big as Swanny. Apart from being shorter, he had a lighter build.

They were easy to handle except for when they were harnessed to the wagon and you first started. Then they were hard to hold. You had to stand up and brace yourself for the first mile before they settled down to a slow trot. As a physically mismatched pair, they looked comical, but they were good horses.

We mustered Toorangie in two days. We'd got the bulk of the sheep the first day, and on the second, we picked up the stragglers. The blokes were poking the mob along the bottom fence line to Mungeltha Bore, and I decided to go back to the Yangee Bore area to double-check – there were no sheep there. Instead of turning back, I rode in to give Pitch, my other horse, a drink. I was standing beside him as he drank. He lifted his head and held the last mouthful before swallowing. The dregs slopped out as he champed on the bit and flicked his tongue and sighed. We were both feeling very relaxed – and enjoying ourselves. It was one of those quiet, peaceful moments that crop up now and then. Just as I decided to get going again, I saw something move beside the top end of the trough, next to the cover over the ball valve. We were at the bottom end, twenty feet away. I took a step closer and whatever it was moved. Then I saw it was a very big bungarra, about five feet from the tip of its nose to the end of its tail.

We could have you for dinner, I thought. I picked up a solid stone between the size of a golf ball and a cricket ball and took aim and threw it – hard. The bungarra didn't move. It was as if it was waiting for the stone. The missile hit it fair and square on the head. The bungarra jerked a couple of times and collapsed. Crikey, I thought, that was a bloody good shot – bit of a fluke. I walked up to it, leading Pitch. Was it alive or dead or what? It seemed to be lifeless. I cautiously took hold of it by the tail. It didn't stir. Bloody hell, I thought, I've killed it. I lifted it up by the tail and it was limp and loose.

Pitch was very unhappy, especially when I wanted to mount and carry the bungarra at the same time. He was squirming around, keeping his head turned, trying to keep his eyes on it and screwing away at the same time. He was unwilling, but I managed to get him to accept the bungarra on his off-side, dangling from my right hand and arm, which were stretched over his wither. It wasn't easy, but I climbed up and into the saddle. Try getting on a horse when you can't use your right hand to grip the pommel. My right forearm was braced against the pommel to give me leverage. The bungarra's head and shoulders were on the ground, which meant it wasn't swaying around during the process of getting on. Once we were moving, I had to lift it up so it didn't drag. Then it wobbled around in the air. Pitch still wasn't happy. He was toey and ready to bolt. After a while, the weight of the bungarra took its toll on my arm and I experimented with trying to lie it across Pitch's wither. He wouldn't have a bar of it. He protested at any contact, even though it was dead.

Except – it wasn't dead. There I was, with this five-foot bungarra that was going to be on the menu for dinner that night, holding it out and away from Pitch's body – and all four of its feet started twitching and scratching in mid-air, inches away from the horse's ribs. We'd gone about a mile and a half, and we had nearly two more to go. My right arm was already aching from the strain of holding this bungarra outstretched. Pitch was more and more agitated, and I was more and more determined to keep a hold on it – and Pitch.

I wasn't game enough to speed up the trip by trotting. Pitch would be even harder to hold. We rode on, in a state of mutual tension and apprehension, as the bungarra became more and more alive. Fortunately, Pitch settled down somewhat, which was a relief. Thirty minutes later we were within yelling distance of the camp. The blokes had put the stragglers into Mungeltha paddock and, as usual, were sitting around the fire drinking tea and smoking. When they heard me and saw my predicament, the bastards, typically, started laughing. 'Come here and give me a bloody hand,' I shouted. 'Get off your arses.'

Jackie knew what to do. He sauntered up and reached up and took the bungarra by the tail. He walked over to a big mulga and swung the bungarra around and cracked its head against the trunk of the tree. To Frank's and Tony's dismay, we ate bungarra baked in the ashes and coals that night, with boiled potatoes and onions.

18

Yalgar Pool

Next morning we moved camp to Barro Well, at Yalgar paddock. The paddock gets its name from the Yalgar River, which meanders in from the east to meet the broad-swathed Hope River charging up from the south and on to meet the mighty Murchison on Moorarie Station. Not far south from where the Yalgar joins it, the Hope has a permanent pool, called Yalgar Pool. It is about half a mile long and about sixty or seventy yards wide. Out in the middle it is quite deep, maybe nine or ten feet. The west bank slopes steeply down to the water and big white river gums run along its length and beyond. Like most of the paddocks in that area, Yalgar paddock is about five miles from east to west and about six miles from north to south. There was more vegetation than in the previous paddocks we'd mustered, so we would have to adjust to the reduced visibility.

We parked the wagon under a big mulga fifty yards from the windmill and the tank. That evening I decided to take over all the cooking. These men never washed their hands, not just when they had to cook, but at any time. The body odour was really starting to annoy me. When the three were close together, the odour was noxious. I took to standing upwind if I had to talk to them as a group. Persuasion and argument hadn't worked. I decided to do something about it, but I couldn't think of the answer right then.

If I let it simmer for a day or so a solution might emerge, I thought. It usually did.

The next day's mustering was made more interesting by the country being divided in different ways by the two river courses and by the higher country at the north end. Mulba and Pitch gave me great pleasure. They were the best horses in the camp – best in the sense that they were more willing, more capable. They were both quick, although speed was only rarely a factor – for instance, when a mob broke and the breakaways had to be headed and turned back into the mob. Your dog can often do that, but sometimes the breakaways are tough to handle and you have to give your dog a hand. Mulba was about 16 hands and Pitch about 15.2 or 15.3. They were both around eight years of age and they'd been doing stock work for about four years. Whoever had broken them in had done a good job and whoever had ridden them subsequently had also handled them well. Knowing I had the best horses gave me a good feeling. It enhanced my confidence and status, although I doubt that the three men cared a hoot. Those horses were enjoyable to ride and enjoyable to handle. Along with Jiff, they were good company. There were times when I thought that riding a top horse, with a top dog trotting beside, through interesting, constantly changing country, with birds all around, was about the best possible life a young bloke could have. The weather was good. The nights were cold, and although the days were not what you'd call hot, it was quite warm in the early afternoon.

Curiosity was niggling at me, so I veered across to the area where the Yalgar meets the Hope, and then I found what I was really looking for – Yalgar Pool. What a sight! It was a much larger body of water than I thought it would be. As I made my way along the west side, I startled two emus, which took off at full pace straight over the bank and into the water. I reined in Pitch to watch. I had never seen emus swim, and swim they did. Their bodies were not totally immersed: all those feathers probably gave them more buoyancy. Their necks and heads stuck up out of the water like periscopes. They swam strongly, all the way to the east bank, which had a gentle slope. They walked out of the water and, without looking back, trotted up the bank and disappeared into the scrub.

Towards the end of the day, in order to catch a killer, we penned all the sheep we had mustered in wire yards close to the mill. We looked them over with a view to selecting a large wether in good condition. Jackie said to me, 'That one over there. Look at his ear markings. He from Trilbar. No good killin one of ours if we can kill one of theirs.'

Fair enough, I thought. 'Tony,' I said. 'Grab that big bastard over there with the short horns. We'll do him.'

Tony climbed into the yard and waded through the mob to the one I'd pointed out. He grabbed the wether by his little stubby horns and swung his leg over his back and straddled him as if he was going to ride him. He walked him over to the gate.

'Don't lose the bastard,' I said. 'Walk him over to that mulga and we can hang him on the gambrel there.'

Tony walked him over and flipped the wether onto his rump, the wether's head in his crotch. He tied the wether's two front legs together with one back leg and laid him on his side. We then turned the mob out into Boolgaroo paddock. Killing and dressing the wether was routine, and the carcass was soon suspended in the air, hanging from the gambrel. The only problem was that we were out of meat and the carcass had to hang overnight and set before we could butcher it and use it. Jackie said, 'Thas OK. We can eat the liver.'

'Eat the liver?' I said. 'You can't eat it straightaway, can you?'

'Course you can. He's better when he's fresh.'

I accepted Jackie's advice, but I was reluctant. I didn't like liver. Cooked liver was always dry and hard, and a mouthful took all the saliva and moisture from my mouth. It was like chewing a hard block of blotting paper. Why my father loved it so much was beyond my comprehension. My mother refused to eat it or cook it. So he cooked it. Getting dinner ready that night, I made a comment about how I felt about eating liver and Jackie said, 'Let me cook im.'

Willingly, I let Jackie take over. The first thing he did was peel and slice two onions. These went into our large frying pan, along with a big spoonful of mutton fat. When the onions softened and started to brown, Jackie placed slices of liver into the pan, with the onions all around. The coals were hot and the pan was soon spitting. In less than a minute, he flipped the slices of liver over and a minute later tipped them out of the frying pan and onto a tin plate. He then mixed water and flour and poured that into the frying pan and stirred it into the remaining fat until he had a thickish light-brown gravy. The cooked liver pieces and the onion went back into the pan and were stirred around in the gravy. Then the pan was quickly off the coals and we were all helping ourselves. I cut a piece of liver in half and inside it was pink, with traces of red in the middle. 'This bloody liver's not properly cooked, Jackie,' I said. 'I can't eat this.'

'You try im,' said Jackie. 'I reckon he's just right.'

Tony and Frank weren't too sure whether to eat it or not. They watched me. I decided to give it a go – a piece of liver with a dash of gravy and a touch of onion. When I chewed, I found it was sweet and moist, with a delicate flavour that had no resemblance to the liver my father served. Tony and Frank followed suit and the whole pan of liver was quickly polished off, together with some boiled potatoes. We washed it down with the regulation billy tea. We all agreed it was good tucker. As we were sipping our tea, there was a lull in the conversation and I said, 'Tomorrow's Sunday and I reckon we can clean up the stragglers by lunch time. When that's done, I'll have a surprise for you.'

'What bloody surprise?' asked Frank.

'If I told you now it wouldn't be a bloody surprise tomorrow, would it?'

Next morning we were away to an early start. Not that the blokes were keen to get the work over so they could find out about the surprise. Tony and Frank gave me the feeling they were very dubious. Frank, in particular, seemed apprehensive. Jackie was indifferent. At one o'clock we ran the mob of sheep we'd gathered through the cocky gate and into Boolgaroo. I told the men not to unsaddle, just tie the horses up to the fence, give them a small feed and get some lunch. Lunch was the usual: grilled chops with a thick slice of damper generously doused with tomato sauce. That done, we roused the resting horses and I led them off in the direction of Yalgar Pool. Twenty minutes later we were there. I dismounted and started unsaddling my horse.

'Off you get,' I said. 'Unsaddle your horses and take off all your clothes and your boots.'

They looked at me incredulously. 'You're fuckin jokin,' said Frank.

'No joke,' I replied. 'We are going to ride our horses bareback into the pool and swim them out into the middle. Today's the day we are going to have fun.'

Jackie obligingly stripped and humped himself over his horse's withers and crawled onto its back. I said to Frank and Tony, 'Come on, you bastards. Get moving.'

Tony couldn't help himself. 'Shit, it's cold.'

'Never mind about that,' I said. 'Let's go.' I gave Mulba a thump on each side with my bare heels and she willingly slid down the bank. Mulba and I charged right in. If Tony had thought it was cold at the top, he was about to discover real cold. Mulba was swimming and I was perched on her back, hanging on to the reins with one hand and her mane with the other. I turned her around to see what was happening with the men. All three were sitting on their horses, on the bank, watching. 'For Christ's sake, come in,' I shouted as loud as I could.

They started and, as they did, I began laughing. Coming down the steep bank, they were sliding around on their horses' backs, hanging on like monkeys. Tony and Frank were petrified they were going to fall off. But in seconds they were all in the water and swimming out to me. Their horses had their heads poking up out of the pool, their ears pricked, snorting spray from their nostrils. 'Righto, Frank,' I yelled, 'this is where the fun starts!'

Frank was shivering with cold, and I swam Mulba alongside him. I put my arm around his waist and pulled him off his horse and into the water. He went right under and came up spluttering and swearing, especially when he saw Tony and Jackie laughing at him. Then I grabbed Tony and pulled him in too. It was on for young and old then. They ganged up on me and pulled me in. The horses were swimming round in circles, snorting and puffing. The men were climbing out of the water and back onto their horses' backs, only to slide off again or be tipped off.

'Bloody hell,' Tony yelled. 'This bloody horse is as slippery as a butcher's prick.' The activity took everyone's minds off the cold, and that, combined with their pleasure at giving me a dumping, got everyone enjoying themselves.

Ten minutes was enough. The horses were tiring. We rode out of the pool and tied them up. Before the boys could get their clothes on, I took two bars of soap out of my saddlebag, tossed one to Frank and the other to Jackie, and said, 'Before you get dressed and since you've got used to the water, you can go back in the pool and soap yourselves all over, hair included.' The response was unprintable.

Soon enough, all four of us were standing in the shallows, soaping ourselves and rinsing with clear water. Like four dogs, we shook the water off. We gingerly made our way, barefoot, up the bank and across the stony and prickly ground to our clothes and boots. We finished drying ourselves with our shirts and used the legs of our trousers to wipe the mud off the soles of our feet.

We rode back to the camp at a leisurely pace, stirred up the fire and put the billy on. By this time, the day was fading and the temperature was dropping and everyone was happy to cluster around the fire and sip their tea. I watched closely. Maybe it was the result of an invigorating cold bath; maybe it was the exposure of three whitefellas and one blackfella all being naked and fooling around together, everyone equal in the pool; maybe they were glad it was all over – whatever it was, there was a new tone in the camp. We had not turned a big corner, but where there had been caution and distrust, the mood was now less cautious, less distrustful. Did they enjoy the experience overall? I reckon they'd have said 'sort of'.

Next day, Jackie introduced us to a Yamatji delicacy – bardies. At lunch camp we met at Toorangie Well and lit a fire for the quart pots. Before we could start on our leftover cold mutton and the damper, Jackie said, 'You fellas ever tasted bardies?'

'What the bloody hell are bardies?' someone asked.

'I'll show ya,' Jackie said.

He slowly gathered himself together and picked up a stick with a pointed end and mooched around the curara bushes that were scattered about. Curaras are spindly shrubs that grow from six to eight feet in height. They have needles instead of leaves and they are very prickly if you brush up against them. Jackie sat down in the dirt under the thin branches of a bush and started digging. We drifted over to watch. Very quickly, he dug a hole about six inches long and two inches wide. He went down about three inches and uncovered a root. He cleared around the root so he could get his hand underneath, and then he lifted and broke the root at one end. He broke it off at the other end and showed us. The root had a big bulge in it, about two inches long. Jackie broke the root open, and inside the bulge was a white grub with a small orangey brown head. Jackie held it between his forefinger and thumb, holding it by the head, the body dangling down. The display ended when, without a word, he popped it in his mouth and bit it off just below the head. Tony said, 'I feel sick.'

'Nah,' said Jackie. 'I'll get some more and I'll cook em for you. You can dig some up too.'

He showed us narrow cracks in the surface of the ground a foot or so out from the trunks of the curaras. 'Where you see them cracks,' he said, 'is where you'll find a bardie.'

A few minutes later, we were spread everywhere, all sitting on the ground under curara bushes, all digging, with someone yelling out every now and then, 'I've got one.' I thought, if Jack Henderson comes along now, he'll think we're all idiots – and he'd be right. After about twenty minutes, I called everyone back to the camp. When each man added his harvest of bardies into Jackie's upturned hat, it was half full of the squirming white grubs. They did not look appetising. Jackie made a long bed of hot ashes and rolled the live bardies into it and gave them a thin covering of more hot ashes. He gently moved them around with a stick, and when they were really hot, one by one, small holes burst in their sides. To Jackie, sitting on the ground beside the fire, that was the signal they were cooked, and he scratched them out of the ashes and offered us one each. I looked mine over and sniffed it. It reminded me of caramel.

'Eat im,' Jackie said.

Holding it by the head, I slowly put it in my mouth. I had no idea what to expect. What I found was that it had a flavour similar to peanut butter but it was softer and creamier than peanut butter. It wasn't bad. It wasn't great.

'Best if you blokes eat im on a bit of damper,' Jackie volunteered.

One by one, we followed his suggestion, and we actually liked them like that. The damper toned down the intensity of the flavour. I suppose eating them on their own was no different from eating peanut butter straight out of the jar.

From then on, every lunch camp, if I was the last to arrive, none of the men would be sitting by the fire. They would all be scattered around, grubbing away like miners looking for gold under curara bushes. At the end of a week of doing this we all got sick of it and gave it away, which I thought was a good thing. It seemed to me to be ludicrous for grown men to be sitting in the dirt scratching around to find grubs to eat. We reverted to chops and damper, or cold mutton and damper, standard tucker.

* * *

It was now eleven days that I had been in the mustering camp. I had mixed feelings about it. The work and the lifestyle were enjoyable. The country was all new to me, and I enjoyed that. But I did not like checking on the men to make sure they were doing their job. This meant doubling back across the country they were mustering to see if they were paying attention to what they were doing. On one occasion I saw Tony riding past a small mob of sheep over to his left. I cantered up behind him and found he was reading a book as he went.

After the second day at Barro Well, Jack turned up to find out what we'd done. I gave him the stock numbers and reported on their condition. I also told him again that I was not impressed with the men – and why. Jack listened and, although I couldn't be sure, it seemed to me he wasn't giving me his full attention. It was hard to tell if he was listening, or whether his mind was on other things, or whether he simply thought I was a whinger. I was still talking to him as he got in his ute and slammed the door and started the engine. The window was down and he had his right elbow in the opening. Now he looked me straight in the eye and, in an offhand way, said, 'Well, Ian, you're the boss.' With that he put the ute in gear and drove off, leaving us to mount up and take the horses to the next camp.

Over the next two weeks, we mustered six more paddocks, pushing the sheep into two paddocks closer to the homestead. From there, they were within striking distance of the shearing shed, and other stockmen would bring them into the holding paddocks as they were needed. Our routine was the same every day. Yet as the days wore on I could feel something slipping away. My hold on the men was never strong and it was steadily loosening. I could feel it and I wondered if they were getting tired and bored. Maybe they were, but I knew it wasn't just that. The problem was me, and I did not know what to do about it. Maybe they just thought I was a bumptious young upstart. Maybe I was. But there was nothing wrong with my daily decisions: there were not too many options, and even choosing a different option would not have been wrong, simply an alternative. I was finding it harder and harder to get them moving. They were slowing down, incrementally. It was difficult to see a difference between one day and the next, but I could feel the difference between the start and the end of a week. There was nothing specific I could put my finger on, except a touch of disdain from Jackie now and then. No-one challenged me face to face. No-one refused to do anything I asked. There was just a pervasive indifference to the work – and to me. Indifference is amorphous and, as such, difficult to deal with. And I did not know how to deal with it.

When we finished cleaning up the six paddocks, we moved into the homestead and stayed there for a few days before moving down to the southwest paddocks some twenty-five miles away. In this country the paddocks were named Yalgaroo, Oilba and Bubbamollie; and there were windmills called Birrabubba, Coodoo and Coolawandie, and one prosaically called Cattle Camp Well. These paddocks were bigger than the ones on the northern boundary and we were to be there for two weeks. Then we were to muster in closer to the homestead. I was concerned about how I was going to handle another three weeks with these blokes out in the bush. I decided to talk to Jack.

We sat in the office, which looked out onto the broad thoroughfare between the two rows of buildings. Jack listened patiently as I ran through the faults of the men in the camp. I told him I wanted to sack all three and start again with a new team. He let me run on until I had nothing more to say. I looked at him expectantly, anticipating words of reassurance and understanding. Instead, Jack leaned back in his chair and spoke slowly. 'You can sack these blokes if you want. You can go in to Meekatharra and hire three more, but I'll tell you this, the three new ones will be no better than the ones you've got. And at least these blokes know the names of the windmills and the paddocks and don't get lost when you send them somewhere.'

I digested this and said, 'These are fair dinkum lazy bastards. They annoy the shit out of me. They make it so hard to do the job properly.'

'I know that,' said Jack. 'I know what they're like. I know it's hard. Just remember, things are never so bad they couldn't be worse.'

That finished me off.

19

A day of reckoning

The day before we were to ride out to the new camp, I replenished the tuckerbox from the station storeroom. The storeroom was long and large, with a small window at each end, each so dusty and grimy that the light was battling to penetrate. The single bare light bulb powered by the station generator was not much more than a glow in the dark. The shadows under the benches were deep and black. It felt the way I imagined a dusty, gloomy mausoleum might. There were benches down the long walls, with shelves above and wooden storage boxes beneath. There was a long table in the middle, nearly covered with wooden boxes. Dust was thick everywhere, except on the storage bins and boxes that were most frequently used. Despite the boxes and bins of stores, the silence made the place feel empty. Nothing stirred. I had it all to myself.

Methodically, I collected a supply of all the usual: flour, tea, sugar, powdered milk, jam, tomato sauce, Worcestershire sauce, potatoes and onions. Then I started exploring, opening lids, looking in boxes and containers. One large box contained dry, pale-coloured shreds of something I couldn't identify. I scooped up a handful and took it over to the window, where I could see more clearly. I stirred it with my finger and looked closely. Then it dawned on me. I was looking at dried vegetables: carrots, parsnips, beans and some I couldn't name. That'll do me, I thought, and I filled a large paper bag. More snooping revealed sago, custard powder and tins of coffee, all added to the collection. Knowing how spartan the tuckerbox had been when I took over, I had the feeling I was stealing. I even found tins of fruit and tinned meat, but I wasn't game enough to take those. Feeling pleased with what I was carefully packing up, I had an abrupt jolt of fear when Jack walked in. He strode over to a shelf, picked up something – and then inspected what I was packing. 'Bloody Christ,' he said. 'What do you need all this for?'

'For the camp,' I said. 'You know, for the camp. I thought it'd be a good idea to vary the diet a bit.'

'And why do you need coffee when you've got tea?'

'Well, just for a change.'

'Bloody hell.'

He looked in the paper bag of dried vegetables. 'And this?'

'I reckon it'd be good to have something other than potatoes and onions. I'll stick a couple of handfuls in the stew, the next time we make a stew. We make stews as well as roasts. The men like a stew now and then.' I felt like a small boy caught red-handed in the pantry.

Jack shook his head in exasperation. 'I dunno, you blokes! When I was in the mustering camp we lived on salt beef and damper and that was it. Nothing else! If it was good enough for me it should be good enough for you. You blokes are just too bloody soft.'

With that he turned and strode out and slammed the door. Bugger him, I thought. He might be my uncle, but he can go to hell. My fear had evaporated, and I angrily gathered up all my new-found treats and carted them off to the tuckerbox on the wagon.

When the blokes saw what I was adding to the food supplies, they were bemused. 'Dried vegetables?' 'Sago?' 'Custard powder?' 'Coffee?'

'Yeah,' I said. 'Yeah. We'll make custard from time to time. I know we've got nothing to put it on or to eat it with. We'll just make it with powdered milk and eat it as it is. Maybe you'd like to try it on damper.'

I got the impression they thought I was weird. Perhaps I was.

The few days we had at the homestead were pleasantly civilised after the camp. I had a room of my own, attached to the kitchen block and the workers' dining room. I ate in the manager's dining room with Jack and Lindsay and any visitors who might be staying for a day or two. This room had great character. The dining table was large; the walls were hung with photographs of Sir Ernest Lee-Steere's champion racehorses, two of which had won the Caulfield Cup in Melbourne. We always dressed for dinner, which for me meant showering and shaving before putting on a clean shirt, a tie and a jacket. The evening always started with drinks in the sitting room. All the stations were dry, including Belele, except for the owners and managers: they were privileged. There was no alcohol for anyone else, apart from shearing teams, and their behaviour under the influence made it obvious why alcohol was banned for the rest of the station.

While I had been out in the mustering camp, Jack had hired three new young blokes, general station hands: Andy, Gil and Norm. With shearing getting closer, the station needed more hands – or bums, because they would have to spend time in the saddle as well as working in the sheep yards. Andy and Gil I liked a lot. They had energy and enthusiasm. I wished I could replace my blokes with them. But that was not negotiable. We got on well together, although there was a shadow in their attitude. They too were older than me, and I think it didn't sit right with them that I was the youngest yet I was the head stockman. It was nothing they said, more their tone. It wasn't the same as the indifference of Jackie and Tony and Frank. They simply were not comfortable answering to someone younger. They would also have had an earful about me from Frank and Tony.

* * *

During the two weeks in the south paddocks – Yalgaroo, Oilba and Bubbamollie – Frank's and Tony's indifference increasingly irked me, while Jackie's disdain was clearly apparent. This climate needed to be dealt with, but I still didn't know how.

All this was on my mind when Jack arrived at Coodoo Well, in Yalgaroo, one Sunday morning. Normally, we worked seven days a week. After many weeks of working Sundays, we needed a break. Besides, our clothes were filthy and we were filthy – and unshaven. It was time for a big clean up. The night before, I told the blokes what I had in mind. Next morning there was a chill wind from Central Australia scouring the camp and whipping up dust. 'C'mon boys,' I said. 'Let's get going. We'll start with the clothes, then we'll do ourselves.'

'Fuck that,' said Frank. 'I'm not getting me gear off. It's too fuckin cold.'

'Ohhh . . . stop bitching,' I said. 'Get on with it.'

Frank was right, it was cold. But there was no turning back. It was one of those days when I had a sour taste in my mouth. I was tired. I was fed up with the attitude around me. It was cold. And then Jack turned up. He stopped the big International twenty yards from the camp. I got up from where I was washing a shirt in a basin, and I thought, this's all I need. Then out from the passenger side a long, lanky bloke emerged. He had what I thought was a silly grin on his face. He strode manfully across the dirt and stepped right up to me, thrust out his right hand and said in a very cheery voice, 'You must be Ian. Hi. I'm Ernest Lee-Steere.' And then he nearly shook my arm off. I thought, what a dickhead – why don't you just piss off and go back where you came from? Visiting fuckin royalty, that's what you are.

Well, I was wrong yet again. Ernest was a thoroughly decent, genuine bloke. Months later, I met him again at the homestead when I was in a better mood, and I couldn't help but like him. At dinner, he took great pleasure in talking about the racehorses featured in the photographs on the dining room walls. He was very well informed – and proud of his father's achievements. He took an interest in me in a very genuine and down-to-earth way.

We moved camp to Ten Mile Well in order to muster the biggest paddock on the station – Chittamundra. Station fences generally run north–south and east–west, and they're usually rectangular or square. Chittamundra was an odd shape. It was roughly rectangular, about fifteen miles from north to south, but it was five miles wide at the top end and ten miles wide at the bottom end. It was far too big to muster in a day. The challenge was to get all the stock in three or four days. Adding to the challenge was the Mingah Range, a rough collection of hills that were home to abandoned mines: Chesterfield and Big Ben.

On our first day at Chittamundra, the Big Ben mine site was like a magnet to three young whitefellas, and, with Jackie in tow, we met at the mine to check it out. The mine was up in the ranges, in a wide depression. The enormous structure, built from thick timber beams, with giant iron wheels at the top, towered above the landscape. Scattered around were corrugated-iron buildings in various stages of decay. Some corrugated-iron panels were missing; some were loose and flapped in the wind. Flywire doors made a harsh scraping noise on the concrete floor as they swung in and out. Every building was empty. Even though it had been abandoned for many years, something about the total absence of human life, the emptiness of the buildings and the landscape, and the silence broken only by creaking doors or the flapping of corrugated iron gave me the feeling we were trespassing. Undeterred, we kept exploring, and found several shafts that looked as if the soil and rocks had been sucked straight out of the earth, leaving deep holes that were impressively precise in dimension and form. Some of them had rickety ladders still in place.

Our curiosity was too much for us, and Frank and I climbed down one of the shafts all the way to the bottom, about forty feet. There we found tunnels heading off in three directions. There was light coming into one of these tunnels, and I headed in that direction. The floor of the tunnel was a foot deep in fine, white powdery dust, and it billowed as I felt my way through. I thought, shit, this's no good. We could be in trouble here. What if one of these tunnels collapses? I suddenly felt a burning sense of urgency to get out of the tunnel and up the shaft and onto the ground above. I headed back the way I'd come. When I got to the shaft with the ladder, I climbed up, testing each dried and decaying rung before putting my weight on it, and soon emerged into the open air and the bright light.

Frank was already there, covered in white dust from head to foot. I looked myself over and I was the same. We shook ourselves and patted our clothes to get rid of some of it, but we still looked laughable. Tony was highly amused. Jackie was manifestly bored. We had now lost any interest in exploring deep holes in the ground and we resumed our mustering work.

The next day started out like any other. The weather was still cold; banks of clouds in the east were obstructing whatever warmth the sun had to offer. The breeze was brittle and chilly. We wore our jackets. We mounted and went our separate ways, according to my plan. I didn't set eyes on anyone until we met for lunch at Six Mile Well, which was inside the paddock – that is, not on a fence line. Tony and Frank had a mob of about 600, resting. After lunch camp I asked them to move them over to the northeast corner, where they could let them go in the holding paddock down from the homestead. Then they were to ride back to the camp at Ten Mile Well. Jackie went off in the westerly direction I asked him to, and I continued to scour the hills in the centre for whatever small mobs I could find.

Late in the day, I arrived back at the camp, without having found any sheep. Tony and Frank were already there and had the fire going, and a billy was on. There was no sign of Jackie. I joined them at the fire and started preparing dinner. By now it was getting dark; the sun had done its job and had headed off over the horizon. At the sound of a horse's shod hooves striking the stones as it walked in towards the camp, I looked up and saw Jackie on his grey mare emerging from the gloom. He too was empty-handed. I stopped what I was doing and walked over to where he was unsaddling his horse. I went right up to him. 'Where have you been? You should have been back a long time ago. Did you muster where I told you to?'

Jackie half-turned and glanced at me out of the corner of his eye. 'I don' give a fuck where you tell me to go. I go where I wanna go. You don' fuckin know what you doin.'

'Is that right?' I said.

'Yeah, thas fuckin right.'

With my left hand I grabbed his shirt front, and with my right hand I landed a punch on the left side of his face. My fist connected with his left jaw and cheekbone at the same time. I hit him a second time, as hard as I could, this time more on the jaw. He fell out of the grip of my left hand and sprawled on the ground.

'You fuckin kill me, you bastard,' he said.

'I'll fuckin kill you all right,' I replied, and I reached down, pulled him to his feet and punched him a third time. He fell down again and tried to crawl away, but I went after him and grabbed his collar and pulled him over onto his back and hauled him up on his feet. He tried to collapse again, but I wouldn't let him. I managed to get another heavy punch to the side of his head, and I felt the jar and the pain all the way up to my elbow. This time I let him go. He was groaning. In between groans he swore at me. I stood and looked at him half-sitting, half-lying in the dirt. He seemed to be choking but he managed to say, 'I'm leavin. I'm not stayin in this camp with you. I'm goin tell the boss what you done.'

Jackie got on his hands and knees and laboriously stood up. 'I'm goin now.'

'Go for your bloody life,' I said.

Jackie kept his eyes on me, wary that I might belt him again. He refixed his saddle. He led the mare away from the fence. He put his foot in the stirrup and struggled to get his body off the ground and his right leg over his horse's back. Is he laying it on? I asked myself. I mean, I only hit him four times. Jackie walked his horse away and then started to trot, heading straight up the track to where it joined the main road, and then on to the homestead. He would probably be there in an hour or so.

Tony and Frank were standing by the fire, taking it all in. I walked over to them – taking one thoughtful step after another. I felt calm and intensely aware, although I was slightly shaky. Even though what had happened was spontaneous and was all over in less than a minute, it felt longer than that. There had been no anticipation, no premeditation. It was an instinctive reaction and I did it without any consideration of the consequences. Now I had to think about the consequences.

Frank asked me if I wanted a mug of tea. I looked at him. What was this? Frank offering me a mug of tea? 'No,' I said, 'I'll get it myself.'

'I've been lookin after the dinner. It's nearly ready,' said Tony.

'The horses'll be finished their feeds. Now that Jackie's gone, I'll untie them and do their hobbles and let them go. And if they eat Jackie's horse's feed, it'll be too bad,' said Frank.

'Yeah, righto,' I said, thinking, what's going on?

I gave Jackie about half an hour's start. I saddled Mulba and rode off to the homestead. The main road was soft in some stretches and I lifted her into a slow canter and we loped along at an easy pace. The night was still. The sky was clear. The stars were bright and sharp as razors. Mulba had a beautiful rocking canter, and sitting in my big stock saddle was like lounging in an easy chair. Except that no easy chair pulsated with the vitality of the life between my legs. We got to the homestead at eight o'clock. I put Mulba in a yard at the stables and eased the saddle off her and gave her a small feed. There was no sign of Jackie, but that didn't surprise me. Jack was in the living room, and, as soon as he saw me, he dropped what he was reading, left his chair and came out the door. 'We can talk on the veranda here.'

'You've seen Jackie?' I asked, apprehensively.

'Yeah, I've seen him.'

'Well, I want to tell you what happened.' Jack didn't interrupt. He heard me out.

'OK,' he said. 'Well, Jackie's quit, so I'll take him in to Meekatharra tomorrow. He also wants to report you to Sergeant Carr. He wants Reg to charge you with assault.'

He looked for my reaction, but I didn't give him any. I was waiting for the rest of what he might have to say.

'I'll send Gil out to replace Jackie, but that'll only be for a day because by then you'll be finished with Chittamundra and coming in. He won't get there in time for mustering tomorrow, so you'll have to make do without a fourth man. Use him in the muster the next day and then pack up to come in the following day.' There was a pause. 'Do you want a beer?'

I did. Jack got me one. I drank it quickly. Feeling relieved, I went to get Mulba to ride back to the camp. We walked into the night and stopped so I could mount in some wanderrie country where the red soil was soft and sandy. As I bent over to go through the routine of tightening the girth and surcingle, she swung her neck and head around and gave me a nudge with her nose. I straightened up and stood beside her head, put my right arm around her neck and rubbed her face with my left hand. And I said to her, 'What a lovely bloody horse you are.'

The next morning I found that Tony's and Frank's change of attitude the night before was still in place. Overnight, their indifference had evaporated. I no longer had to ask them more than once to get anything done. They even volunteered to do various chores. I thought, this is bullshit. Putting aside what Jackie had done to Mark – and the whitefella at Leonora, if that was true – I thought, I shouldn't have to give some blackfella a hiding just to earn respect from you bastards. I wasn't proud of what I had done to Jackie. If it was a win, it was very hollow. You couldn't call it a fight; Jackie made no attempt to hit me. In any case, given the differences in height and build and reach, Jackie was no match. Nor was he really a match for Mark, unless he had a weapon and could use the element of surprise, quickly followed by flight. With me, Jackie was the one who was surprised – shocked, really. My reaction was the last thing he expected.

As I thought about it over the following two days in the camp, I wondered if I had gone too far. I remembered the stories of Ernest Potts at Mount Augustus, how they said he'd sooner have a fight than a feed. I thought, I don't want to have to do that to get you blokes to perform. It's true that I did not enjoy the punch-up with Jackie, but I did enjoy a degree of satisfaction at getting the best of him – although I would never have admitted that to anyone at the time.

The mustering team rolled into the homestead in a cloud of dust. Frank was driving the wagon and he used all his weight to bring the horses back from a trot to a walk. The house staff and the new station hands and the little black kids all came out to watch us pull up. Andy came up to me. 'Gidday, Ian,' he said. 'You want me to unsaddle your horse?' I declined the offer.

Norm came over. 'Want me to start unloading the wagon?'

'Bugger off, Norm,' said Gil. 'Soon as I've put me horse away, I'm doin that.'

Everyone was 'on the broad grin', as they say. They were so cheerful and friendly it disgusted me. It made me feel awkward. At the same time, I couldn't help thinking that life on the station was going to be a lot easier. With all this new-found respect and authority, I thought, I'll have to be careful not to swagger.

A few days later, when I caught up with Jack at morning smoko, we sat on the veranda and drank our tea, with biscuits made that morning in the station kitchen. We talked about this and that, and then Jack said, 'Oh, by the way, I took Jackie into Meekatharra and dropped him at the blacks' camp, and then I went to see Reg Carr.'

'Yeah,' I said, 'then what?'

Jack gave such a long-drawn-out 'Yeah' it was more like a reflective sigh. 'Y-e-a-h. Well, I told Reg you'd had a blue with Jackie Stevens and that Jackie was going to report you. As you'd expect, Reg knows Jackie, knows him pretty well. I said to Reg, "You need to know Ian gave Jackie a hiding." And Reg said, "That's all right. If he comes to me to complain, I'll give him another one."'

Jack raised his teacup to his lips, paused and looked at me over the rim. It was difficult to hold back a wisp of a smile, so I didn't try.

From that moment, I accepted my new identity. I had crossed some sort of bridge and I liked being on the other side. I still asked the men to do things, rather than gave orders, but my asking now had a new edge. What I did not like was the way in which I had earned my new status.

PART FIVE

OVERSEER

In charge of all of a station's workers;
one step down from the station manager

20

Jack Henderson

We were back on the north side of Belele, pushing the sheep, paddock by paddock, closer and closer to the shearing shed. We gathered the mob in Mungeltha to transfer them to Bundle Bubba, and I sent Frank, Tony and Gil to scout for stragglers while I moved the 3,000 head along the fence line to the gate into Bundle Bubba. There was just me, on Pitch, and Jiff. A mob this size is not difficult for one man and a dog to handle – once they're settled down. The herbage was lush. The sheep were in good nick. The sun was shining. The breeze was cool. The branches of the mulgas moved half-heartedly. It was a day like so many others. Yet I was enjoying one of those moments when you feel exhilarated for no clear reason.

Then Jack turned up in his International. He came up from the south, his right elbow out the window as usual. He drove slowly, wide of the mob and around behind me. He turned off the engine, got out and walked towards me. I halted Pitch and dismounted. He knew we were coming with a big mob and I wondered what his visit was in aid of. We said our giddays and the 'how's it all goin?' business.

'I thought you'd be about here,' he said.

'Yeah?'

'I couldn't wait to come out and see. How many you got?'

'Just over three thousand.'

He had a smile on his face. 'You know, that's the biggest mob of sheep anyone's seen around here for over a year. Shows you what can happen when there's decent feed around.'

Jack's smile broadened into a grin. His gaze scanned the sheep. 'Yeah,' he said. 'The mob looks good, doesn't it?'

I continued walking behind the sheep, leading Pitch, giving Jiff a direction now and then. Jack strolled beside me.

We walked on together.

'You like that horse?' he asked, after a while.

'I love this horse.'

'Good. So you should. Look after him.'

By now we were 150 yards from the ute. Jack put his hand on my arm and stopped me. We stood, facing each other. He smiled again. 'It's a good time to be alive, isn't it?'

I too smiled. 'Yep,' I said.

We looked at each other silently – then Jack turned and strode back to the ute. 'See you later,' he called.

'Yeah,' I said.

To give Pitch a rest, I walked on for another half-mile. Then I remounted and got ready to meet the other blokes in the corner with whatever they had, if anything.

The shearing team was a PLB (Pastoral Labour Bureau) team. A young wool classer named Mike was in charge. The expert was a small, older man, Don, quiet and reserved. The wool presser, Gordon, was a tall, strong bloke in his thirties. The reputations of the PLB teams were not as good as those of the private contractors, like Harry Finlay, whom I'd met at Landor. Harry and the other private contractors prided themselves on doing a good job. They depended on repeat business and word of mouth. They had strong personalities and kept their shearers and rouseabouts in line. Their teams stayed pretty much intact from season to season. This was much less the case with the PLB teams.

Poor Mike had his hands full with his team. They had him

bluffed when it came to the evening ration of beer. They were allowed one big brown a night. But that didn't stop them coming back to him two hours later and demanding another, insisting that they hadn't got one earlier.

'Well, on my list, it says you got one at six o'clock,' Mike said.

'Well, the fuckin list's wrong.'

'No.'

'I'm tellin yer it is. Gimme me fuckin bottle of beer.'

And Mike capitulated.

'What can I do?' Mike appealed to me later.

'Tell them to bugger off,' I said.

'What? And get a fistful in the face?'

He could not relate to the men in the team, so we spent most evenings together. For one thing, I knew the rudiments of wool classing, which gave us a common interest. Some evenings we watched what Don was doing. Don was an amateur entomologist. He went out into the night, some distance from the shearing shed, laid a sheet on a bare patch of ground and placed a Tilley lamp in the middle. Within seconds, insects appeared out of the night and bashed against the light. An hour later he returned, picked up the lamp, gathered up the sheet and bundled up all the insects that had gathered – most of them dead. He returned to the empty dining room and spread the sheet on a table. With a long-handled pair of tweezers, he sorted his catch. The pile was an inch and a half high in the middle and nine inches across. The range and variety was beyond anything I imagined it could be.

He sat at the table until after ten o'clock every night, the light glinting on his magnifying glass. He made meticulous notes. He kept a few samples, which he carefully pinned in little boxes, and threw out the rest.

Don rarely spoke. He worked alone. He put up with Mike and me for short periods, providing we didn't ask too many questions. It turned out that Don was renowned and, in fact, had discovered some previously unknown species that were named after him by the state museum.

Next morning, after the cook, he was the first one up. At 6.30 you'd hear the diesel engine thump-thump-thump into life and then settle into a steady thrumming. Don would be there in the engine room, sharpening the combs and cutters on the emery wheel, the sparks flashing off orange and red in the gloom. Then he distributed the newly sharpened tools in tins along the shearing board. At 7.15 the shearers arrived to oil their handpieces and fit the combs and cutters. They yarned. They lounged. They stretched. They flexed their backs and arms and wrists, and cracked their knuckles. They leaned over the gates into the pens and assessed the shearability of the sheep. At 7.29 they were ready for the bell. When it rang, the race was on. Sheep were dragged from the pen on their backsides. A front leg was tucked up under the shearer's left armpit. The rope was yanked, and the handpiece kicked into life and was snatched from the floor before it could jump around. With all eight stands in action it was exciting.

Every shearing team had a man in charge of the engine that drove the shearing plant, usually a Lister. He sharpened the combs and cutters. He was called the 'expert'. If the engine broke down, it had to be fixed quickly, so good experts devoted time to preventative maintenance. Don was a top expert. All the shearers respected him. Because of his quiet air of authority, no-one dared confront him. They depended on him. They didn't depend on Mike, though. His work didn't affect them directly. And he was too young, too lacking in experience and maturity to be respected.

A few mornings into the run, the shearers refused to start work. They called a meeting with Mike and complained about the pickles. There was always a cluster of sauce and pickle bottles on the dining room tables. But the pickles were not the brand they liked. There would be no shearing until the unacceptable pickles were replaced with the approved brand. Mike argued. The shearers stood their ground. Mike threatened. That made matters worse. Mike conceded defeat. He went to the homestead and spoke to Jack.

Jack fired up the ute and disappeared down the road to Meekatharra, thirty-eight miles away. Less than two hours later, he was back. He pulled up at the shearers' quarters. He picked up a carton of pickles from the back of the ute and placed it on a dining room table. The shearers gathered. One of the shearers cut the carton open. He withdrew a jar. It was the approved brand. He displayed it for all to see. One of the other shearers said, 'Are they all the same?'

'Of course they bloody are,' said Jack, with just enough edge in his tone.

'Can we get back to work now?' asked Mike.

The shearers shuffled off. Don was waiting in the engine room. He started the engine. The place hummed back to life again. The rouseabouts flung fleeces on the skirting tables. The rouseabouts threw the skirtings and the bellies in the right bins. The rouseabouts ran for the tar pot when it was called for. The rouseabouts were on the go all day. Mike methodically checked the fleeces and bundled them and threw them in the AAA or the AA or the BBB or the BB bins. Gordon, the wool presser, had gone to work at 7.30 as usual. The shearers being on strike for two or three hours gave him a chance to catch up some ground. Otherwise he'd be working long after the final bell that ended the day.

Like shearing, wool pressing is piece work, but unlike shearers, a wool presser is not bound by unionised working hours. For a presser, limited hours of work are not practical since a shed with, say, eight shearing stands, like Belele, produces more wool than a single presser can bale in an eight-hour day. Shearers are competitive with each other, so they must be constrained to the same working hours. A wool presser generally works alone – and works longer hours to keep pace with the shearers.

Three weeks of shearing at Belele and 23,000 sheep were shorn. The team moved on to the next shed.

When shearing was in full swing, I was based at the homestead. From there we rode out and fetched each day's requirements of sheep to be shorn from close-in paddocks, and then moved the shorn sheep to other nearby paddocks. There was a lot of time spent in the yards. We pushed the sheep through one holding yard after another and on up the ramp into the shearing shed. Inside the shed, we restocked the holding pens. Good yard dogs made the work easier. Some kelpies were adept at running across the backs of a tightly packed mob to bark at the ones in front when they baulked at a gate. Jiff didn't do that, but he was a great yard dog.

Some say mustering dogs are no good in the yards, and yard dogs are no good in the paddock. Some are better at one job or the other, but I believe good dogs can do both jobs. When it came to counting sheep, I preferred to have just Jiff working with me than any combination of blokes. To count a mob, we ran them from one yard to another and counted them as they ran or jumped through the gateway. The art lies in keeping the mob pointed at the gate – and Jiff was the master. He worked from the back, of course, but he continually came around the side to see how the front was going and to see if I wanted him to do something else. The last animal through the gate was always the black dog, wagging his tail and looking at me for further instructions. More often than not, the communication was a point with my chin or a tilt of my head. Jiff knew that meant go around there, or over here, or wherever. He knew exactly what was expected of him. He loved his work. If there was work to be done, Jiff was on his feet in an instant, eager to get moving. The relationship that can develop between a man and a dog when they both have work to do can be sublime.

Jack and Lindsay quite often had visitors. Occasionally, they were other station people. Mostly they came from Perth or the eastern states; sometimes they came from overseas. Usually, it was just a couple – husband and wife. Invariably, they knew nothing about station life or the outback. Shortly after shearing, a couple of friends of Ernest Lee-Steere's, a husband and wife, came for a week. I was introduced to them when we gathered in the living room for drinks before dinner.

It felt good to be freshly showered and shaved, wearing my best gabardine trousers, a woollen tie and a tweed sports coat. Jack introduced me. 'I'd like you to meet my nephew, Ian Parkes. He's the overseer here.'

The overseer? This was the first I'd heard of that. Since when was I upgraded from head stockman to overseer? Jack hadn't spoken to me about that. Was it a slip of the tongue? As the weeks rolled by, if it was necessary to identify my status to anyone, he continued to refer to me as the overseer. At no stage did we discuss it. He'd made a decision. He'd made me aware of it, in a backhanded way, and that was the end of it. So, I thought, I haven't yet turned twenty and I've done what my grandfather did – become overseer at nineteen. All right, you might say it was nepotism, but knowing Jack, I doubt it. He never cut me any slack. He gave me more and more responsibility and expected me to work it out for myself.

It was only in private that he let his guard down and showed me any feeling of affinity. The visit in Mungeltha, when he met me bringing in 3,000 sheep, was a particular moment. There were many others, such as when we discussed horses and men, alone together. And I felt there was an extra dimension to his support when I had my sorting out with Jackie Stevens. Otherwise, I could feel him appraising me when he looked at me. Jack wasn't much for explaining anything. I had to understand how he felt by the way he looked at me and by his tone.

When there were visitors, my position was to replenish drinks and let Jack have the floor. That wasn't hard to do, but it was difficult to dissemble when Jack started telling tall stories about station life. With a straight face, he could ramble on with outlandish stories that had elements of truth and just enough overall potential for credibility for someone to be taken in. It amused him.

Leg pulling was a common practice among station men. It was playful. It was a form of teasing. Ideally, the person whose leg was being pulled woke up in due course. Sometimes they didn't, and they repeated the story as gospel. Jack was a master of the art. His imagination was impressive.

Jack enjoyed shocking some people with a blunt, raw description or comment. It was always said in an offhand way that fell short of being offensive. He was in his element if he could tell a story that was rough on city-bred nerves – and stretch the truth somewhat.

The friends of Ernest Lee-Steere were especially susceptible. 'I've heard that dingoes are a big problem on sheep stations. Is that right, Mr Henderson?' asked the man.

'Not too big a problem here in the Murchison. But I once managed a station for the Lee-Steeres further north, in the Upper Gascoyne, where the dogs were a lot of trouble. The station was called Elliott Creek then. It's now called Wanna.'

'What exactly was the trouble? Do they only kill lambs? Or do they attack fully grown sheep?'

'They kill sheep. And they kill calves.'

'So why didn't you just go out and shoot all the dogs? Wouldn't that be the answer?'

'Wild dogs are cagey. They hear you coming from miles away, so they usually disappear into the bush. It's bloody rough country out there. They head into the hills and you can never find them. And they mostly hunt at night. The best way of getting them is poison baiting – oh, and trapping.'

'Poison and traps? Isn't that rather cruel?'

'Depends on your point of view. Dogs are not only cagey, they're tough bastards. I've seen front legs left in traps after the dogs have chewed them off.'

'Chewed their own leg off? Can they survive with only three legs?'

'Not for long.'

'Do they ever come near the homesteads?'

'Yeah. I've even seen a wild dog come in and mate one of the station dogs on the back veranda. I chased the bugger off, but you know what happened, the dog and the bitch were knotted. He was a bloody huge dog, and he dragged the poor little bitch halfway across the paddock until his dick came out, and then he bolted. That's how the Red Cloud breed of dogs got started, you know – kelpie bitches mating with wild dogs. That's why so many Red Clouds are yellow.'

The couple looked at each other. 'Amazing. That's so interesting, Mr Henderson. You can learn something every day, can't you?' the wife said.

'I think we should go to the dining room and have dinner,' Lindsay said.

Lindsay led the way, followed by the visitors. I held the living room door open. Jack winked at me as he went through. Everyone clustered on the veranda while they waited for me to get to the dining room door and hold that open. As they went in, I overheard the woman whisper to her husband, 'What did he mean about the dogs being knotted?'

Fencing contractors had been booked to start work on replacement fences, but the station had to supply the mulga fence posts and the star pickets. That meant we had to cut the posts and cart them to where they were needed. There were six of us in the post-cutting team and one of them was a bloke called Lofty. We worked in pairs and I worked with Lofty. We got started on a Wednesday, and on the Friday night all work stopped for the weekend. The following day, Meekatharra's October race meeting was on. In the morning, I drove the team into town and left them to it and took myself off to the races.

On Sunday, it was time for everyone to get back to the station and, at about two o'clock, I drove to the Railway Hotel and stopped outside. The pub was set a bit lower than street level, and hanging under the veranda there were cages with very colourful parrots. The Railway was known to all the locals as The Three Pees. This stood for parrots, prostitutes and piss. It was not a high-class hotel.

Outside in the wide street, people were loading cars and fetching runaway children for the long drive home. Separating one side of the street from the other, there was a strip down the middle with seats in which idle station hands waited for the Sunday afternoon session. The day was very warm, but inside the Railway it was cool. The green door at the front opened into a darkened lounge, which led to a passage. There was an office, where the licensee was counting money. He was a confident man, quick in his actions, with alert eyes. He was small but he had the sort of manner that would make you think twice before arguing with him. I asked him, 'Where will I find Lofty Stevens?'

'Number fifteen – if he's there.' He didn't look up.

I clomped off down the passage, my high-heeled boots making a hollow sound on the concrete floor.

The hotel was very old, probably one of the first in the Murchison. The low mud-brick walls had been whitewashed over and over until the paint peeled off in quarter-inch-thick flakes. At the end of the passage, I turned right for a few yards and then left. Halfway down this passage I found number fifteen. I knocked. There was a yell. 'Come in.'

I opened the door and peered into the gloom. In the opposite wall was a tall window, which was almost covered by a blind. There was a table under the sill and a bed on either side. On each bed a man was sitting, while another was squatting on the floor. It took a few seconds to see that Lofty was the man on the right-hand bed. 'Ready to come back to Belele?' I asked.

'Nah!'

'What do you mean, nah?'

'Let's wait a while and have a few drinks.'

'We're making tracks now, Lofty. We're going to be back at Belele for tea.'

Lofty's tone was indignant. 'What's the hurry? Let's stay for the session and go home after that.'

He swung his legs over the side of the bed and his gangling height was suddenly more pronounced. His long limbs were clothed in dirty khakis and his grimy bare feet made a scuffling noise as he rubbed his big toes together. He was thirty-odd – and slightly drunk. On the other bed, a middle-aged man wheezed and belched. He hadn't shaved for days – his face and chin and throat were covered in grey stubble. He smelled of stale beer and sweat. Or perhaps it was the room that smelled like that – there were empty beer bottles littered everywhere. Tobacco tins turned into ashtrays were buried under heaps of ash and butts. Old Westerns, beer glasses, matchboxes and newspapers were lying about on the floor and the table and the beds. The third man stood up and poured beer into a quart-pot mug. He grinned at his companions.

'This is Clarrie,' Lofty said. 'He's dumb. He can't talk, so don't worry if he never says nothin. You oughta seen him last night – he cleaned up two jokers and never even bruised his knuckles. Two blokes! Not bad, eh?'

Clarrie sucked his knuckles and looked eagerly at Lofty. He was almost bald, and his eyes were surrounded with smooth skin, not a wrinkle anywhere. He blinked incessantly. I wondered what it would be like to fight a man who had no voice. Would he grunt if he was hurt?

'That's George,' said Lofty, as the man on the bed on the left sat up with an effort and stretched a black-haired hand towards me. I stepped forward and took it and felt the stumps of two amputated fingers dig into my palm. His eyes were slits between puffed lids. He looked as if he'd been drunk for a week. 'How do?' he asked.

I returned to leaning against the doorjamb, thinking of the three days before the races, working with Lofty and the other men. Lofty was vociferous and temperamental, which was why I'd had him work with me – no-one else would put up with him. He talked about the managers he'd bluffed, the fights he'd won and the unfairness of a world that prevented him from getting his rights. He was underprivileged, underpaid, under appreciated. He vowed that one day he'd change the order of things. Even if he had to organise all the station hands in Australia from Cape York to Carnarvon, he'd pull them all out on strike. Even if he had to do it by himself, he'd see that justice was done to the long-suffering working classes.

In my experience of him, he was lazy and not dependable. The only way I could get him to put in a full day's work was to turn it into a competition. He fancied himself as a top man – and with an axe he was. I set the hottest pace I'd ever worked, and Lofty swung his sinewy arms fast enough to be in front of me at the end of each day. I couldn't care less that he bragged about being able to beat me.

'Lofty,' I said. 'I'm leaving in five minutes.'

Out of the blue, George said, 'You look just like my son,' and he fell back on the bed, making a terrible noise of sighing and clearing his throat. I waited for him to recover and lend his support to Lofty.

'Ah, come on, ave a beer,' Lofty pleaded.

Clarrie dragged the top from a bottle by holding it against the edge of the table and striking down on it. The beer frothed out and foamed over his hand. It dripped on the floor and then he quickly raised the bottle and drank several inches. He poured some in a glass and offered it to me. I waved it aside.

'No thanks. Look Lofty, we're not staying for more beer, session or no session. We're going back to Belele for tea.'

'Yeah, but there's a two-up school this arvo behind the bakehouse. I reckon I can win a few quid.'

'We're going now.'

I began to wonder how I was going to make that happen. It was getting to the point where I'd have to sack him – or use force. Use force? With Lofty? Lofty was a lot taller and stronger than I was. And Lofty with two sidekicks, especially the formidable Clarrie? My heart began to thump. My mind groped for a solution. Lofty reached for a glass and sloshed it full of warm beer. He was pointedly deliberate and purposeful. He drank the lot in one swallow. He cleared his throat and spat in a corner of the room. He looked at me disdainfully as he lay back on his bed, arms folded under his head.

'Lofty, are you coming?' I was starting to despair. The old, frayed curtains drifted into the room with a small puff of wind. The blind snapped. I waited, and I felt the anger rising from deep inside.

'Course he's goin.' The voice was George's. We all looked at him in surprise.

'Lofty,' said George, 'Ian's your boss, isn 'e?'

'Yeah.'

'He's a good bloke, isn 'e?'

'Mmm, yeah.'

'He's got a job to do – same as you.' George belched a long belch. 'He's got orders – and you're not makin it any easier for im.'

Lofty slowly sat up. He listened – and looked at the floor. Clarrie flicked his glance from one to the other. I waited.

'Do ya think Ian here wants to go back to work? Course he don't. Give im a go. He's got a job to do. You should help im out, on account of 'e's a good bloke.'

Lofty slowly bent over and dragged a small suitcase from under the bed. He said nothing. He slipped on a pair of greasy sandshoes. He tucked two bottles of beer under his arm and walked out the door. His face had a sour look. I remembered the rule of no grog on the station. I decided to let it slide. I was too grateful to George to worry about small details.

George stood. He proffered his hand. 'Good luck, boy,' he said. 'You do remind me of my son, you know. Only wish I had a picture I could show you.'

Suddenly, I felt very sorry for him. I shook his hand and said, 'What do you do?'

'Me? I work on the railway out to Nannine. I come up here to write a book twelve years ago and I haven't even started yet. The old booze has fair caught up with me. But I s'pose I'll write it one day.'

There was a silence. 'See you later,' he said.

I walked out of the Railway Hotel into the bright sunlight. Lofty was waiting, hunched, in the cab. Ten miles from town he was asleep. I drove along the rough, dusty road with a feeling of affection for the man who'd helped me in a way that I would never have imagined. Through the miles of quiet and loneliness, Lofty bounced and snored alongside me.

By the end of the following week, I was fed up with Lofty's high-handed, temperamental ways – and I sacked him.

21

New challenges

There had been a good winter season. Rainfall for the year was below average, but 80 per cent fell when it was most useful. The sheep were enjoying the benefit. So too were the cattle – they were in good condition. Jack decided it was time to bring them into the homestead stockyards for marking and to castrate the calves and the micky bulls. Because of the poor seasons, they hadn't been mustered for two years. I spent a few days at the homestead, getting ready. There were going to be eight of us in the camp. It was December. The days were hot, but the nights could still be cool.

After breakfast one morning, Lindsay took me aside and said she wanted to see me at morning smoko. That made me wary. The relationship I had with Lindsay was nothing like the rapport I had with Jack. With me, Lindsay kept a polite distance. It didn't help that she and my mother didn't get on.

It was a pleasant day, a good time to be outdoors. We met on the veranda. Lindsay was a very tall woman, trim and quite stern looking. She was always well groomed. She was a good stepmother to Penny and totally committed to Jack – somehow you were always aware that he was her property. Lindsay took her responsibilities as the wife of Belele's manager very seriously. She was respected and liked by the Aboriginal women who worked in the kitchen and the house, but the men, especially the white ones, were quite guarded with her.

She poured the tea. I waited. Then, with no preamble or change of tone, very smoothly, she said, 'Ian, I want you to understand that Belele is not big enough for the two of us.'

I sipped my tea – and reflected. I was surprised – yet, in a way, I was not surprised. The sentiment was unsurprising. It was just the delivery that was unexpected. What do I say to that? I thought. 'So, what are you suggesting?'

'You know exactly what I'm talking about, Ian.'

She sat still and observed me. She was composed and waiting – waiting for what? Waiting for me to agree? Surely not. Argue?

In the distance I heard the blokes banging things around on the mustering wagon. There was a burst of laughter from the women in the kitchen. The windmill creaked and slopped water. The crows in the white branches of the trees beside the vegetable garden croaked with that excoriating rasp that slowly softens and fades mournfully away.

Bugger you, I thought. Why should I tell you what I think? 'Mmmm,' I murmured. 'Well, Lindsay. Thank you for the tea. I think I'd better get back to work.'

I picked up my hat, placed it deliberately and carefully on my head and, taking my time, walked down to the stables as if nothing had happened. But something had happened. I was incredulous. One part of me was saying, what a joke. Another part was saying, Lindsay, you just don't understand the relationship that Jack and I have. Yet another part said, Lindsay, you are a fool: how could you take the risk that I might speak to Jack about this?

Of course, I didn't tell Jack. And Lindsay and I never returned to the subject of that conversation. We swept it under the carpet. But from that point forward, the relationship between Lindsay and me was a shade cooler. When our eyes met, there was challenge.

* * *

A week before the cattle muster, Jack told some of us that a station owner from southeast of Meekatharra had asked his advice about a difficult gelding. He was a thoroughbred, and the station owner had tried to race him in Perth. The problem was being able to keep a jockey on his back. So he brought him up to the station to educate him to stock work. That didn't work either, because no-one at the property could handle the horse. They changed his name to Tossum and wondered what to do. The owner told Jack, 'It would be a pity to shoot the bugger, because he is such a nice-looking horse.' Jack said he told the owner to bring the horse to Belele, where Ian would sort him out. Thanks, Jack, I thought.

Two days later, the owner arrived in his truck with the horse in the crate on the back. Everyone was curious and gathered around to meet the horse that was too hard for anyone to handle. Tossum stepped off the truck calmly and led easily into a yard. He was tall – a bit over 16 hands – but he looked taller because he wasn't carrying much condition. He wasn't skinny, just wiry looking and athletic. He was a pale bay, slightly yellowish – maybe he hadn't seen any good feed for a while. If he had an outlaw streak in him, he wasn't showing any sign of it.

The first time I rode him, I treated him with great respect. I put him in the round yard and brushed him all over and talked to him. He took the bridle and the saddle with barely a flick of an ear. When I eased onto his back, I set myself. Tossum shivered, like someone putting their foot in a cold bath, and he stood there. I put my heels in his ribs, and he offered me a few stiff-legged pig-roots – and that was all. I walked him round the yard, almost brushing the legs of the spectators sitting on the top rail waiting for a spectacle. They had plenty to say about their disappointment.

We had three days of sheep work before we went out to muster the cattle, and I rode him each day. After the first day, I began to take him for granted. He wasn't the bogeyman everyone said he was. But on the third day, as I put my toe in the stirrup, he reared and spun away, sending me sprawling on my backside in the dirt.

One of the men caught him and brought him back. When I mounted this time, I paid more attention to what I was doing. He thought about repeating the trick, but I had control of his head – and I was quicker slipping into the saddle.

Two days after finishing the sheep work, we were packed and ready for the cattle muster. We were heading out to Ebal paddock, on the west side of Yalgar paddock. We were to make camp at Nanular Bore. The mustering wagon was loaded and the two horses were harnessed and anxious to go. The driver was standing up, bracing himself to hold them. Six riders were mounted, ready and waiting, their horses jerking at the reins. The entire population of the homestead, adults and children, were gathered to watch the departure and wave goodbye. This included two families of part-Aboriginals, the Frasers and the Walleys. Doug Fraser and his son Mervyn were two that I later worked with. The crowd was sitting on the top rails of the yards; they were standing around talking; they were squatting, leaning up against the stockyard fence.

Everyone was waiting for me and Tossum. The bay thoroughbred with the reputation was a big attraction. I was aware that all eyes were on me, and I was feeling a bit cocky. Casually I put my foot in the stirrup and swung up. Before my backside was anywhere near the seat of the saddle, Tossum reared and jumped away to the right. He sent me flying as though I had been catapulted. I sailed through the air – backwards. I landed flat on my back, right up against the chook-yard fence. The chooks scattered, squawking and flapping their wings. My back was badly jarred and it hurt, but not as much as the humiliation. Obviously, I'd forgotten the lesson he'd taught me a few days before. As I got to my feet, I pretended I was OK. Someone brought Tossum back and I took the reins. Well, I thought, you're a cur, aren't you? An unpredictable, untrustworthy cur!

This time I shortened the reins to stop him swinging his head away. My stockwhip was in my right hand as it gripped the pommel when I mounted. Then I was on his back and seated and ready. Nothing happened. You bastard, I thought. If you want to buck, then buck. I doubled my stockwhip and wrapped it around his belly on each side – whack, whack. He humped his back and half-heartedly made two little props. He swung his head from side to side, and I could see the whites of his eyes. That's regained a bit of authority, I thought.

He didn't catch me unawares again, although he thought about it. From time to time he unexpectedly put in a few bucks when I asked him to canter, out in the middle of a muster. But he wasn't a serious buckjumper. His efforts at bucking were tame. I was puzzled why others found him hard to handle. He was by Manolive – and Manolive threw offspring that were sneaky and mean, no matter how good looking they were. And sneaky and mean was the worst I could say about Tossum at this point. He had a totally different temperament to Pitch and Mulba – and most other horses.

Out in the mustering camp, the effects of the fall at the homestead became apparent. Lying on my back on my stretcher, I couldn't sit up without putting a hand behind my neck to push myself up. I was in pain. I'd lost strength in the muscles in my back. Whenever I had a leak it came out white like milk. There was nothing I could do about it. We were committed to the cattle muster and I couldn't take time off. I was up at four, sending someone with a hurricane lamp to find the horses, while I kicked the fire into life and filled the biggest frying pan I'd ever seen with mutton chops for breakfast. By 5.00 or 5.30, we were in the saddle and on our way, picking up cattle tracks and splitting into pairs to find different mobs. We followed the tracks of a mob until we saw the ground chewed up by their hooves, with spatters of dung on trunks of trees. They usually smelled us before we saw them – and they cleared out. We galloped after them, hard on their heels, following the tracks until we caught up.

There were other times when it was quite different. Three or four micky bulls, up to two years old, might stand their ground, watching us from thick scrub. We saw them, facing us, with their ears pricked. They snorted, flicked their tails and struck at the ground. Before we could make up our minds what to do, they charged. They had horns nine inches long, and they were solid and sharp and potent, and they pointed straight ahead. Each bull weighed half as much again as a horse, and when such a beast galloped straight at me, it looked unstoppable. It *was* unstoppable. With its horns aimed directly at me and my horse, the adrenaline surged. We spurred our horses and evaded them. The bulls turned and came back at us. There was a wild mêlée, the dust swirling, the whips cracking, the riders swearing. Sometimes they closed right in alongside, bulls and horses twisting and turning, side by side, all mixed together. We belted them around the head with the whip handles, which had no effect. We frantically extricated ourselves and cracked our whips and yelled and turned them and made a mob of them. Our faces and arms were a dirty red, caked with sweat and dust. Our horses were heaving. The bulls were panting. As the bulls' aggressiveness subsided, we gradually got control. Reluctantly, they followed a rider, and we kept them together and we made our way to the yards.

At the end of the muster, we'd gathered the big mob of cows, steers, calves and mickies in the northwest corner, and we were moving them down the west fence. Two-thirds of the way down, we had to cross a creek, a tributary of the Yalgar River, way off to the east. There was a long pool of water, which was shallow at the fence end but deeper a hundred yards into the paddock. It was a much smaller version of Yalgar Pool.

The cattle stalled at the crossing. All eight of us were working to get them across when a micky bull peeled off and trotted east. The scrub was thick along the north bank of the creek and, further down from the fence, there was a six-foot drop from the top of the bank to the water. I cantered off on Tossum to work this bull back into the mob. He wouldn't turn – he kept diving past me, ignoring my stockwhip. In our close-combat struggle, we worked our way through the thickets, towards the creek bank, until Tossum and I were right on the edge, parallel to the creek. The bull changed tactics – he charged. I had nowhere to go. The scrub was too thick in front.

There was a six-foot drop on my left. There was no room to turn and no time to get out of the way. The bull dropped its head, and the horns slipped beneath Tossum's belly. The bull heaved with its head and shoulders and lifted Tossum and me into the air and over the bank and down into the water. The bull's momentum carried it on, and it too finished up in the water, on top of us. The creek was deep. We all went under and came up spluttering and dripping. I got back on Tossum, and he swam the few yards to where he found footing. Out on the sloping sandy shore on the south side, the bull made another decision. This time it decided enough was enough – and it meekly trotted back and rejoined the mob, which, by now, had crossed the creek. That little drenching took the sting out of the bull, I thought, and probably Tossum too.

When we packed up the camp for the whole entourage to move in to the homestead, all but one of the team went ahead with the cattle. I stayed back with young Joe Gilla to help bring the spare horses. Joe was a part-Aboriginal lad of about fourteen, and he was worth his weight in gold. As usual, the horses cleared out and Joe stretched out along his horse's neck as he raced to head them. I cantered sedately behind, conscious that Tossum was still young and lacking experience. Without any warning, Tossum dropped his head between his front legs and bucked, really bucked, for the first time. I slapped against the knee pads and bounced to the back of the saddle. I settled in to try to get control. He careered under low-slung mulgas. The branches whipped and whistled all around. I ducked my head this way and that. Tossum was out to get me one way or another. As I leaned far forward, the branches snatched at my shirt. Tossum threw his head back and smacked me in the face. Blood flew everywhere, and when my head stopped buzzing, I was boiling angry. I yanked the reins and pulled his head in and stopped him. I roared at him. And I whacked him with the doubled-up stockwhip. I was so angry, I was shaking. After that I didn't have another problem with him – and I got to like him. He was fast. He was clever. He was handsome. And now we had an understanding.

For one thing, he taught me not to make assumptions about unpredictable horses.

Back at the homestead yards, we branded and cut the bulls and the calves. Some of the old steers were so tall I couldn't see over their withers. With that job done, I was still in pain from my fall and still urinating white. Jack drove me to Meekatharra to the doctor, who diagnosed the problem as bruised kidneys. The doctor prescribed tablets and a week off work. Jack's idea of a week off was to send me out to work with a part-Aboriginal fellow whose name was Henry Lefroy. He was out in the bush with his wife erecting a windmill. Henry was a top man, very honest, very professional. He was my boss for this job and his instructions were clear and concise. And he had a good, relaxed sense of humour. My time with him and his wife was enjoyable, though I was glad to get back to the homestead and the real action on the station.

When Jack decided I was recovered, he sent me out with the team to move the stock out of Danthroobubba into Woombada. My team was Frank, Tony and Andy. Andy was one of the three young blokes Jack hired just before shearing. Woombada was mostly watercourse flats and Jack reckoned the feed was stronger there. We rode out from the homestead and headed for the southwest corner of Danthroobubba. It was about an eight-mile ride. Mervyn Fraser was to bring our swags and camping gear out in the truck and leave them at Danthroobubba Well.

Two days later, we had completed the muster and the sheep were all in Woombada. Sitting around the fire, drinking tea, Tony said, 'Why don't we get in the truck and shoot a few roos?'

That was a popular idea, so I agreed, even though I knew Jack would disapprove. His view was that we were in the mustering camp to work, not play around with guns and shooting. Andy was especially keen. He had a sawn-off .22 he could handle like a pistol, and he was dead keen to use it. We decided to drive down the track beside the west fence and intercept the roos that might be coming to the well to water. Sure enough, the headlights of the truck picked up five. They immediately turned tail and headed back the way they'd come. Without having a clear-cut plan, I gunned the truck and raced after them.

Andy was sitting beside me in the cab, with his fancy .22 in his lap. The other two were on the back, ready to lean on the roof of the cab to brace their rifles when it came time to shoot. Knowing how trigger-happy they were, I told them it was no use trying to shoot while the roos were hopping and the truck was bouncing along the rough track. I thought that maybe the roos would stop when they reached the south fence and, if we were close enough and quick enough, I would stop the truck to give the boys a clear shot. But while I was thinking this and concentrating on my driving, Andy's gun went off. I thought, you silly bastard. Why are you shooting now? Fifty yards further down the track, Andy said, 'Ian, can you stop the truck? I've just shot myself. I want to have a look in the headlights.'

I left the engine running and we went round to the front. Andy undid his belt and dropped his trousers. There was a dark blue, small round wound on the inside of his left thigh and another on the outside of his thigh. The bullet had gone straight through and then punched a hole through the door. Fortunately, it missed the femur. The gun had been in his right hand, resting on his right thigh, loaded and cocked and ready to use – and with his finger on the trigger. When the truck went over a bump, Andy involuntarily squeezed the trigger. Now we were in a pickle. Jack would be livid when he found out – if he found out.

We suddenly lost interest in shooting roos. We went straight back to the camp. We boiled water and laced it with Condy's crystals. Andy bathed the wounds while we all sat around wondering what to do next. Our main priority was to keep the whole incident under wraps. Hopefully Andy's wound would heal and no-one would be any the wiser. If only it had been that simple.

The next day we packed up the camp and Mervyn drove our gear back to the homestead while we rode in. Over the next few days, Andy's wound became increasingly painful. After four days, his thigh opened up along the path of the bullet. He now had a wound that was three inches long – and it looked bad. Obviously, medical treatment was needed. That meant Jack had to be made aware, so Andy could be taken to the doctor in Meekatharra. There was no mention of the roo-shooting expedition. Accidents like this can happen just sitting round the campfire. They can, can't they? After all, Bill Moxham nearly shot me when we were cleaning our guns at Winnininnie.

22

Over the horizon
and out of sight

In early January 1955, we received four inches of rain in three days. The land was like blotting paper, and then the soaked country opened its heart and produced beautiful, lush grasses. At the same time, there was plenty of runoff water that flooded the watercourses and filled the pools. Jack was excited. 'As soon as the roads are driveable, you're going to Wurarga, the other side of Yalgoo. You're gunna muster the sheep we've got there on agistment,' he announced.

One week later we were on our way. Before we left, we could see why he was so enthusiastic – the grasses were already bursting through. There was another reason I was enthusiastic. Wurarga was about 260 miles from Belele, and we would be there for at least a fortnight. So far from home – out of sight and out of mind, or so I imagined.

The sheep were agisted on two stations – Barnong and Gabyon. They were in paddocks close to Wurarga, which was a railway siding with a tiny pub. My team was Frank and Tony and Gil, and we were to drive down in Belele's Commer truck, just like the one at Mount Augustus. I was to phone the owner of Barnong, find out where to camp and be ready to collect our horses when they arrived at Wurarga in a railway cattle truck.

When we left Belele, we took the forty-mile short cut that bypassed Meekatharra. This was a station track along the Hope River watercourse, through Annean Station and then out onto the Great Northern Highway, at which point we turned right and headed southwest. About ten miles to our left, up the highway, were the remnants of the Nannine mining town site, in a corner of one of Annean's paddocks. All that remained was a tiny post office, a railway siding and a handful of pensioners. Nannine was to be a staging post for getting the agisted sheep back to Belele.

We were to send the sheep from Wurarga by train, in several shipments. Jack had arranged for Jim Evans, the manager of Annean, to unload them and let them go in the paddock. Later, we were to come back, muster them and drove them to Belele.

Our route took us through Tuckanarra, Cue, Lake Austin, Mount Magnet and Yalgoo. There was one bloke in the cab with me and the other two were on the back. It was a long drive. We were curious about the places we were passing through and we had that feeling of having been let off the chain.

The day was over a hundred degrees and we were thirsty. It was mid-morning when we stopped at Tuckanarra to test their beer. The highway ran parallel with the railway line, and on the other side of that there was a side road where there was the pub and a short string of fettlers' cottages. The beer was cold. The bar was cool. We had a few quid in our pockets. Life was pretty good. There were just the four of us in the bar, enjoying ourselves, when the door opened and a tall, middle-aged, grey-haired, part-Aboriginal man walked in. He had an air about him that was a curious combination of authority and diffidence. He carried himself with dignity, and he addressed us with an attitude that suggested he'd known better men than us. He wasn't arrogant, but I couldn't help getting the feeling that he saw us as being beneath him. Maybe it was his age and his depth of experience. He passed the time of day with us and introduced himself. After a period of talking about nothing of consequence, he got to the point of his intrusion. 'I've got a daughter over in one of the cottages. Are yers interested?'

I didn't understand what he was getting at. 'Interested? In your daughter?' I asked.

'Yeah, young blokes like you – been out bush a long time – been a bit lonely, eh?'

There were quick glances among the four of us. We didn't know what to say.

'Come on. Come an ave a look,' he said.

Gil looked at me and said, 'Whaddaya reckon? I reckon we should at least have a look.'

We finished our beers and the man led us out across the road and over to the line of cottages. We passed three and stopped at the second last. There was an enclosed veranda. He opened the door and held it for us. We went in. There was a pleasant-looking teenage girl sitting on the edge of an iron bedstead, with a grubby mattress and a dirty grey blanket.

'Whaddaya think?' he asked. 'It'll only cost yer ten bob each.'

At that point I'd seen and heard all I needed. 'Come on, you blokes,' I said. 'I'm going. And you're comin with me, unless you want to walk to Wurarga.'

I brushed past the old man on my way out. I was embarrassed. And I was annoyed, although, at the time, I couldn't say exactly why. I couldn't look at him. He started to say something. I ignored him. I kept walking. The other three followed me. We went back to the truck and continued on to Cue, where we stopped at the famous Cue Hotel and had a few more beers and reflected on the incident at Tuckanarra.

At Mount Magnet we turned off the Great Northern Highway and headed west along the Geraldton–Mount Magnet Road. Late in the afternoon we arrived at Wurarga. It was just a place where trains could drop off and collect railway trucks. But it was to be our base – for one thing it was the only place where I could get phone contact with Jack. Jack, on the other hand, would sometimes send a message through the owner of Barnong. The message was usually, for Christ's sake, get on the phone and tell me what's happening.

By now we were hungry, and the pub had rare delicacies to offer, like tinned herrings in tomato sauce and tinned peaches and tinned cream. We opened the tins with our pocket knives, and we leaned on the bar and ate from the tins with our knives, and we drank beer. Then I remembered I had to phone the owner of Barnong. He gave us directions, and, reluctantly, we left the pub and drove for about five or six miles on a bush track that led to a windmill at the bottom of a hill. We arrived just as the last of the light disappeared.

When we woke in the morning, one look around was enough to make all of us despondent. The country was totally different from the top end of the Murchison. The windmill was in an open area, but beyond the perimeter, the scrub was thick and the visibility nonexistent.

'How the fuck are we gunna muster in this country?' said Frank. 'Yer can't ride a horse through this shit.'

'Right now, I dunno what we're going to do. But I'll work it out,' I said.

We drove back to Wurarga and found out the horses were due to arrive that afternoon. I phoned the owner of Barnong and he offered to come to see us at the mill.

Two hours later he turned up. We made a billy of tea and he explained. 'Generally we trap the sheep at the mills. But there was a big fire through here last summer and it burned out large acreages of country. With the winter rains, there's been some herbage and the sheep often graze in the open. Shouldn't be too hard for you.'

I was dubious.

After lunch, we went back to Wurarga. The horses hadn't arrived. We whiled away the time in the bar, yarning with the publican. About four o'clock the train slowly pulled in, and the railway truck with our horses was uncoupled and placed on a side track alongside a ramp. Frank, Tony and Gil saddled their horses and, leading mine, rode out to the camp, while I drove back in the truck.

In the morning we went out to see what the owner had told us about. On the west side of the clearing round the windmill, the scrub was thinner than elsewhere. We rode through at that point and, after five minutes, suddenly found ourselves in a desolate, vast open space with blackened tree stumps, tangles of blackened branches on the ground and a meagre veil of green across the soft, sandy land. In the distance, a mob of sheep, dark grey from constantly brushing against charcoal-black tree trunks, was grazing quietly. We rode out into the open towards them. The moment they saw us they bolted. They dived straight into the unburnt scrub and vanished.

'Shit,' said Gil. 'This's gunna be lovely.'

We tried riding through the thick scrub. Sometimes we could, but we could never go in a straight line. We had to detour around obstacles – fallen dead trees and groups of trees with branches so low that only the sheep could get through underneath. We could not muster the way we did in the Upper Murchison. New tactics were needed. Our main technique was to patrol the wide, open, burnt areas. When we saw sheep, we rode flat out to cut them off before they could escape into the scrub.

The fence lines were a big help. The land was cleared three or four yards on each side, partly to make erecting the fence possible, partly to provide dirt tracks for vehicles. We chased the sheep through the scrub to a fence line, which blocked them. Dogs were invaluable, but we had only one, and that was Jiff. We moved the sheep along the track but, inevitably, the mob spread into the scrub. One or two horsemen, yelling and swearing, crashed through the bushes and prevented the sheep from spreading too far.

The timing for ordering the shipments was critical. Having nothing to feed the sheep, we could not confine them in the holding yards for more than a day, followed by another feedless day and a night on the train. The starting point was when the goods trains were running – and they didn't run every day. The availability of trucks was not a problem, because we'd ordered sufficient to ship at least 2,500 head. The trucks sat at the siding on a side track, and we had to push however many we needed to the loading ramp – which we did by hand. To get a truck moving, we used a crowbar and jammed it between one of the steel wheels and the steel track and levered it until it moved. Once it moved a little, the four of us put our backs into the truck and usually kept it going until it was in position. Stopping it was another issue. Handling the railway trucks took a huge amount of effort. It was tough on our leg muscles, especially our thighs. Fortunately, the Wurarga pub was only a few yards away.

On the fourth day, we were finding small mobs of sheep in different places. We split up but I had a good idea of where the other three riders were. I caught glimpses of them occasionally. Then I lost track of Frank. In the afternoon, Tony and Gil and I came together, each of us with a small mob, which we combined. None of us had seen any sign of Frank. We put the sheep in the holding yards and rode back to the camp. Frank was already there, lying on his stretcher, with his boots off, smoking. I unsaddled my horse and I went over to him. He looked at me from where he was lying and drew on his cigarette. 'How long have you been here?' I asked.

'A while.'

'How long?'

'A few hours.'

'Why the fuck did you stop mustering?'

'I'm sick of it. I hate this fuckin country.'

'You bastard! You can't stop work, just like that.'

'Pig's arse! I'll stop when I feel like it.'

I bent down, grabbed the edge of his stretcher, heaved it up and tossed him on the ground. At the same time, I said, 'Don't give me that bullshit. I'm gunna teach you a lesson.'

Before I could lay a hand on him, he leaped up and raced off, barefooted, into the scrub. I was fuming, but I wasn't going to chase after him. Tony and Gil stood there, wide-eyed, not saying a word.

'Well, come on, you blokes. Get the bloody fire going,' I said. 'You feed the horses, Gil. I'll start getting dinner ready.'

They stayed silent for an hour or so. By then I'd simmered down. 'What about Frank?' Tony asked.

'What about him?'

'Well, where is he? What about his dinner?'

'I don't bloody well know – and I don't bloody well care.'

I lay in my swag and wondered when Frank would come back. He had no boots or coat – and the night was cold. There was no point in trying to look for him. There were thousands of acres of thick scrub and he could have gone in any direction. I doubted that he'd be silly enough to get lost.

At first light next day, I raised my head and looked in the direction of Frank's stretcher. It was still on its side, his swag on the ground. I got the fire going and put the billy on. 'Tony,' I said. 'I want you to feed the horses, and then you and I are going in to Wurarga to see if Frank is there. You stay here and mind the camp, Gil. And tell Frank where we've gone – if he shows up, that is.'

Tony and I drove in to Wurarga. It was too early for the pub to be open. There was no sign of him outside. 'Let's go to the siding,' I said.

The siding was a small weatherboard shed, open on the side facing the railway line. It was painted cream and it had a corrugated-iron roof. It had slatted wooden benches around the walls, where people could sit while they waited for the train. I walked into the shed and there he was, hunched up on one of the benches. He cowered when he saw me.

'Come on,' I said. 'Get in the truck and I'll take you back to the camp.'

'Only if you promise not to hit me.'

'Oh, for Christ's sake, Frank. You'd moan if a shithouse fell on you. We're here to do a job. Let's get on with it. We can't get the job done if you're gunna play silly buggers.'

With his bare feet, he walked gingerly across the gravel and got into the truck, and we went back to the camp. We ate breakfast and went back to finding and mustering the sheep. Frank pulled his weight from then on.

The whole exercise of mustering and dispatching the sheep tested my ability to coordinate. I had to juggle the booking of the train with having sufficient sheep to ship. We did it in three bites. After that it was time to celebrate. We were frustrated with the country and we were fed up with fighting our way through blackened tree trunks and branches. Our clothes were filthy and so were we. By now, we were bored with Wurarga. We'd heard about the pub at Pindar, thirty-odd miles down the Geraldton–Mount Magnet Road. We'd heard it was a one-horse town, and when we got there, we thought that was an exaggeration. Still, the Pindar pub was a double-storey building, which gave it a presence in the flat, empty landscape. As at Tuckanarra, the pub wasn't right on the main road. The main road ran beside the railway line and there was a crossing over the railway line to another road that ran parallel. The pub was readily seen from the main road and it was a magnet for us.

We swung right over the railway crossing, then right again to the pub. Like you do at most outback places, we pulled up, nose to the kerb, at a slight angle. We sauntered into the bar. There were three other blokes, perched on stools. The barman recited the usual welcome. 'Gidday, boys. What'll you ave?'

What'll we have? Beer, of course.

Oh, were we pleased with ourselves! We'd mustered 1,500 sheep in godforsaken country and we'd manhandled bloody great railway trucks and we'd shipped the whole lot off and Jack had to be impressed with us. Our next move was to Gabyon. But before that, we were going to reward ourselves and find the inspiration to tackle the new challenge. 'Four schooners of beer, mate,' I said. And the four of us breasted the bar and leaned on our elbows and looked around. There were shelves on the wall behind the bar and they were laden with bottles of exotic liqueur. The most prominent was Vok's complete range of the stuff they drank in Europe.

We introduced ourselves to the other drinkers. They brought us up to date with the news. This meant what was happening with the cricket – the Poms were in Australia for the summer, current wool prices, and feed conditions in the various parts of the country. We shared jokes. We shared yarns.

We were not drinking hard. Just quietly drinking and taking our time. After a while, Tony left to go to the dunny. He'd been gone about twenty minutes when Gil started to nod off and, in slow motion, his legs folded beneath him and he slid down the front of the bar and stretched out on the floor. I looked down at him and I said, 'We can't leave the bugger there like that. Give me a hand, you blokes. Somebody grab his legs and we'll put him on that iron bed out in the passage.'

Somebody got off a stool and helped me. We dumped him on the bed, and we stood back and admired him. He was out cold, lying on his back with his mouth open. 'Tell yer what,' I said. 'Let's make it interesting for him when he wakes up. Grab the end of the bed and we'll take him out and leave him in the road.'

We did that, and we thought he looked very peaceful, lying on the bed, out in the sun in the middle of the road. He was quite safe. There was next to no chance he'd get run over – not in Pindar. When I went back in the bar, there was still no sign of Tony, so I went looking. My first port of call was the dunny – and that's where I found him. I opened the sit-down dunny door and there he was, slouched on the can, trousers down around his ankles, sound asleep, with his mouth open. I thought he too looked peaceful, so I left him.

Back in the bar, after two more drinks, Frank called it a day, and he too passed out. Bugger this, I thought, I'm not going to make him comfortable too. I got one of the other drinkers to give me a hand, and we lugged him out and threw him on the back of the Commer. The tray bounced up and down and the truck rocked a couple of times but Frank didn't feel a thing.

I was still in pretty good shape, and I wasn't ready to pack up and leave – not yet, anyway. The Vok liqueurs caught my eye and I asked the barman to tell me about them. He grabbed a bottle of yellow stuff and said, 'This is advocaat. It's a Dutch drink. It's made from eggs.'

'Since we haven't had any lunch,' I said, 'the eggs might do me good.'

The barman poured me a shot. 'Actually,' he said, 'advocaat and cherry brandy mixed together is the real go.'

'I'll try this first,' I said.

I downed the drink and waited for something to develop. There was no effect. 'Better give me another,' I said. 'But no cherry brandy.'

I sipped this one. It was quite tasty, like drinking sweet custard. I looked around the bar. I saw the time on the clock. If I was feeling a little groggy before the advocaat, I was feeling stone-cold sober now. 'Is this stuff supposed to sober you up?' I asked the barman.

'Well, the Dutch reckon it does,' he said. 'The Dutch are world champions at drinking beer and they finish off with advocaat. Except, they add the cherry brandy.'

'Bugger the cherry brandy,' I said. 'Look at the time. We've gotta get back to the camp. Give me a hand to get my blokes in the truck.'

The barman came out from behind the bar. He was a burly bloke and it was easy to chuck Gil on the back with Frank. We brought the bed inside and went out the back to the dunny. We gathered up Tony and packed him in the front of the Commer. Then I drove the thirty-odd miles back to the camp at the windmill. When we got there, I woke the three of them enough to stagger to their swags.

Next morning, we packed the truck, and Frank and Gil saddled up to take the horses. Tony went with me in the truck. We said our goodbyes to our Barnong camp site, hoping we'd never have to return. On the way through Wurarga, I phoned the Gabyon manager to tell him we were heading in his direction. He said he'd meet us at Black Tank Well, where we were to camp.

The scrub in this part of Gabyon seemed even thicker than at Barnong – but there were no burnt-out areas. Trapping was standard practice. About forty or fifty yards out from every windmill and the trough, a brush fence was built in an arc from one paddock fence to the next. The area inside was clear; no doubt the scrub had been cut down to make the brush fence. In the middle of the brush fence, there was a ramp on either side to enable the sheep to get to the water – and get out again. Trapping was simple: remove the inside ramp. Sheep coming to water were used to walking up the outside ramp, and, with the inside ramp removed, they jumped off and into the enclosure.

If trapping was the easy part, managing the mob once they were released from the enclosure was the hard part. The sheep were usually keen to race off into the scrub. It took us three days to get all the sheep we could find – 1,023. We drove them to the siding and dispatched them to Nannine.

After that, we felt we'd earned a decent feed. The nearest town was Yalgoo, and Yalgoo did not have much going for it. We decided to head for Mullewa, a further eighteen miles on from Pindar, making it a fifty-odd-mile drive all up. Mullewa was in farming country and had more facilities than Yalgoo. Heading out from Geraldton, it was the last stop before you entered the outback.

We got there in plenty of time for lunch at a café. We stuffed ourselves with grilled steak, onions, chips, salad and thick slices of bread smothered with butter. We felt a bit conspicuous: outback stockmen in a wheat-belt town, in our moleskins, high-heeled boots and broad-brimmed hats. Our success in mustering the sheep and sending them away on the trains gave us reason to swagger. We finished the food and leaned back in our chairs and cheeked the waitress. The other blokes made a show of rolling cigarettes one-handed and lighting them with wax matches struck on the soles of their boots. Our talk was a little too loud and we laughed a little too often. Eventually, we got tired of showing off. We paid the bill and clomped out to the truck. We felt pretty happy and carefree. In the mood of the moment, the four of us were all best mates.

The next morning we packed up and drove back to Belele. It was now early February and we had been away a bit over two weeks.

Later, in March, Gabyon Station was about to start shearing, and Jack shunted me back there to pick out whatever Belele sheep had been left behind when we mustered. Small numbers get missed, especially in the country around Yalgoo. Some sheep get through fences into neighbouring paddocks. As the sheep were assembled at the shearing shed, they were sorted by age or by sex, by running them through a drafting race. When sheep were brought in from areas adjacent to where the Belele sheep had been agisted, my job was to stand beside the bloke working the gates and claim the ones with Belele ear markings.

The sheep were funnelled in one end of the race, and at the other end, there were two gates, which pointed in to the race. This provided three options for drafting: push both gates to the right and the sheep had to go into a holding yard on the left; push both to the left and the sheep had to go to a yard on the right; or push the left gate to the left and the right gate to the right and the sheep had to go straight through the middle.

I've seen drafting races that had three gates, but you had to be pretty slick to manage those. The bloke on the handles had to be quick to direct the traffic one way or another. Generally, the sheep came through the race at a run. My old notebook records that by 17 March 1955, I had picked out a total of twenty-seven sheep. I wondered if it was really worth it. Jack thought it was. At least he was satisfied to learn that that was probably all we'd missed.

Yard work was usually first thing in the morning or at the end of the day. For the rest of the day I struggled with boredom. I hung around the shearing shed, ready to help out if someone needed a hand. It was no good sitting around twiddling my thumbs while I waited for the next batch. The Gabyon manager was happy to have me to help in the yards and around the shed.

Even though the shearing took three weeks, I was there for only a week. There was no point my being there when they brought in sheep from paddocks far from where the Belele sheep had been. And one week was more than enough for me. The shearing shed and the shearers' quarters were close to the homestead. Between the two, there was a machinery shed, which had a room sectioned off at one end that I could use. I ate with the Gabyon station people. After the first night, I was invited to join the shearing team for a yarn and a beer. Not having any beer of my own, I declined to drink theirs, because I couldn't return the favour. But I sat around and joined in the talk.

Three of the shearers were older men. They were good shearers and responsible blokes. They had families to support. They stayed sober. One of them, a bloke called Murray, raced motorbikes with sidecars at Claremont Speedway when he wasn't out bush shearing. He was big for a shearer, but he was the gun. He was the one who all the other shearers looked up to. The rest of the shearers were young – and two of them were wild. These two drank to the point where they could hardly stand up – and then they started looking for trouble. Shades of Bill Moxham, I thought; I'll try to keep out of their way. But I was too conspicuous – I was an outsider. Being a stockman and not a shearer, I was a lower class of human being.

One of these blokes, Curly, a little older than me, had short-cropped blond hair, which was why they called him Curly. He was muscular and strong and, in his blue shearer's singlet, his physique showed. When it came to being pugilistic, this bloke was in a different league from my Winnininnie mate. Unlike Bill, this bloke got dirty, really dirty. He confronted me: 'I'll betcha not a member of the AWU.'

I tried to avoid answering, because I knew it wouldn't stop there. He was persistent. 'Come on, fuck yer, answer me.'

'No, I'm not,' I had to say.

'No what?'

'No, I'm not a member of the AWU.'

He looked at me in disgust. 'What a bloody maggot.'

I shifted to the other end of the veranda to talk with Murray. Five minutes later, Curly staggered up to where I was leaning against a post. He thumped me in the chest with the base of his right hand and challenged me to fight him. 'I don't want to fight you,' I said lamely.

'Fuck you. You'll fight when I fuckin tell you to fight.'

'No. I've got no reason to fight you.'

'Listen, you maggot, I'll fuckin give you a reason.'

He turned and walked a few yards down the veranda. He picked up an empty beer bottle by the neck. He broke the base off by cracking it against the edge of the veranda floor. He turned back to me and thrust the jagged end in my face. 'If yer don't fuckin fight, I'll jam this bottle straight in yer fuckin face. Then yer'll fight.'

It was something to think about. Would he really do that? Or was it just show? I didn't budge. I didn't take my eyes off Curly's eyes. Curly glared at me, swaying, his anger rising. I'd better do something quick, I thought, before it's too late. The jagged end of the bottle was waving inches from my eyes. I stepped quickly off the veranda and backed away, watching Curly and the bottle. He started to come after me. I kept backing away, increasing the distance between us. Then Murray, who hadn't moved from his chair, said, 'Drop it, Curly. Just drop it. You're a fuckin pain in the arse. So drop it.'

Curly started to argue. Murray raised his voice. 'Sit down and shut up. If you don't settle down, I'll deal with you. I'm sick of your bullshit.'

After a few steps of retreating backwards, I turned and walked to my room. Curly yelled abuse at me from afar. 'I'll fuckin get yer later, you prick.'

The next evening, I stayed in my room and read. At about eight o'clock, I heard shouting at the shearers' quarters. I stepped outside.

There was a commotion on the veranda. It was a scuffle between three or four blokes. Two were going hard at it. From where I was, I couldn't tell if Curly was one of them. I thought it was odds-on he was. Back in my room, I closed and locked the door.

For the rest of my time at Gabyon, I avoided the shearers' quarters at night. During the day, there were no problems. Curly and I passed each other several times, going to and from the shearing shed. We looked each other in the eye and said 'Gidday' and 'How y'goin,' and it was as if the incident with the bottle had never occurred.

23

Back to Belele

When we returned from mustering the agisted stock at Barnong and Gabyon, I drove in to the homestead at Belele just before sunset, with a feeling of relief: it was so good to be back on home territory. And good to be back where I could soak myself under a hot shower, where I could luxuriate in a real bed in my own room, where I could sit at a table and eat good meals, with vegetables. Not having to cook the food myself and then chase blokes to clean the dishes and the pots and pans felt very civilised. The euphoria lasted a whole twelve hours.

At breakfast the next morning, Jack said, 'Now I want you to bring the agisted sheep back from Nannine. You'll take your gear on the mustering wagon and camp one night on the way over. It'll take as long as it takes to bring the stock back, so grab sufficient rolls of Ringlock and steel posts to build a fence around the mob at night. You can get going today.'

Today? Oh, shit! Righto! Can't wait to tell the boys. They'll all say, 'Whoopee.' We've only been out in mustering camps for six months. It'll be good to be back in the bush again. They'll love me. Yeah.

'OK,' I said despondently. Then I brightened up. 'If Pitch is in the horse paddock, I'll take him. I've missed that horse.'

Pitch was the best horse on the station, just edging out Mulba. He was well bred. He was solid. He had a kind eye – big and brown and soft. And he was a mighty walker. He could throw in a buck occasionally. The only time he ever beat me was when I hopped on, bareback, to chase some horses into the camp, and he put his head down and sent me sprawling on the biggest and roughest quartz outcrop on the station. I didn't lose him, because I kept hold of the reins. For two miles of trotting and cantering, Pitch pulled like a train. He worked his head lower and lower, inch by inch, as he gathered himself to let me have it again. I tightened my grip with my legs and wrenched his head up with all my strength, and we stayed together until we caught up with the other horses at the mill. I loved him. He was so full of life – not a nasty bone in his body.

We left just after lunch and we got as far as Minniearra Well, about fifteen miles from the homestead. At Minniearra there were brush yards where we could hold the horses overnight. The next day we arrived at the windmill where we were to camp. It was on a fence line about two miles from Nannine.

Nannine had been a famous mining town in the early 1900s, when its population peaked at around 3,000. It had breweries, a newspaper and a railway station, and you could still see where the streets had been laid out in a grid. A few lonely stone fireplaces were all that remained on the outskirts, but when we were there, the post office was still active and there were several old prospectors, surviving on the pension, each with his own camp on an abandoned mine site. Fresh supplies of food were delivered by train once a week.

After we made camp, we rode in to the remains of the town and met a couple of the old prospectors and the family running the post office. It was a Saturday and they were listening to the wireless commentary of a football match in Perth. It was incongruous – a lonely, windswept, desolate, barren part of the world and there were four people huddled around the radio inside, listening to frantic, overexcited commentators.

Around Nannine the country was open and the vegetation was sparse. The visibility was excellent. What a contrast to Barnong and Gabyon. Even though the paddock was about four miles by four miles, we could see we would be able to muster all the sheep in less than a day. We gathered up the 2,500 ewes. Our timing couldn't have been worse. The ewes were dropping lambs and the mob was growing. And, of course, the lambing would slow us down.

We had the mob at the top fence, ready to push them through the gate and start the trek. Jim Evans, the manager of Annean, arrived on his motorbike to take me for a check of the far corners of the paddock to make sure we had left no stragglers. It took us an hour to skirt the perimeter and crisscross through the watercourses, where the scrub was thickest. We were relieved to see that the paddock was clean. When I got back to the mob, the blokes were sitting around, smoking. The sheep were standing and lying – waiting. Jiff was lying under Pitch's belly.

'That bloody dog of yours is pretty good,' Gil said.

That puzzled me. No-one was allowed to work my dog. I didn't think he'd work for them, anyway. 'What do you mean?' I asked.

'Well, while you were out on the motorbike, the mob started to break up, and we called Jiff. "Git away back, Jiff," we called. We whistled the way you do, and you know what? He dropped his head and wouldn't look at us. He went over and lay under Pitch. And we couldn't get the bugger to move, no matter how hard we tried.'

All three of them were grinning. Tony said, 'Yeah, a bloody one-man dog. And that's bloody good, isn't it?'

'Yeah, I hope you're happy now,' I said sarcastically.

'Yeah, I am,' said Gil. 'I reckon it's good he's like that.'

Good on yer, Jiff, I thought.

We opened the gate and ran the sheep through and headed them towards Belele. It was difficult to stop them from spreading too wide. These sheep hadn't seen lush grass like this for months. The feed at Barnong and Gabyon was almost eaten out. Then they'd been locked in yards and they'd been crammed in railway trucks, and all they wanted was for us to open the gate and let them eat. We got about a mile down the track and called it quits. We bunched the mob, all 2,500 ewes plus the growing number of lambs, and hastily erected the Ringlock yard before they walked away. They'd had no water, but our priority was to keep the mob together.

When we let them go at six the next morning, they spread out and went west. Each stockman had a dog, and by 1.30 all the dogs were knocked up and refused to work any more. By then we had managed to assemble the mob again, but we hadn't made any progress towards Belele. From then until after dark, we covered about two miles. Fortunately, sheep tend to stick together at night, and I left the blokes to hold the mob while I cantered through the moonlight to the camp at Cement Tank Well, where Tony was waiting for us, getting dinner ready. I yanked the saddle off Pitch while Tony harnessed Swanny and Reg to the wagon to take the Ringlock to the mob. We were all set to go but the horses wouldn't budge.

I got down off the wagon and pulled them by their bridles. They shook their heads. I pushed them from behind. They champed their bits. We both yelled. We let fly with the stockwhips. I was gasping and panting when they suddenly took off. I only just managed to clamber up onto the driver's seat with Tony. We flew at a flat gallop, in the dark, down the track, more off than on it. The wagon was rattling and shaking as though it was going to fall to bits. The further we went, the harder the horses pulled. We flew straight past the mob, which I realised only when we'd gone half a mile too far. Somehow, we stopped the horses, turned them around and brought them back. We erected the fence in the pale light. We went very slowly back to the camp and we sat down to our evening meal at one o'clock in the morning.

The next day, at five o'clock, the same thing happened. The sheep went everywhere. We cantered and galloped all morning, trying to stop the wings from spreading, trying to stop the leaders from getting too far in front, trying to keep the tail moving. The mob became so scattered that there were never more than ten or a dozen together. We yelled and screamed. We cracked our stockwhips. It made no difference. It was as if we were mere phantoms. They walked straight past us, across the front and behind our horses – even straight under the horses' bellies. We totally lost sight of one another. I couldn't hear anyone. I was hoarse from yelling and bellowing. The others probably were too. Jiff gave up and lay under a bush and only moved when I got too far away – then he followed at a very slow jog. But Pitch was still willing. Pitch was still ready to go.

At noon I decided to give up. I rode around until I found the others, and told them. There was scarcely a sheep to be seen anywhere. It seemed they'd vanished off the face of the earth. I wished they had. We went back to the camp and put the billy on. When all else fails, make tea and have a think.

At 1.30, I resaddled Pitch, told Jiff to stay behind and rode for the homestead. I can't say exactly how far it was – certainly well over thirty miles. We arrived at the homestead at seven o'clock. You might say that was hard on the horse – we'd been on the go since five in the morning, and the only time we stood still was when we stopped at the camp for half an hour. Mostly, I let Pitch pick his own pace, which was a jog. To cover long distances, a fit horse can keep it up for hours and hours. Pitch was fit and Pitch was a goer. He was still on the bit and still going when we swung into the stables at the homestead. What a horse. Later I worked it out, and I reckon we covered eighty miles on each of the last two days.

Once again, I roused Jack from his comfortable sitting room and told him my story. We agreed the only sensible solution was to leave the sheep where they were for a couple of weeks. Let them get their bellies full. Let them finish dropping lambs. Then go out and muster them. There were Annean sheep in the same paddock, so we'd have to sort them out. To my relief, Jack said he'd send out the truck and trailer, and truck the sheep back, however many trips it took.

Next morning we drove out in the International and told the blokes to come straight in to the homestead.

By the end of February 1955, we were back at the homestead, having a weekend off. I had a slightly odd feeling. For one thing, I'd been out in mustering camps for several months and it felt strange to be at the homestead. For another, the look of the country had totally changed. The feed was already halfway to our knees and the scrub was sprouting fresh foliage. Being at a loose end was also an odd feeling.

In the yards, a magnificent dark liver-chestnut gelding caught my eye. The moment I went near, he raised his head, arched his neck, pricked his ears, snorted and pranced around the yard. Where had he come from? I wondered. At lunch I asked Jack. He looked at me as if I'd asked a really stupid question. 'That's Chester, for God's sake. What's the matter with you? You know Chester.' And he continued eating his lunch.

Yes, I knew Chester, but the pale Chester I knew was ancient and hollow backed and too slow to die a sudden death. 'I know I know Chester,' I said, 'but that horse doesn't look the faintest bit like the horse I know.'

'Well, Chester's an example of what happens to stock in this country when we have a summer season.'

Jack chewed and swallowed another mouthful. 'And that's not the only thing that happens in a summer season. With all this feed, the sheep are scouring. And with the heat, the blowflies are everywhere. So, this coming Sunday, I want you to take your blokes out to Brown Bore to muster for crutching. You'll muster Bindingwah, Toorangie, Mungeltha and Mulyalgarra. I've got two blokes coming out to do the crutching. There're yards at Brown Bore and there's a bit of a lean-to bough shed where they can set up their plant. OK?'

So we were out in the mustering camp again. Trees were few and far between in the vicinity of the mill – and wood for a fire was even scarcer. We had to make camp a hundred yards from the mill and the tank. This was a real pain in the backside, because we had to lug our water supplies in buckets all that way. A full bucket of water gets very heavy after the first thirty yards – and it's no longer full by the time you get to the camp.

Apart from the heat and the flies and the complaints of the blokes doing the crutching, the first week went reasonably well. But then the sky turned dark grey with heavy clouds and, just to make sure the grasses and the vegetation would keep growing, the heavens gave us another two and a half inches of rain. The country was flooded. The water was about three inches deep right through our camp. There was no dry ground within cooee. There was nothing for it but to stay put and make the best of it. We stayed dry at night by taking refuge under our groundsheets. The campfire was another matter – we found a spot where the water was only about an inch deep, and we built this up to make a little island in the inland sea. We gathered firewood and leaned it against the wagon to dry. We kept the fire going even when we didn't need it, because it was too much hassle to keep relighting it with damp sticks. In our spare moments, we sat around on our wire stretchers and tried to dry our boots. It continued to drizzle and at night we listened to the rain pattering on our groundsheets. If there was enough light, I filled in time plaiting a bridle for my cousin Penny.

The heat and humidity were suffocating. It was worst during the middle of the day, when we were mustering. The sky was always heavy and overcast. The ground literally steamed. Just from riding around mustering, we were drenched in sweat from head to toe. Our clothes were soaked. The horses were dripping from all points. The saddle blankets were a soggy mess. Everything leather was slippery – the saddles, and the reins. We choked on the heavy-laden atmosphere when we tried to get a lungful of air. What had I done to deserve this? I felt desperate.

The ordeal went on, day after day. After four days the waters subsided. Instead of water coming in the tops of our boots, we had the relief of trudging through mud. The blokes doing the crutching earned every penny they were paid. Apart from the weather conditions, they had to deal with hundreds of sheep that were already flyblown. It was enough to make you vomit, cutting away wool clogged with faeces, with hordes of maggots squirming over the sheep's skin. Loose folds of flesh around the sheep's backsides made the job much harder. The crutchers had to grasp a fold of flesh and pull it tight so the shearing handpiece had a clear run. Once all the wool was removed from the sheep's crutch and wherever the flies had struck, the area was sprayed with Cooper's Dielfly. This killed the maggots and provided a period of protection from further strikes. Hour after hour, day after day, the crutchers bent their backs and sweated their way through sheep after sheep. They complained bitterly, but they stuck to the task, and they toiled till the last sheep was set back up on its feet and sent on its way. How I would have loved to sit down with those blokes at the end of the last day and sink ice-cold beer until we couldn't stand up. It was no good even thinking about it. There was no beer, let alone cold beer – just a barely cool water bag.

When the crutching was over, Jack told me to take a mob of 400 to Rogo paddock, two paddocks across from Brown Bore. He sent the other blokes off with a bigger mob elsewhere. My route took me across Mungeltha and into Boolgaroo. I was to make camp at Boolgaroo Well, in the middle of the paddock, in the Hope River watercourse. The next day I was to take the mob into Rogo and ride home. Mulba and I were nearly across Mungeltha when we came to a watercourse. The sheep stopped at the water's edge and drank – and wouldn't cross over. I yelled and Jiff chased and we raced from side to side. I had to ride through the centre of the mob to force the leaders to step into the water and start swimming. Then I had to get back quickly to gather up the ones that were drifting off in all directions. It took twenty minutes, but we got them across. I could never have done it without Jiff. He was a black-haired tower of strength.

As the last sheep entered the water and swam to join the bedraggled mob standing around on the other side, I walked Mulba to the steep bank and started down. The ground was so muddy and slippery she lost control and slid straight down into the water. To my astonishment, it was much deeper than I'd anticipated and we both went right under. Mulba never touched the bottom. She came up snorting. I came up gasping – and looking for my hat. As Mulba stumbled out of the pool on the other side, the water poured out of my saddlebag. She shook herself vigorously, the saddle flaps flapping and the stirrups jerking this way and that. Jiff shook himself too. I thought, I haven't been this cool for a hundred years – I wish it would last.

My swag, my stretcher and my camping gear were waiting for me at Boolgaroo Well. It was situated in a bit of a depression, where the feed was thick and green. There was a thicket of curara bushes on one side, forming a loose, open kind of hedge. I settled the mob down close to the thicket and hobbled Mulba. It was a comfort to get my campfire going. I ate dinner by it in the last of the light.

There was not a whisper of wind. The heat and the humidity were intense. It was too hot to get into my swag. I lay on top. Within seconds the mosquitoes arrived. Never had I seen mosquitoes so big. When they landed, they almost left a bruise. I swatted and brushed. This's no good, I said to myself. I got up and lifted the groundsheet that was over my swag, and settled myself beneath it. Instantly the sweat gushed out of me. I couldn't breathe. I tried lifting my knees to make an internal prop to provide some air space. It was even hotter under there – and airless. I tried placing my head close to the edge and lifting the groundsheet a touch so I could get the outside air that wasn't so hot. My attackers found me instantly. I slammed the groundsheet down. After ten minutes, I needed air – I had to fling the groundsheet up and away. I was fully clothed and wearing my boots, so I spread a towel over my arms, hands and head, leaving a tiny opening to breath through.

I lay there and I wished I wasn't there. I tried to sleep. Although I was dog tired, I was too restless. I dozed; I woke; I sat up and checked that the sheep were still there. Before the sun was up and before the sheep were up, I was up. I went to the trough and splashed water over my face and neck. I felt the lumps of the mosquito bites all over my head and arms. There was nothing to be gained by hanging around. A billy of tea and a chunk of dry damper was breakfast. I packed up the camping gear and rolled my swag. By now the sheep were on their feet and starting to move. I saddled Mulba. It was only a couple of miles to Rogo and I couldn't get there fast enough. It didn't matter what I wanted – the sheep made their own pace and it took three hours. The final test was for Jiff and me to get the sheep into Rogo. Threading the mob of 400 through the twelve-foot gateway was a battle of wits, but once they started to pour through, the rest were anxious to follow and not be left behind. With great relief, I closed the gate and we walked the fifteen miles back to the homestead.

24

Time to play in the outback

Twice a year, around April and October, there were race meetings in Meekatharra, Cue, Mount Magnet and Yalgoo – a week apart from each other. This was the Eastern Goldfields Racing Round. Unlike the Landor Races, these races were not for grass-fed station horses. They were more professional than Landor – many of the horses also raced in Geraldton, Carnarvon and other major centres. The jockeys rode full time or part time; some of them had ridden in Perth.

When the races were on, the atmosphere in Meekatharra completely changed. People came from hundreds of miles away, days before the actual race meeting. The main street was lined with cars. The hotels were fully booked. In many of the back streets and alleys, there were yards where horses were stabled. At night, the lights from the main street barely filtered between the buildings. Walking along the lane that ran parallel to the main street, I sometimes passed small men, jogging alone, leading compliant horses. They were hard, silent, enigmatic little men. They were intent. They knew their business. They always looked as if they knew something that I wished I knew. They disappeared into the mysterious, quiet darkness of a back yard. The faint clop-clop sound of hooves padding along in the deep dust faded away into the night. Sometimes it was so soft I wondered if I had actually heard the clop-clop or whether I was putting a remembered sound to what I saw. The quiet and peace all along the lane was accentuated by the noise in the main street and the pubs.

By twelve o'clock on race day, the east wind was up, collecting red dust and flinging it at the town. Doors and windows were shut and sealed. But the insidious wisps of dust crept between the cracks and the red film settled on everything. That did not deter the racegoers. Nobody spoke about the wind and the dust, as if ignoring them made it easier to endure. Women stood in groups, each with one hand holding her hat, the other holding down her skirt, handbag in the crook of an arm. Men wandered from the horse stalls to the bar to the saddling paddock to the bookmakers. At every fresh gust of wind, people turned their backs and faced the way the red dust swirled through the racing club building and across the hills into town.

At 1.45, the crowd was ready for the running of the first race. So was I. Without discussing it with me, Jack, who was a prominent member of the racing club committee, volunteered my services as clerk of course. There it was in the April 1955 race book: 'Clerk of Course – I. Parkes'. There was no fancy attire, such as the clerks of the course wore in Perth. Spotlessly clean white moleskins, equally clean blue shirt, polished high-heeled boots and a broad-brimmed Akubra were correct attire in Meekatharra. I received only the vaguest instructions and was told to 'get on with it'.

It was an education. Behind the barrier, the horses were jostled around to get into position. The jockeys threatened each other. With the tension before the start, the yelling as the horses jumped out, there was more excitement – and more animosity – than I had anticipated. I loved it. I cantered behind them and got to the straight in time to lead in the winners.

As darkness gathered, Meekatharra started pulsing with life and the volume of noise went up several notches. The lights came on. The bars filled. The hotel dining rooms struggled to cope with the crowds. The main bar of the Commercial Hotel was packed tight.

The place was roaring. I was with a group that included a bloke whose name was Bill Broad. Bill was about six foot three – and solid. He came from a station called Wagga Wagga, on the Mount Magnet side of Yalgoo. Bill was probably in his late thirties or early forties. There was a woman with us who was the girlfriend of one of the bookmakers. Her name was Mavis, and she was in her middle to late forties – and good looking. She was petite, about five foot one in her shoes. What she lacked in height she made up for with chutzpah. She was mature, she was lively and she was cheeky. There was so much noise, we had to bend to get our heads a touch closer so we could hear each other. There was a bit of chitchat between Bill and Mavis, and then Bill said, 'Hey, Mavis, what about sleeping with me tonight?'

Mavis took half a step closer, her head level with Bill's chest. She tilted her head back so she could look right up into his face. 'Oh, I dunno,' she said. 'We wouldn't be able to talk to each other.'

Later in the night, people congregated in one of the hotel dining rooms for the presentation of prize money and trophies. A table at one end glittered with silver plate. Owners and trainers and other connections sat on hard chairs around the walls. The climax was the presentation of the main trophy. The prominent pastoralist who had donated the trophy struggled to his feet and just managed to get to the table without falling over. Like most of the men, he'd enjoyed the refreshments all day. He swayed; he muttered; he fumbled. The waiting recipient of the trophy shifted his weight from one leg to the other. The audience whispered. After a moment of deep silence, the presenter, still battling to stay upright, thrust the trophy at the winner and said, 'Here – take it!' And he sat down on the nearest chair. Everyone applauded more enthusiastically than usual, relieved that the moment was over. They quietened down to listen to the winner make his humble acceptance speech.

Two weeks later we were at the Mount Magnet races. It was Meekatharra all over again. I travelled down with Jack and Lindsay, but I spent my time with the young blokes I knew. I also knew one of the racehorses – Bunty. It gave me a big thrill to see my beautiful horse from Mount Augustus. I spent time with him in his stall. He was the same personable horse he always had been, and being with him again simply heightened how much I missed him.

He was entered in the last race. During the afternoon, I failed to pick a winner, and I was broke. As at Meekatharra, there was wind and there was dust. The Silver Fox, Harry Finlay, the bookmaker, was there but by late afternoon he was the red fox.

Two minutes before the start, I checked the odds and Bunty was four to one on – why would anyone wager four quid to win one? The rest of the field were at worthwhile odds, but they clearly were not winners. I was desperate to back Bunty – but not at four to one on. Five minutes before the start, I was hanging around the betting ring, no money in my pocket, my favourite horse in all the world about to win the last race, and I couldn't get a bet on. Harry was watching me. 'What's the matter, Ian?' he asked.

'I want to back Bunty – but not at those odds.'

'Tell you what,' he said. 'I'll give you two to one on.'

'Thanks, Harry, but I've run out of dough.'

'How much d'you want to put on?'

Seeing that Bunty was a certainty, I thought I should go for broke. 'Thirty quid,' I replied. Thirty pounds was nearly three weeks' wages. For me, it was a big punt.

'Right,' said Harry. 'I'll give it to you on tick. OK?'

I was really grateful – good old Harry. I put the betting ticket in the breast pocket of my shirt and walked quickly to stand on a bench in front of the grandstand. A mate, named Jimmy, joined me just as the race started.

The jockey on Bunty bustled him to the front immediately and had him running six lengths clear when they turned the corner for home. Halfway down the straight, a mare called Delmar was gaining ground rapidly. Fifty yards from the post, she collared him. Locked together, they went over the line, with Delmar a head in front. In the blink of an eye, I was thirty pounds in debt. My stomach churned. My mind was dazed. I thought, you bastards. That was a setup. I wondered if Harry knew.

The next challenge was how to find thirty quid for the settling the following morning. I had no intention of asking Jack. The obvious answer was the two-up school. But first I had to raise some capital. Jimmy said he'd lend me five quid. I needed more than that. We went into town and bumped into two brothers we knew, Bill and Charlie Gillespie. They had a bit of a rough property out east, and they were a bit rough themselves. They agreed to lend me ten quid between them. Then, at about ten o'clock, we ran into another bloke Jimmy knew. His name was Kev. He was big and bulky and half-drunk, but friendly. He threw in a fiver. I confidently told all of them that they would get their money back, plus a bit more.

When the bars closed at eleven o'clock, Jimmy and I watched the drunks stagger out. There was a chill in the air, and it hit every man hard. Already a handful of blokes had passed out on the pavement, causing people to step over and around them. Jimmy and I walked back in and along the main corridor to the large side room where the two-up school was being set up. The secretary of the race club was the ringkeeper. Only three others were there before us. A large table covered with a blanket filled a third of the room. Close on our heels, more men came in, a little noisy and a little drunk. They settled down and the ringkeeper got the game going.

Tails betting was my game, doubling up when I lost. In fifteen minutes my bankroll had grown from twenty quid to forty, so I was twenty quid in front already. It was quickly obvious that four men in the school were there for the benefit of everyone else. The four blokes weren't aware, but everyone else quickly cottoned on. They bet haphazardly in large and indiscriminate amounts, sometimes losing a hundred on one spin and winning twenty on the next. One was a bookmaker, who good-naturedly lost 600 quid. A big, surly, middle-aged storekeeper from another town and a young publican lost heavily. The fourth was a wealthy pastoralist who lost a roll that would choke a bull. Nearly everyone had had too much to drink. I was sober.

When the dice came to me, I put five pounds on the table. It was quickly covered. The bloke on my left asked how many heads I'd spin. I said four. Don't ask me why I said four. It just came out. He said he'd back me in. I spun the first set of heads, then the second. Out of the corner of my eye, I saw Bill and Charlie arrive. I whispered to Jimmy to tell them to keep clear of me.

No-one had spun three sets of heads in a row for some time. The table was excited, especially the heads betters. I rattled the cup and blew in it. I blew in it once more for luck. The table was hushed. I threw the dice. They rolled across the table. They were all heads, my third set. By now I had forty quid on the table. Now I could stop, or take some and continue. I took twenty and left twenty. The bloke on my left increased his bets. I spun the fourth set of heads. I raked the centre and quit. I was shaking.

My winnings were seventy-five pounds. Including the original twenty, I now had a roll of ninety-five quid. I needed thirty for Harry, twenty to repay my backers – and another twenty to say thank you. Jack was standing at the back of the room, watching. I went over to him and handed him thirty pounds. I said, 'Hang on to that for me. I need it for the settling tomorrow.' I put forty quid in my hip pocket and twenty-five quid in my left-hand side pocket.

Protocol required that I should not walk away the moment I had a big win. I went back to the table and played for another thirty minutes, lost ten quid and unobtrusively withdrew. At two o'clock in the morning, Jimmy and I slipped out. The others discreetly followed. We met at Kev's truck and I surprised my backers by giving them back double their money. Kev had bought beer before the hotel closed. We knocked the tops off the bottles and stood in the yard and celebrated. Then we sat in the dirt and leaned our backs against the wheels of the truck. We passed the bottles around and we laughed till we couldn't laugh any more. Then we discovered that Kev was asleep. We tried to wake him up, but he groaned and told us to piss off.

Jimmy knew where he was camped. Those of us who were capable half-carried and half-dragged him to his swag and left him.

The following week, Bunty trounced Delmar in the Yalgoo Cup – at ten to one on. So much for the four to one on at Mount Magnet.

The next morning I collected my thirty quid from Jack and at ten o'clock I turned up at the settling. Betting on tick was common, and a small crowd gathered, some to pay their debts, some to collect winnings.

Over the days and weeks that followed, I reflected on how I had gambled and lost – and then gambled and won. I had sneaked out of trouble by the skin of my teeth. The feeling of success was sweet. I was amazed at my confidence in the two-up school. I was also proud of myself for quitting when I did – after spinning four sets of heads – and for my timing at leaving the school. There was no temptation to think I could do it again. It was sheer luck that enabled me to escape with the win – and luck is a treacherous friend.

25

In sole charge

After the races, Jack sent us to the southeast corner of Belele to muster wethers in Berringine and Podyne. These paddocks were hinged around an old outcamp called Four Corners. We were to bring in 3,000 head to the homestead to be shorn prior to being shipped overseas. With wool the price it was, there was no point in exporting sheep carrying good fleeces. The mustering team included Norman and Joe Gilla, the two part-Aboriginal brothers, who were about fourteen and fifteen. They were good horsemen, willing workers and easy to have in the camp. In fact, they were far easier to work with than the white stockmen, who always needed a shove to get going and who sat back in the traces and who always found something to whinge about. For two skinny lads, Norman and Joe punched way above their weight.

One of their enthusiasms was cooking. Not only that, they were adventurous with it. They asked me if they could make a trap to catch pigeons. 'Go for it,' I said.

We were camped close to the old Four Corners outcamp hut. We didn't camp in the hut, mainly because it was too small but also because there was no firewood nearby. Norman and Joe had been over to the hut and found scrap chicken wire. They made a cylinder about two feet in diameter and about four feet long. Both ends were closed off, but one end had a wide-mouthed funnel at ground level. The boys staked the trap near the windmill, where there were always pigeons and other bird life. They scattered oats around the opening and inside. Then they sat in the shade a few yards away and waited. They didn't have to wait long. Birds have sharp eyes. As soon as two or three started pecking at the feed on the ground, others flew down and joined them. They followed the feed trail through the funnel and into the cylinder. When the boys judged there were enough inside, they ran like the dickens to the trap, shouting and waving their hats. The birds inside tried to fly, and the wire cylinder became a mass of flapping wings and bouncing bodies, and nearly lifted off the ground.

The boys removed the funnel and reached inside for the birds, one by one. As Joe took out a bird, he handed it to Norman to wring its neck. I watched all this from the camp and congratulated them when they proudly showed me their haul of pigeons – and white cockatoos and galahs. 'You're not going to cook these bloody parrots, are yer?' I asked.

'Course we are,' Norman said. They boiled a big pot of water and did the plucking and the cleaning. They peeled onions and started them going in a large bedourie oven, using a big dollop of mutton fat. Then they placed their catch of twelve birds in the oven and let them cook for an hour. They prodded them with a fork and decided it was time for the next stage. They added water and stirred it in with the fat to make a gravy. Wonder of wonders, we had a bag of carrots, so in went some of those, plus the ubiquitous potatoes. They mixed flour and water, and made dumplings and threw them in too. The final touch was two handfuls of dried apricots that I'd stolen from the store. The other blokes in the camp were wary about all this. 'Bloody pigeons and bloody parrots!' said Gil. 'What's wrong with a leg of mutton?'

There's an old saying about eating galahs and cockatoos: you put a brick in the pot with the birds, and when the brick is soft you eat the brick and throw the birds away. Like most old sayings, it was not far off the mark. The pigeons were only just edible, and the galahs and cockatoos were as tough as leather. We did our best to eat them, gnawing on the stringy flesh. But the spuds and the dumplings and the dried apricots were good, although the white blokes thought the apricots were strange tucker. Regardless, I was impressed with Norman and Joe. Nothing daunted them.

Some of the Aboriginal people at Mount Augustus and Belele were born and raised there and they had an inalienable right – not rights enshrined in law, but a moral right to believe that where they were born was 'home'. This was respected at Mount Augustus and Belele, as it was at most of the stations that had Aboriginal people. Those who were born 'nearby' and who were related to some or all of a resident population were entitled to call a particular station 'home' too.

Thus there was a strong feeling of family, which managers like Jack and Lindsay Henderson fostered. But this kind of family relationship, with its attendant responsibilities towards women and children, did not extend to itinerant Aboriginals and white employees who drifted in and drifted out, although they were well treated. Jack showed everyone equal respect, whether they were black, part black or white. If he was hard and demanding, he was that to everyone.

It had struck me that Ernest Potts provided the Yamatjis at Mount Augustus with leadership and direction. It seemed to me that he related to all of them and they respected him. Jack Henderson was the same. At Belele, home to families like the Frasers and the Walleys, the people also looked to Jack for leadership.

The population at Belele was different from Mount Augustus's in that the people at The Mount were primarily full-blood Aboriginals. At Belele, apart from Jackie Stevens, I don't remember seeing any full-blood Aboriginals. Instead, they were what were called half-castes. This is no longer an acceptable term. The preferred option is Aboriginal people, regardless of their being part white.

In the 1950s, on the stations where I worked, it was not derogatory to refer to a person as a half-caste; it was not a racist pejorative. Although I know that in other situations it was used as a slur. But in my experience using the term was no different from identifying a person as Japanese or English or American. Such identification highlights a possible cultural difference that one might need to take into account. To say that Bill van Rijn was Dutch sends a signal.

There was an old view in the bush that you could judge the attitude of the management of a station by the reception you received from the station dogs. The dogs at Belele barked, half-heartedly, but they were never threatening. As you got out of your vehicle, the dogs that greeted you wanted to sniff your trouser legs and boots. And then they wagged their tails and cocked their legs against the wheels of your vehicle.

Jack arranged for three part-Aboriginal shearers to start work on Monday, 9 May. Their names were Alec, Horace and Herbie. They were itinerant, part-time shearers. Alec was in his thirties, solidly built and the best shearer of the three. Both Horace and Herbie looked frail. I wondered if they would survive the contract. My job was to run the whole shooting match. That meant I ran the shearing shed. I was the organiser, the expert, the wool classer and the presser. Norman and Joe and a couple of other blokes were rouseabouts. Stockmen were delegated to bring in wethers as they were needed and then relocate them when they were shorn. Watching and learning from Don, the expert, when the PLB team did the shearing the previous year meant I knew how to run the engine and sharpen combs and cutters. I understood enough about wool classing to make a reasonable fist of allocating the fleeces to the right bins – they were mainly AA and BB. Bellies and skirtings and pieces sort themselves out. As the bins filled, I had to press a few bales to make room. I'd also done a small amount of shearing – enough to know how to do it, not enough to be productive.

Jack figured the three shearers would clean up the 3,000 wethers in two weeks. That's 300 a day. These blokes were mediocre shearers, but a hundred wethers a day each wasn't asking much – not when you remember that a really good shearer can turn out more than 200 a day, depending on the size of the sheep and the condition of the fleeces. On the other hand, I was under some pressure. I rotated from making sure the shearers' supply of wethers was maintained to being the expert, to doing the wool classing, to pressing the bales – all the time keeping an eye on the shed hands and liaising with the stockmen. But I got into the rhythm of it and enjoyed it. There was also some fun when my cousin Penny and a couple of her school friends came to watch. The first week of shearing was the last week of their school holidays. This was one of those rare occasions when Penny and I had any contact. Usually when she was home for school holidays, I was out in the mustering camp or off the property.

At twenty years of age, was I interested in a trio of sixteen-year-old schoolgirls? Well, no, but after weeks and weeks in mustering camps, these girls, young as they were, were a sight for sore eyes. And I indulged in showing off when I was pressing wool. It is hard, athletic work, and even though it was May, and cool, I worked with my shirt off. I vigorously tramped the wool into the pressing boxes. I worked the long wooden lever up and down to compress the wool in the top box into the bale in the bottom box. I stretched the flaps at the top of the bale pack and pinned them down to close the bale. As I unclamped the side of the pressing box, I hoped my audience would notice how effortlessly I rolled out 400-pound bales and tumbled them to the side and out of the way. I was as fit and trim as I had ever been. I felt like a young bull. But not quite as heavy as those 800-pound mickies we mustered in Ebal. It seemed to me that I got the girls' attention, though a young bloke could never know for sure.

At the end of the first week of shearing, Jack and Lindsay took Penny and her friends back to Perth for the new school term at

Perth College, and Jack took the chance to have ten days off. Before he left, we sat in his office and he gave me instructions. For the first week, I would be busy finishing the shearing. For the start of the second week, he gave me a list. When the wethers were shorn, they would have one week in the paddock to recover from nicks and cuts before the trucks arrived to transport them to the port. Overall, I was in charge. The twelve people working on the station answered to me. Apart from Joe and Norman, I was the youngest. Doug Fraser was more than twice my age – but he was a good bloke, and he and his son Mervyn were easy to get along with. Actually, both Doug and especially Mervyn were very much on side. I wish the same could have been said for the shearers.

On the Saturday morning that Jack and Lindsay and the girls left, the three shearers took off for Meekatharra. On the Sunday night, only Alec and Horace returned. The message from Alec was that Herbie was drunk and wouldn't be coming back. As I couldn't leave the shed to go looking for him, and as no-one else had any authority he might listen to, I decided to make the best of it and press on.

On Wednesday night, Alec and Horace disappeared. Thursday morning, there was no sign of them or Horace's ute. Alec's car was still parked behind the shearers' quarters. I waited until midday, and then I jumped in the Commer and drove to Meekatharra. I went straight to the corrugated-iron shantytown just outside. This consisted of two straggly lines of shacks, roughly parallel. There was a thoroughfare between them, and I drove straight in. I stopped and inquired after Alec and Horace. 'Further down,' someone said. I stopped at a likely spot. Alec staggered out from one of the shacks on my right. I stayed in the truck. I kept the engine running. 'Come on, Alec. Get Horace and come back to work.'

'Horace isn comin.' Alec swayed and nearly toppled over.

'Well, get in the truck and let's get going.'

'Fuck you. Git outa the truck so I can punch your fuckin head in. You bloody fuckin white cunt.'

315

Instead of provoking me, Alec's language made me go cold. It would not resolve the situation if I got out of the truck and took him on. Alec was drunk and I was stone-cold sober. What would I do with him if I managed to flatten him? What about the people inside the shacks looking out through the glassless windows? There was one simple answer to all these questions.

'Git outa the fuckin truck. You're just a white piece of shit.' Alec reached out to grab the door handle. 'I said – git outa the fuckin truck.'

I slammed the truck in gear. 'I'll come back for you later.'

I dropped the clutch and took off. Alec had his hand on the door handle. He spun away and fell heavily and rolled over in the dust. I watched him in the rear-vision mirror. He lay there and lifted his head to watch me leave.

I drove back into town and stopped outside the Commercial Hotel. At that hour of the day it was quiet. Only two old blokes in the bar. I ordered a schooner. It didn't touch the sides. I ordered another and sat down at a table in a corner by myself. The time was now 2.30. I decided to hang around until about five – and then go after Alec again. But I wasn't going to spend the afternoon drinking. Instead, I window-shopped at the Elders showroom. I made a note of the gear we didn't have at Belele but should have had. Then I went over the road to McAleer's store, where it was rumoured that you could still buy clothing he'd taken into stock before the war – still at prewar prices. I called in to Alf Sallur's chemist shop and chatted with his daughter Lorraine. At 4.30, I couldn't stand it any longer. I drove out to the shanties.

There were very few people about. Outside the shack where Alec had been, two lads were sitting on the ground, leaning against the wall. 'Where's Alec?' I asked.

'He inside.'

'Can you tell him I'm here to take him back to Belele?'

'Nah. He sleepin. You won' wake im up.'

I turned off the ignition and went to the shack. 'Show me.'

One of the kids slowly got to his feet and led the way inside. Sure enough, Alec was asleep, on a wire stretcher. The kid said, 'See, he won' wake up.'

'I hope he's not dead,' I said. 'I need him.'

I shook Alec by the shoulder. There was no response. I thought for a second he might be dead. 'Get your mate outside to give me a hand. We're gunna put this bloke on the truck. I'm takin him with me,' I said.

We struggled. Alec was nearly six feet – and burly. The three of us half-carried, half-dragged him to the truck, and we heaved him up. The boys grabbed his bag and threw that on. One of them brought out six bottles of beer, and I put them in the cab beside me. I gave the boys five bob each and left. I thought, how many more times do I have to cart passed-out drunks on the back of a truck, like I'm a drunk collector? How many more times do I have to put up with idiots who want to fight me?

Halfway to Belele the radiator boiled. It had a small leak, just below the top. I had to stop. There was no water within cooee. When the radiator cooled, I knocked the tops off three of Alec's bottles and poured the beer in. It frothed up, but there was enough liquid to get us going. Nine miles from the homestead, it boiled again. The last three bottles of beer were just enough to get home. At the shearers' quarters, the blokes were sitting around waiting. They gave me a hand dumping Alec on a bed. We left him as he was. I thought of pulling his boots off, but I decided he could go to hell.

Next morning, Friday, I was apprehensive about what Alec's state of mind would be. But he was as meek as a lamb, very respectful. He looked terrible, but he went back to work. I was now down to one shearer, with more than 1,000 wethers to go – and a deadline to meet. I gathered my troops. 'Can anyone shear?'

Norman and Joe and Mervyn said they could. 'Well, let's git goin,' I said.

We worked the four regulation two-hour shifts and got through about 350. I made them all go back to the shed after dinner and shear by the light of Tilley lamps. We knocked off another hundred. We still had 600 to go, and I didn't want to be still shearing wethers when Jack arrived back on the Tuesday. I told everyone we would work through the weekend.

At six o'clock on Saturday morning, I went to the shed to get the engine running and to sharpen the combs and cutters. The first thing I noticed was that Alec's car was gone. So too, of course, was Alec. By 7.30, Joe and Norman and Mervyn were hard at it. But they were all beginners, all inexperienced, all as slow as a wet week. I wasn't any better, but I found another handpiece and joined them on the shearing board. Every now and then, we stopped and threw the rolled-up fleeces on the table and skirted them, and I classed them. The kitchen brought lunch over to the shed and did the same for dinner. We continued shearing by the light of the Tilley lamps until eleven o'clock. We'd done about 310 between the four of us, and we had 290 to go.

We worked all day Sunday and we finished the last at ten o'clock that night. I turned off the engine and went back to the board. Without the drumming of the engine it seemed extraordinarily quiet. Small sounds were not only audible but loud.

I looked around and took stock. Rolled-up fleeces were lying everywhere – in the corners they were stacked on top of one another. Norman was stretched out on the floor and Joe was taking a swig from the water bag. Mervyn was sitting, leaning against the partition between the shearing board and the sheep pens, rolling a cigarette. We were too drained to say anything. We just sat in the pool of light, the background of the vast shed vague and deep and dark and foreboding. We barely even looked at each other – we had nothing to say. But we knew we were sharing a special moment. We'd done it. We had finished the shearing. We were a team. My gratitude to Norman and Joe and Mervyn – and the station hands who did their bit – was huge. They were such a contrast to Alec and Horace and Herbie. Where Jack had found those shearers, I don't know – but, for my money, they were the pits.

We cleaned up the shed on Monday and I finished the wool pressing on Tuesday morning. There were thirty-one bales, with an average weight of 418 pounds. The heaviest was 672 pounds, which was made up of pieces. The next heaviest was 565 pounds, composed of locks. Pieces and locks are from very low down on the sides and underneath the sheep, where they collect dirt and faeces. On the other hand, the fleece bales, being clean wool from the backs and sides, weighed as little as 362 pounds.

When Jack and Lindsay arrived back on Tuesday night, Jack had to be told what happened. For one thing, there was the matter of paying the shearers for the sheep they'd shorn. I had the tallies. 'OK,' said Jack. 'You did get the whole 3,000 shorn, didn't you?'

'Yeah, of course.'

'And the wool pressing?'

'Yeah.'

'Good. Well now – I want you to keep going with that list I gave you. Don't waste time on it. I'll need you and Mervyn and Gil to spend a week cutting more fence posts. I've got fencing contractors coming in two weeks.'

26

Dark days

A diet lacking green vegetables and fruit often led to boils. In my case, they had erupted on my thighs and backside before the shearing started, and they were still making life uncomfortable when we started cutting mulga fence posts.

On Monday, 30 May, we went to Rogo paddock, where there were good stands of mulga. We cut Monday, Tuesday and Wednesday. At the end of each day, we loaded the truck, brought the posts in to the homestead and stacked them behind the workshop. On Wednesday evening, Jack told me to go to Meekatharra the next morning to get a load of chaff for the horses. The break from cutting posts was welcome, because pain had developed in my lower chest and up the middle to my throat when I bent to swing the axe to cut at the base of a tree.

That night, at dinner, David Wilcox was with us. He was an adviser from the Department of Agriculture who was visiting for a few days. He was in his twenties, quite tall and solidly built. He had experimental patches of plantings dotted around Belele, and each day he wandered off in his ute to inspect the progress. He had a high regard for Jack and Lindsay, and they for him. With his dry sense of humour and his wry smile, he was excellent company at dinner.

Next morning, the chest pain was back. While I was in town, I went to the chemist to see if Alf or Lorraine had anything to ease the discomfort. 'I reckon I've got indigestion or something,' I said.

Alf asked a few questions, went to his dispensary, made a concoction, put it in a small bottle and said, 'Here. Try this every morning and every night.'

I took a dose straight away, and a short while later, the pain had diminished. Then it was back to Belele to round up the blokes to help unload the chaff.

The next day, Friday, the pain was back to where it had been before – and Alf's special potion had no effect. On Saturday morning I struggled to get out of bed. Driving out to Rogo in the truck, I wondered if I was going to make it through the dark day. The sky was ominously overcast; there was a fine, wispy drizzle. As the day wore on, I wore out. Bending over to swing the axe was savage. Frequently I had to stop to let the pain subside before starting again. Mervyn and Gil did nearly all the loading, but I was still able to drive the truck. Unloading the posts was beyond me, and I had to bow out and leave them to it. I struggled to shower and shave, and when I was back in my room, I lay on my bed and there I stayed. Getting up was too hard.

When I failed to appear for dinner, Jack sent David to see what I was up to. As far as I was concerned, I was up to nothing. David was solicitous and reported to Jack that I was pretty crook and wouldn't be eating. After dinner, Jack came to have a look. 'Dunno what's the matter with you. We'll see how you're going in the morning,' he said.

In the morning it was worse. The pain in my chest was searing. Later, Jack paid another visit. 'There's been more rain this morning, and David's leaving before the roads get too wet and he gets stuck here. He's offered to take you to the hospital in Meekatharra on his way through. Let's see what Dr Ekstein says.'

With David's help, I shuffled to his ute. Jack and Lindsay came out to say their goodbyes, and David carefully drove out onto the road to Meekatharra. The sky was still overcast and this day was dark too. There were occasional showers. He drove with a tender concern for my comfort. About a third of the way into town, on a long, straight stretch of road, there were patches of water, not deep enough to be pools but deep enough to make the surface slippery. We started to slide and then we stopped. David revved the engine and the back wheels spun. We weren't really bogged, just stuck. He tried again – the tyres still didn't grip. 'David,' I said. 'Lemme get behind the wheel while you go round the back and push.'

David was reluctant. 'I can't let you do that. I'm taking you to hospital.'

'Just get out and go round the back – and push when I yell "push".'

I slid behind the steering wheel, engaged first gear and caressed the accelerator pedal. I tipped my head through the window and called, 'Are you ready?'

'Ready!' said David.

I tried a few modest revs. I gave it some more until I could feel the wheels wanting to spin but not actually spinning. 'Now push,' I yelled.

With David's encouragement, the ute inched forward onto ground that hadn't been churned up. David jogged up, panting. I slid over to the passenger side and David climbed in. 'I'm sorry, Ian. I'm so sorry,' he said, still panting.

'Don't worry about it, mate.'

'But I'm taking you to hospital and this shouldn't happen – I'm terribly sorry.'

And with that, David drove slowly and carefully to town, but he was anxious about every wet patch on the road and he kept glancing at me out of the corner of his eye. Was there ever a man so considerate?

David walked with me into the hospital and saw me safely into the custody of Dr Ekstein. Out came the stethoscope, and the examination went on and on. 'I don't know,' he said. 'I don't know.'

Ekstein had recently arrived in Australia from Czechoslovakia. 'We put you to bed and see what tomorrow,' he said.

This Meekatharra Hospital was old. It was spread on a rise a quarter of a mile out of town. The front was built up on piles and there were steps leading up to the main door. It was timber framed and most of the internal walls were whitewashed hessian. A nurse led me to a ward on the right of the entrance hall. There were eight beds but only two were occupied. The best thing this place had going for it was the matron. Her name was Barbara Smith and, believe it or not, I knew her. She was the sister of my mate from Errabiddy days, Gerry Smith.

When Barbara came on duty next morning, she was astonished to see me lying in the ward, all limp and useless. She was an older woman, I'd say around thirty, and I thought she looked pretty good in the tight-fitting uniform that accentuated her femininity. With a flowing cape behind her cap and with white shoes, she commanded attention. She sat by the bed and extracted all the information she could, and stood up. 'I'll bloody find out what's going on. Trust me,' she said.

There was no option but to lie there – and wait. In the opposite bed, there was a bloke called Cedric. He snored with his mouth closed, his head a shadow on the pillow. During the day, he woke and stared unblinkingly across the room. I said, 'Gidday, Cedric,' but got no response. Someone told me he had been brought to the hospital to die. He was slipping into death like a small creek flows into a swamp. It was gentle, so imperceptible you hardly noticed the change each day. It seemed to be easy – this slipping away, no apparent distress, slowly sinking. Not like me. Not like the pain I had in my chest.

The pain was something I was forced to think about. I had to find cunning ways of shifting and moving – from my back to my right side, then to my back again, without sending the pain surging up through my chest and into my throat and into my eyes and over through my left shoulder and down my left arm. The days and the nights wore on. Dr Ekstein said there was an infection, that they would use penicillin. They hoped this would fix it.

Through every day and night, I was repeatedly jabbed in the buttocks or the thighs with more and more penicillin. Yet steadily the pain increased. Please, I thought, stop it. What little I had to do I did with the least effort I could manage. I reduced my breathing in quantity and frequency. I couldn't eat. Nobody heard me, but I thought I cried out, again and again, and railed against not being able to do anything about the pain. I did my best to will it away. Instead it grew worse.

Then it got so that I didn't care. It hurt more than ever, but it didn't seem to matter. I lay awake for days and nights and thought about Cedric dying in the opposite bed, or I tried to see the man in the end bed, who talked and mumbled in his sleep.

Meekatharra Hospital smelled of carbolic and cleanliness. And it smelled of warmth. Maybe this was because winter had not really set in. Maybe it was because of the thin walls and the exposed position. Warmth came through the doors and windows, and sieved through those whitewashed hessian walls inside. It lingered for a while after the sun went down, and I could smell it, the warmth. It was a good smell.

Lying through each night, I concentrated on breathing minimally to avoid exacerbating the pain. I checked the passing of each night with the rounds of the night nurse and I smelled all the smells and I listened to all the sounds. Sometimes I thought I might be like Cedric – dying. But I did not think that very often.

To turn in bed from one side to the other was an expedition. It took thirty minutes of manoeuvring with the utmost caution, fractions of an inch at a time. Then it got so I didn't know how long it took, because my watch stopped. The watch was powered by a tumbling mechanism, which moved with every movement of my arm and kept the watch wound. I stopped moving. The watch stopped. And for me, time stopped. The days and nights merged.

I had no idea how much time had passed when Matron Barbara came and whispered, 'We're changing from penicillin to cortisone. They've flown some up from Perth.'

I closed my eyes. I didn't care any more. Do what you want. I closed my eyes and it shut out the light. It shut out the white, sterilised world of the ward. It shut out everything except the pain. I closed my eyes and I saw what I wanted to see. And mostly what I saw was mist, mist that gently flowed and wafted – and it was soothing, soothing like the music I remembered from my wireless, but softer. Hands touched me, moved me, injected me. Though I was conscious, I was only vaguely aware.

My parents came and they sat and they watched. They spoke softly to each other and to Dr Ekstein. Their voices were barely audible, and I couldn't hear clearly enough to understand what they were saying. I had the impression that they came to the hospital two or three times, but I wasn't sure.

Some days after they had gone, I was lying on my left side, barely breathing. I drew in a soupçon of air, just a wisp – and something in my chest seemed to give way, as though something had burst. I kept inhaling, but slowly. And the pain did not increase. I breathed out – and I cautiously breathed in again – and in and in. The experience animated me. One of the nurses noticed. She came quickly. She bent over. 'What's wrong?' she asked.

'Get matron,' I murmured. 'Just get matron.'

Moments later Barbara was there. She sat in the bedside chair and put her face close to mine so she could look into my eyes. 'What is it?'

'I can breathe,' I said. And I looked at her looking at me and my eyes flooded and I wept. She stroked my forehead and my cheeks with the back of her hand, and she said, 'It's all right. It's all right.' And I fell asleep.

When I woke, I found that moving was easier. I was still in pain, but it was not the way it had been, and it steadily diminished. Dr Ekstein and Barbara came to see me. They sat down, one on either side of the bed. 'You are making big improvement,' Ekstein said.

'The cortisone is doing the trick. You see, you have pericarditis. This is very serious. You are here now three weeks. In one week you will fly to Perth to hospital and the heart specialists. Then you will recover. But it will take time.'

Ekstein asked questions about how I felt and what I thought. I wasn't interested in his questions. I wanted him to clear out so I could talk to Barbara. Eventually he did go, and I caught Barbara's eye – and she lingered. 'What's this bloody pericarditis business?' I asked.

'Well, I've never heard of it before now. And neither had he until he rang Perth for help.'

'OK. So what is it?'

'It's an inflammation, an infection, in the outer covering of the heart called the pericardium. It develops fluid, which shouldn't be there. We thought you were going to die. They sent the Flying Doctor plane to bring your mum and dad to see you. I'll tell you what, Ian, Dr Ekstein was shit-scared.'

'So what caused it?'

'It's hard to say.'

'Could it have been infection from boils? I had heaps of boils a few weeks ago.'

'Maybe. I don't really know.'

'Now what?'

'You'll find out when you get to Perth. You'll be in the hands of the specialists then.'

Barbara then told me how no-one apart from my parents had been allowed to visit me. No Jack or Lindsay. No mates. They had even spread the word in town that if anyone who knew me was visiting the hospital they were to enter through the back door instead of the front, in case I saw them and got excited.

The day I left the hospital, they weighed me. I tipped the scales at ten stone. Three weeks before, I had been twelve and a half stone.

* * *

Ensconced in the Mount Hospital, in Perth, for two months, in a private room, I was in the care of a heart specialist. He informed me that the only known cure was complete rest. The probable timeframe? Many weeks! For the first two weeks, I wasn't allowed to feed myself – I had to be hand fed. I even had to use a bedpan lying down.

As I recovered and my strength slowly returned, I dwelt on my life so far and what I might want for the future. Pamela wasted no time in coming to see me. She visited frequently and she introduced me to the man in her life – Robert Juniper. Bob was teaching art at Hale School and was on the threshold of becoming a world-renowned artist, represented in every major Australian gallery and many overseas. The three of us talked about art and music and literature, and, when I talked about wanting to write about my experiences, they both encouraged me to start putting words on paper. Bob and I became friends, and we are still friends, even though his relationship with Pamela is long gone.

Another regular visitor was Ian Bridson. It was a curious coincidence that he and Bob Juniper were teaching at my old school. We continued our seamless discussions about books that started in the bush camp at Towrana. He too encouraged me to write, just write, write anything, get started. See where it led. Sometimes he brought friends and we talked long after visitors' hours ended – the length of my stay seemed to entitle me to special concessions.

Across the passage, I discovered a law undergraduate, John Samuel, who was recovering from a cartilage operation on his knee, the result of a rugby union game. He had a coterie of friends who were law students and rugby players, and they opened up fresh avenues of thinking for me. Sammy, as he was known, became a firm friend.

As if all that was not enough incentive to think about living in Perth, I fell in love with a young nurse called Rebecca. She was a darling and she personified an essential ingredient that was missing from outback sheep stations. She was lovely to look at, lovely to be with. This was so good I wanted more and more of it. How could I go back to the bush for months and months, up to a year or so, before seeing her again? What on earth would I do in the meantime? So, towards the end of my time in hospital, I seriously contemplated working in Perth – but doing what? I wanted to write but I had to earn a living.

Influenced by all the hours listening to my radio in the bush, I thought radio announcing might be the go. And it just so happened that Sammy's father, Bryn Samuel, was general manager of 6IX, the top-rating radio station in Perth by a country mile. Would young Sammy talk to old Sammy on my behalf? Of course he would. Soon after I left hospital, I met Bryn Samuel, and he referred me to his program manager, Stan Gervas. Stan demolished my visions of being an announcer but gave me a job as a copywriter.

Before I started work at 6IX, I returned to Belele to collect my belongings – and Jiff. Where I was going to live in Perth was no place for a dog, especially a big dog, so my parents looked after him, which reunited him with Smokey.

Then, with some uncertainty on my part, I started my new job. I thought it was a big punt on Stan's part too, since I didn't even know what a copywriter was until he explained. Those were the days when all advertisements were read live by the announcers. Recorded commercials came much later. Stan taught me to write advertising copy and, perhaps even more importantly, he mentored me. He encouraged my interests in literature and music, and introduced me to the quality of English newspapers like *The Sunday Times* and *The Observer*.

My work area was a tiny space between a window and a door that opened back towards me – and which was kept open. There was just enough room for a chair and a small desk with a giant typewriter, and there I taught myself to two-finger type, as it is called – except that I used more than two fingers and my thumbs – and produce the copy that Stan vetted.

In my own time, I started writing stories and did a mature-age matriculation to university. But during my year at 6IX, I wavered. At times I agonised. The pull of the bush was strong. But I couldn't tell if it was just nostalgia or something deeper. The lure of life in or close to the city was tugging at me too.

After a year, the relationship with Rebecca was over, and I quit 6IX and joined my parents for a short spell at Moorarie Station, which my father was now managing. It was an opportunity to be back in a station environment and test which of the two pulls was strongest.

After many discussions, an alternative emerged. It was the prospect of working for one of the stock and station firms, like Elders or Dalgety. These companies serviced station owners and farmers by selling their produce and supplying them with the requisites to run their properties. Following that path might give me the best of both worlds: living in a town but spending time on rural properties. So I applied to Dalgety and was accepted. They posted me to Katanning, southeast of Perth. I soon felt stranded. It was a very quiet country town, surrounded by well-to-do farming properties. After experiencing an 800,000-acre sheep station like Belele, 5,000-acre farms were a culture shock. Farmers talked about how they lived in the bush, but their idea of the bush was quite different from mine. The hankering for the Norwest continued to gnaw. At the same time, Dalgety was beset with internal politics, which I disliked. After nine months I resigned.

By now, it was two years since I had left Belele, and the pull of the city was winning the tug-of-war. I decided that a world that revolved around Pamela, Ian Bridson, Stan Gervas, Bob Juniper, John Samuel and people like them was what I wanted. These people were far more interesting and enjoyable than anyone else I'd met in the outback – but that's not to belittle the importance of friendships I made there. Apart from that, in Perth there were the pleasures of young ladies in one's life. Finally, reluctantly, I withdrew from my grandfather's vision of my destiny, although I could hardly bear to tell him. It was time to put the bush behind me. At 6IX, I had met several advertising agency people, and I wondered if I could use my copywriting ability to find a niche in that world.

I made my way to the station my father was managing and stayed with my parents for a week. After a couple of days, I spoke to my mother when my father was out somewhere on the property – I didn't have the heart to speak to him directly. I told her that my procrastination was over, that I had made a firm decision to give up the bush and, this was the most painful part, that they had to stop tying their future to me – we were never going to own a station together. Well, of course, we talked about it over the next few days, but there was no argument, and they did not try to persuade me otherwise.

Like a lizard, I had been slowly growing a new skin. Hesitantly, I climbed out of my old skin and left it behind in one piece.

Epilogue

All those years ago, when I had thought I put the bush behind me, what I really did was put it to one side. Part of me belongs out there and always will. Its legacy lingers and is reaffirmed with every fleeting visit, especially at familiar camp sites. At dusk, as colours deepen and shadows darken, the birds settle for the night. Their calls subside and the twilight hush is soft all around. The flickering firelight entertains and dispels uncertain feelings. Calm prevails. All of this, always.

At the heart of my connection with the bush lies Mount Augustus. Although many places have special memories, The Mount is pre-eminent. It is here that the frisson is strongest. Even to glimpse it from a remote distance quickens my spirit. Climbing at dawn, hand over hand in the steepest sections, pausing to look back across the emerging landscape, I feel a surge of exhilaration. Making my way beneath spreading branches, up the long, sloping gully that leads to the summit, I am in a realm like no other.

Out in the open and climbing the last 200-metre rock face, ledge by ledge, my anticipation of the thrill of being on the top increases, step by step. Then I am there, and it is everything I could wish for. Standing on the peak, almost in the sky, in the swirling air, slowly absorbing the vast landscape in every direction, I am awed. The beauty, the scope, its timelessness, all contribute – and humble me. Even as my human vulnerability lurks in the recesses of my mind, I have a singular feeling of being complete, which I do not feel elsewhere.

Way across the river flats, layer upon layer of ranges, like giant corrugations, ripple to the horizon. Relatively near but barely discernible, that white dot on the edge of the plain is Mount Augustus homestead, the link with the outside world. It is time to return to earth. I do not want to leave. It is consoling to know I will come back.

If this land buries its mark within you, it will be a wellspring forever. It is not visible to anyone – it is a mark that only you can feel, deep within yet always just beneath the surface.

Acknowledgements

In putting this book together, I am indebted to many friends, advisers, guides, correctors and sounding boards. They include: Laurie Bain, Michael Barrett-Lennard, Alan Blood, Janet Bradshaw, Hugh Mackay, Rhonda McDonald, Clive Palmer, Stuart Ridgway, Terry Spence, Ainslie Steadman, David Steadman and Madeline Walley. Their assistance, encouragement and support were unstinting. Their corrections and criticisms were all valid – and some saved me from embarrassment.

In particular, Margaret Kennedy's work with me was invaluable. Always deeply thoughtful, always encouraging, she stimulated me to do the best that I could do.

So too, Vanessa Mickan has contributed greatly.

My thanks also go to the Department of Agriculture and Food for providing me with maps of Belele Station.

Finally, to the one who has lived the journey with me, with unfailing enthusiasm and support, my deepest thank you to Sheryl.

Glossary

agistment
The practice of paying for stock to graze temporarily on a property other than one's own, usually for drought relief

AWU
Australian Workers' Union

bardie
Edible wood-boring grub

bedourie oven
A bushman's round steel oven with a lid that fits right over the base, unlike the lid of a regular cast-iron camp oven, which sits on top of the pot

big brown
A 750-millilitre bottle of beer

blitz wagon
A large four-wheel drive truck used a lot in the Second World War; also known as a blitz buggy or a 4 x 4

breakaway
A flat-topped hill, called a mesa in other parts of the world, with sheer slopes at the top

bungarra
Sand goanna, an Australian monitor lizard that reaches an average
length of 140 centimetres (4 feet 7 inches) and can weigh as much as six
kilograms (13 pounds)

cocky gate
A home-made gate composed of fencing wire and wooden or metal
uprights. A cocky gate is floppy when open but pulls tight when braced
to a fence post.

Condy's crystals
In the mid-1800s, a London chemist, Henry Bollmann Condy, marketed
potassium permanganate as a disinfectant, and the name Condy's
crystals has stuck.

Coolgardie safe
A metal-framed safe for holding perishables in hot weather. On top of
the safe there was a trough of water. Hessian cloths, fixed at one end
in the water, were draped down the sides, gradually becoming wet as
they absorbed water from the trough. If there was a breeze, there was
an instant cooling effect inside, because of evaporation. It was originally
developed at Coolgardie, in Western Australia.

crib
A meal eaten out on the job

dunny
Originally an outside toilet, prior to the availability of septic tanks or
sewerage; usually positioned some distance from the house

girth
A broad strap, usually consisting of a double thickness of leather, with
buckles that fasten to straps on either side of the saddle, underneath the
saddle flaps. The girth keeps the saddle in place.

girth galling
The development of a raw skin wound on the underbelly, caused by the
girth rubbing against the skin

hard feed
Stock feed made up of chaff plus grain and/or cubes of concentrated,
processed hay and other additives

kangaroo dog
A large dog developed from breeds of racing greyhounds

kelpie
A breed of sheepdog unique to Australia; mainly black and tan with a dash of white

killer
One of a group of wethers kept in a holding paddock, readily available for slaughter

making enough water
The state in which a well or bore is able to provide a reliable water supply in the volume required

micky
A young, wild bull

neck reining
A method by which a horse understands that it is being asked to turn right or left, by the rider applying light contact of the reins on one or the other side of its neck. At the same time, the horse is also responding to the rider's seat and legs, which are actually more important than the reins. In the use of this aid, there is no direct contact with the bit.

nulla-nulla
A wooden club

Old Westerns
Short novels set in the American West

pig-root
A mild form of bucking, consisting of a forward leap followed by the horse coming down on stiff forelegs, with its head between its legs, while kicking up high behind with its rear legs

Red Cloud
Basically, a chestnut kelpie. The breed originated in Western Australia, and there are now specialist Red Cloud breeders. Even though Red Clouds are red, yellow-ochre-coloured dogs can be classified as Red Clouds.

Ringlock
A type of wire mesh used for fencing

rouseabout

A general hand on a station or someone who does the menial tasks in a shearing shed, like yarding sheep and sweeping the floor; also called a shed hand

scouring

Diarrhoea in livestock

sheep pad

A narrow path, usually somewhat winding, regularly taken by sheep from out in the paddock to a source of water. The term *pad* can also be used for a path worn by cattle or horses: a cattle pad, a horse pad. The floor of the pad is always soft and loose from the continual passing of hooves.

Stillson

The brand name of a large wrench having adjustable jaws that tighten as the pressure on the handle is increased. The name became a generic term for this type of wrench, even though other brands were on the market. Now it is more usual to refer to this tool as a pipe wrench.

strainer (1)

The end post in a fence line, against which the fence wires are strained and kept tight

strainer (2)

The tool used to strain the wires against the post

the string

A set or a number of horses, usually in one's possession

surcingle

A wide strap that goes over the seat of the saddle, right around the horse, and provides extra security in case the girth breaks (see *girth*)

wheat pickling

The practice of putting wheat through a bath of copper carbonate to combat rust, a fungal disease

windmill round

When someone on a station checks a number of windmills to ensure that they are working and that the troughs are clean

Endnotes

Chapter 5: Ian Bridson

1. William Shakespeare, Sonnet 73, in *The Works of William Shakspeare*, ed. The Editor of the 'Chandos' Classics, Peacock, Mansfield and Britton, London.

2. Robert Browning, 'Andrea del Sarto (Called "The Faultless Painter")', in *The Poetical Works of Robert Browning*, Oxford University Press, London, 1949.

Chapter 7: Two Dutchmen and a Norwegian

1. Laurence Irving, introduction to *Crime and Punishment*, Fyodor Dostoevsky, trans. Frederick Whishaw, J.M. Dent & Sons Ltd, London, 1948.

Bibliography

Evan (Enie) Bain, *The Ways of Life*, Elder Smith Goldsbrough Mort Limited, Perth, Western Australia, 1976.

The Geraldton Guardian, Geraldton Newspapers Limited, Geraldton, Western Australia, 1955; in the collection of the J.S. Battye Library.

P.R. Heydon, *They're Racing at Landor*, Hesperian Press, Carlisle, Western Australia, 1992.

Sir Ernest Lee-Steere, *Be Fair and Fear Not*, Sir Ernest Lee-Steere, Perth, Western Australia, 1995.

Rhonda McDonald, *Winning the Gascoyne*, Hesperian Press, Carlisle, Western Australia, 1991.

Martyn and Audrey Webb, *Edge of Empire*, Artlook Books, Perth, Western Australia, 1983.

Frederick Francis Wittenoom, *A Varied and Versatile Life*, Hesperian Press, Carlisle, Western Australia, 2003.

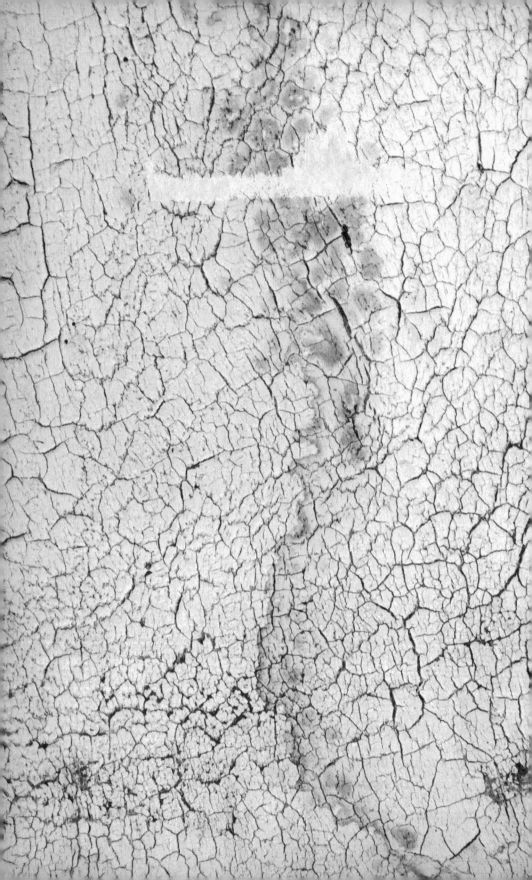